A Nine

B. M. Croker

Alpha Editions

This edition published in 2022

ISBN: 9789356907942

Design and Setting By

Alpha Editions
www.alphaedis.com

Email - info@alphaedis.com

Contents

A NINE DAYS' WONDER
PART I

CHAPTER I

A tall grey-haired soldier, with a professionally straight back, stood looking out of an upper window in the "Rag" one wet October afternoon. His hands were buried in his pockets, and his face was clothed with an expression of almost mediæval gloom. The worldly wise mask their emotions so that those who run may not read, but Colonel Doran had lived so many years among a primitive race that he made no effort to conceal his feelings, and all the world was welcome to see that he was bored to death. To tell the truth, he had been too long in the East to appreciate club life. Other men were undoubtedly contented, interested, occupied; it was different in his case. The palatial dignity, solemnity, luxury of the place failed to stir his pride; even its traditions left him as cold as the marble statue on the great staircase. He would have felt ten times more at home in a Bombay chair, on a brick verandah, with the old Pioneer in his hands and a "Trichy" in his mouth.

The big smoking-room below had presented a most animated scene; groups of old brother officers were discussing various burning questions, and topics ranged, from the new Hussar boot, to the North-west Frontier. Colonel Doran knew a good deal about the frontier, but made no effort to enter the lists. What were possible campaigns to him now? He wandered aimlessly up to the library, and turned over some books; he tried to read—it was no use. Ashamed to appear a sort of no man's friend, and stray, he made his way to the upper smoking-room, which he was tolerably certain to find empty at that hour. He sauntered round it, gazing indifferently at the pictures and mementoes. A sketch of two elephants in a dust-storm arrested his attention. How he wished himself on the back of one of the old beggars—dust-storm and all! At last he strolled over to the window, and as he stood looking out on a dismal vista of wet slates and an iron-grey sky he heaved an involuntary sigh. So this was the end of his career—idleness, boredom, solitude!

The career of Ulick Doran had commenced at eighteen, when as a cadet he had landed in India—that hospitable godmother of younger sons—and the kindly East had adopted and made him her own for the better part of thirty-four years. He had been gazetted as a mere boy to a crack regiment of Bengal cavalry known as "Holland's Horse," and in this corps, his home, he had lived and fought and nearly died: had seen his comrades come and go, marry, and retire. Now it was his own turn. At fifty-two his career was ended, and the curtain rung down. Good-bye to everything he cared for—to the sowars, his children, to the mess, to the horse lines, aye, to the very horses, half of which he had selected—good-bye to all that had made life worth living. Naturally he could not remain in India, that unseemly spectacle, a mere camp follower of the regiment he had so ably commanded, hovering around it like a departed spirit. He must return to England, and range himself decently on the shelf along with most of his contemporaries. Unfortunately Colonel Doran had but few resources apart from his profession; he was a fine horseman, a noted swordsman, a keen and capable officer, and here he stood, a stranded and unhappy pensioner, the very typical dragoon without his horse! What made his position still worse, he was alone in the world. His mother had died when he was a small boy—he scarcely remembered her; his father, on the other hand, had lived to a great age, a red-faced, irascible old gentleman, whose eldest son predeceased him by many years; and thus the family place had come to the Indian officer, after all.

An agent had remitted him spasmodically his somewhat shrunken rents; and recently he had visited Kilmoran Castle, the home of his ancestors, a tumbledown old place six miles from a station, with a defective roof, and a pervading odour of soot and dry rot. He scarcely knew a soul in the neighbourhood: undoubtedly there was good hunting to be had of a somewhat rough-and-ready description that would carry him through the dark winter days; but what of the *evenings* at home? He recalled the cavernous dining-room, with black horsehair and mahogany furniture, the heavy flock paper, the narrow windows, the glowering family portraits, and, above all, the grim sarcophagus under the sideboard that seemed to await, not the plate, but a corpse! whilst the drawing-room, which had been closed for fifty years, was a ghostly apartment, given over to dust and mice, who played weird tunes among the wires of the ancient Broadwood piano. Ulick Doran shivered as he pictured the dim flagged passages, the damp, desolate bedrooms. If he were to live at Kilmoran alone, he would undoubtedly take to drink or cut his throat! The other alternative was London and a bedroom near his club, where he would see the same faces, hear the same arguments, walk the same streets—every day. Oh, he would soon come to the end of that! This great city had no attractions for him. As he stood gazing out on the streaming rain and leaden clouds he was mentally contrasting Pall Mall with the "eye of his heart"—the Punjaub—and wishing he were back under the deep blue sky, with the first nip of the cold weather in the air, and his new Australian thoroughbred between his knees.

Just at this instant the door opened and a brisk little bald man, with a fair moustache and cheery eye, entered the room. He was Major Sutton—or Johnny Sutton, as his friends called him—late of Holland's Horse, a comrade who had retired, married, and apparently lived happy ever after.

"I say, old man," he began, "what are you doing here all by yourself—eh? What's the matter? Down on your luck?"

"Not much luck to be down on, as far as I know," growled the other, turning from the window and sinking into a capacious chair.

"Of course it's just raw to you at present; you miss the old regiment, and, by George! they miss you," said Johnny Sutton, opening his cigar-case. "We all have a sort of lost, end-of-all-things feeling, when we first come home, but we get over it in time and make a fresh start."

"That's all right for the young 'uns, Johnny, but a man of fifty-two has gone over most of the course."

"Nonsense, Pat. I see you are affected by this beastly weather, and your liver—a man of fifty is in his prime! Why, I'm fifty myself, and can walk and shoot with the best."

"You were always a great shikari, Johnny."

"For that matter, so were you."

"Well, there's an end of all that now."

"Why so? Haven't you shooting on your place in Ireland?"

"Shooting!" he repeated derisively. "About as much as is in St. James's Park. Perhaps after a hard day's work I might bag a brace of rabbits and one snipe. It's been poached for years. My father was an old man, and let things slide——"

"Still, I suppose you will go over there and pull the place together a bit?"

"No, I could not stand it for more than a week; the loneliness and dreariness seem to penetrate to one's very bones."

"And you are not keen about living in town—eh? You are like a newly imported remount—everything is strange, and you don't know what to do with yourself?"

"Yes, Johnny, you have hit the nail right on the head; and if you can give me some sort of lead, I'm your man."

Major Sutton puffed at his cigar, removed it from his mouth, examined it carefully, and then blurted out—

"I say, why don't you marry?"

"Marry!" repeated his companion. "What an idea!"

"Yes, man alive, and a good one; people do it every day. You stare as if you had never heard of the institution. Look at me"—and he tapped his waistcoat: "I am married."

"Yes, but I—I am not a ladies' man."

"So much the better; *they* never marry."

"And I'm too old," objected Colonel Doran.

"Bosh!"

"No girl would have me."

"Well, what do you say to a fine young woman of five-and-thirty—or—a widow?"

"I'm not a society man, or in the way of meeting ladies."

"Because you won't go out when you are invited, except among the old married folk of the regiment. I can introduce you to one or two really suitable young women, with good looks, a little money, and no nonsense about them. There is Flora Davey! Why, her father commanded the 25th Bengal Cavalry. You remember him. She was born in Lahore?"

"Yes; and I was at her christening," he supplemented grimly. "No, no! that would never work. Thank you, old man, I believe I'll stay as I am."

"But look here, Pat, you remember when I got that crack on my head at polo and was shunted home—years ago: it nearly broke my heart, but matrimony cured me. I met Maudie on the Riviera my first winter—and she took to me and I to her. You see, I was an invalid, and she pitied me, and talked over her rich old pater. People said nasty things, and it was a lie; I married Maudie for herself only, though money is certainly a power. Now the old man is gone, she has a clear three thousand a year, and I have come into a comfortable legacy. Maudie is a confirmed match-maker, and tries her best to settle her friends."

"Yes, like the fox who lost his tail," remarked the bachelor.

"Bar jokes, come along and dine with us quietly on Friday."

Colonel Doran hesitated; he knocked the ash off his cigar reflectively and then began—

"You are very kind, Johnny, old man, but——"

"Oh, no, I'm not going to make up a match for you on the spot—no fear: but just take a look at me and mine—as a practical illustration of my argument—no party: I want you and Maudie to get to know one another better—she likes you so much——"

"All right, then, I'll come—thanks. Friday did you say?" and he took out a little pocket-book. "Friday, 13th, at 8 o'clock, 402 Sloane Street."

"Now, remember, you are engaged to us to a *tête-à-tête* dinner. I must be off; I'm taking the Mem Sahib to a theatre, and we dine early. You ought to look in yourself; it's rather fun—*The Old Bachelor's Blunder*."

*   *   *   *   *

Major Sutton had been a Benedict for nearly ten years. His wife was a pretty, fashionable little woman, some months—though few suspected this—older than himself. She dressed with taste, had a capable maid, and was, in the eyes of Johnny Sutton, perennially young and beautiful. He had no secrets from her, and told her, like a good boy, where he had been, who he had seen, what they had said. The couple were on terms of delightful good fellowship, and she, for her part, shared with Johnny all the dearest secrets of her dearest friends.

"I say, Maudie," he began, when they were settled in their brougham, "you know my pal, Pat Doran, one of the best fellows who ever stepped——"

"Yes, of course I do; he looks like an unhappy duke, poor old boy."

"I met him to-day, alone and evidently rather wretched. You see, he feels a bit out of it now he is retired; he is like a lost dog. The regiment was his home; now he is out of it. If he had had a clever little wife to exploit him he might have become a brigadier and goodness knows what. Now he is short of a job; he is not even on the club committee, and he has nothing to do."

"And Satan finds, etc. etc.; only he is too old to get into mischief, I should hope. What about him?"

"Well, you see, he doesn't take kindly to London, and he does not care to live in Ireland. He has a fine estate and castle over there. His family goes back to the Flood, and had their own ship."

"Yes, he looks an aristocrat all over," agreed Mrs. Sutton, who, being the daughter of a successful nobody, had a profound respect for blue blood.

"He is one of the simplest and best of men, but all alone in the world. After living years in a mess he can't stand the empty halls of his ancestors, and I've been telling him to-day, that he *must* marry!"

"Of course," she eagerly agreed—"certainly he must marry."

"And you are the proper person to find him a nice wife, Maudie—a real jewel, you know—no paste. I've asked him to come and dine on Friday—quite by ourselves, and you can talk to him—of course, not about matrimony—just to find out his tastes. In fact, I know them—he was desperately in love once, with a quiet fair-haired girl; she had a soft manner, and a charming smile, and married a drunken boor—who broke her heart—and——"

"But listen, Johnny," interrupted his wife, "we have a little dinner on Friday—don't you remember? The Colletts and Sir Fred and Lady Hewson."

"By Jove! Yes—so we have! Then I'll put him off till Sunday."

"No, no, you will do nothing of the sort. I will ask a girl specially to meet him. I know the very one to suit him. What do you say to Julia Barker?"

"Oh," doubtfully, "I don't think she would be his style at all—no—not one little bit."

"Why not? She is handsome, agreeable, well connected—the Hollington-Barkers you know."

"Yes, but I don't admire her; she's too stout and full-blown; too loud, and *I* should say, had the devil of a temper."

"It is not necessary for *you* to admire her, Johnny. Poor Ju has led a life to try the temper of a saint. A spendthrift old father, and since his death she is a sort of wanderer, and wants a home of her own so badly; her life is spent in visits—and she lives in her boxes. Now the Barre girls are growing up she cannot be there so much, and she hates being paying guest."

"Miss Barker has no money," objected Major Sutton.

"But Colonel Doran has, and Ju is wonderful, she can make one penny go as far as two! She will be a capital wife for him, lively, energetic, and managing—and *so* well connected."

"I don't think she will suit, Maudie. He is a quiet, reserved sort of chap, and would like some one of his own caste."

"Not a bit of it: silent men always take talkative wives—every one chooses their opposite—I believe Ju and the Colonel will be an exact match—and here we are!"

CHAPTER II

Julia Barker was the youngest daughter of a needy gentleman of good family who for many years had roamed about the cheaper continental resorts, bearing in his train two dashing good-looking girls—and leaving in his track a considerable number of bad debts. Occasionally, his rich relations came to his assistance; for instance, when Fanny succeeded in capturing the affection of a wealthy baronet, Sir Herbert Barre, the connection provided a suitable wedding and trousseau, and hinted that they looked to Fanny to help her sister in the like manner. It was really discreditable, the way in which old Fitzroy dragged their name about in the dust of Europe; they were constantly encountering people who said, "Oh—we met your cousins the Hollington-Barkers at Spa or Monte Carlo—they *are* your cousins, are they not? Rather a handsome girl, and a thin old gentleman, who gambles a good deal." Sometimes it appeared that the thin old gentleman had borrowed money from these too confiding travellers. However, at last Captain Fitzroy Hollington-Barker's wanderings came to an end; he was accorded (for the sake of the connection) a decent funeral, buried in the ancestral vault; and Julia his daughter had her liberty, the world before her, and one hundred and fifty pounds a year. Lady Barre had exerted herself in every way to "help off poor Ju" as she termed it; but so far her anxious efforts had proved of no avail: on the contrary, poor Ju had sustained several crushing disappointments. Yet Julia Barker was a handsome woman, in a showy dark style; she had bright eyes, a bright, somewhat fixed colour, a fine carriage, and a sustained supply of energy and conversation. Also she was granddaughter of the late Earl of Hollington, and sister to Lady Barre, who entertained so well; but—Miss Barker had no money—was losing her looks and figure, and bore the reputation of a temper, and debts! In spite of her clever manœuvring, and her astonishing aptitude for exacting invitations, favours, presents, and even the use of their carriages, from her circle, Miss Barker's future was becoming somewhat grey. People were beginning to weary of her company, her stories, her assurance, and herself! when Maudie Sutton—to her supreme joy—presented to her the gallant gentleman, whom she subsequently advertised as "her fate." She and Maudie, who had been intimates for years, met at the glove-counter of a well-known shop in Knightsbridge.

"You got my note, Ju?" said Mrs. Sutton. "I hope you are coming on Friday?"

"No, dearest; I am engaged to the Farmers—charades and a dance——"

"Oh, never mind the Farmers, Ju," interrupted Mrs. Sutton; "this little dinner of mine is ten million times more important—and," she lowered her voice and concluded her speech in a series of somewhat breathless whispers.

The young lady over the gloves was curious—evidently something mysterious was afoot! Miss Barker now became all animation and interest, and as she took leave of her friend, she kissed her repeatedly, and said—

"Thank you, dear old Maudie—you are a *real* friend!"

When Major Sutton received his brother officer at the drawing-room door, he said, "Look here, Pat, I owe you ever so many apologies—I guaranteed a family party, and I've let you in for a 'Burra Khana.' Maudie had arranged it before—better luck next time."

There was indeed a large party at 402 Sloane Street, and Colonel Doran was one of the latest arrivals; he looked very distinguished and soldierly, as he talked to Mrs. Sutton, a vision in yellow and diamonds.

"I know you were told we were to be alone," she said, smiling; "but it makes no matter to a man if there are three, or three hundred—not like us poor women, who have to dress according to numbers. Now I want to introduce you to a most particular old friend of mine, Miss Hollington-Barker," and she towed him over to a sofa, on which was enthroned a handsome Juno-like form. "Julia—this is Johnny's comrade, Colonel Doran; you are to be very nice to him, and he will take you down to dinner"; and with an affable smile Mrs. Sutton sailed away and left them.

Colonel Doran stood before Julia, lamely discoursing of the rain and the east wind—whilst she figuratively proceeded to take his measure. When she descended the stairs on her cavalier's arm, Julia Barker had definitely decided that "he would do."

He was neither too old, nor too young—he was good-looking, a gentleman, and a soldier—with a fine property in Ireland; and as to family, her own was of mushroom growth in comparison! Maudie Sutton had given her this splendid chance, and Miss Barker meant to seize it. She had heard all about Major Sutton's distinguished friend—a man without relatives, but possessing immense savings and a castle—who was looking about him for a wife! There was now no occasion for him to seek further than his present companion. As his partner ate her soup, which he had declined, Colonel Doran studied her stealthily.

The lady was dark-browed, dark-haired, with brown eyes, a high colour, a large mouth, and a short straight nose; her age was considerably over thirty, her figure plump; she was remarkably well dressed (in one of Lady Barre's cast-offs), black, with pink velvet, and wore a handsome old-fashioned necklace. Subsequently his eyes travelled round the table and he noted Mrs. Sutton—fair and fluffy-haired, animated and pretty. Sutton was a lucky man! He discovered several attractive-looking ladies; one opposite had dark auburn hair and an ivory skin, whom he admired immensely. And now his own partner began to unmask her fascinations; she was a practised diner-out, and talked well. Little did he guess that on the present occasion she was talking for a wedding ring, and straining every nerve to interest this polite, but unresponsive gentleman. Their conversation really opened with that disastrous catastrophe, the upsetting of the salt-cellar.

"Yes, and it's on a Friday!" she exclaimed, with mock tragic eyes,—"and I've upset it towards you, and will bring you sorrow!"

As he looked a little embarrassed by this jaunty speech, she rattled on to relate the well-known anecdote of an absent-minded gentleman, who, having spilled some salt, instantly poured a glass of claret over it—thus transposing the usual remedy. With sundry excellent, and, to him, perfectly fresh chestnuts, she kept her victim thoroughly entertained—actually so interested, that he forgot to glance at the red-headed girl—or even at Mrs. Sutton—and refused two of the most toothsome *plats*. What a fortunate fellow he was, to have secured such a charming companion! By turns amusing, sympathetic, or serious; he had but to listen, to look into her eloquent dark eyes, admire her white teeth, and her delightful smile. Among other things, she told him how it had ever been the one dream of her life to go to India, and how she still devoured ravenously every book about India that came in her way. She drew him out cleverly about his regiment (his hobby), his chargers and polo-ponies, his tiger-shooting; and presently he found himself talking to the lady as if he had known her for years; they had discovered a mutual Indian friend—one Bobbie Travers, late of the 170th Bengal Lancers, who was Miss Barker's own second cousin, and he—oh, lucky man—now commanded no less a regiment than Holland's Horse. Here was a tie indeed! Bobbie proved not merely a link, but a *chain*, and it was almost in the nature of a shock when Mrs. Sutton gave the signal, and the two enthralled companions were compelled to relinquish an absorbing conversation.

As soon as the men appeared in the drawing-room, Miss Barker made a significant movement of her hand, and as the enchanted veteran ventured to occupy the seat beside her, she began—

"I am longing for you to finish that story about the old sower, and the pariah dog—do, please, *do* go on—you had just got to where he was lying on the orderly-room steps, when Maudie hustled us all upstairs"; and so conversation was resumed precisely where it had been interrupted. "Your experiences are so enthralling!" she remarked, as he took her coffee-cup. "I only wish my sister could hear them—you really *ought* to write a book."

Colonel Doran looked at her doubtfully for a moment: then he laughed aloud.

"Lady Barre is my only sister; I live with her," she resumed. This was not a fact. Julia happened to be staying with her for a few days; but, as the Spanish proverb says, "there is no tax on lies." "Will you come and have tea with us some afternoon?"

"I—I——" He was about to refuse, but she suddenly looked up at him with an appeal in her eyes, and he said "Er—I shall be delighted."

"We live at two hundred and five, Grosvenor Street,—shall we say Tuesday at four o'clock?"

"Thank you."

"You won't forget, will you?" again looking up at him. "If you do, I shall feel so hurt and disappointed."

Colonel Doran, though over fifty years of age, blushed as if he were seventeen; he actually felt his face burning at the implied compliment. How astonishing it seemed that this handsome, charming woman should be interested in a battered old soldier. What *did* she see in him?

* * * * * *

"Fanny," said Julia, as she opened the door of her sister's boudoir. "So you've not gone to bed yet! I am so glad. I've something to say to you, and I want you to help me."

"Yes," agreed Lady Barre, languidly laying down her book. "The girls are out, and Tom is down at the house. What has happened? If it's money again, I really cannot——"

"I've met a man to-night at the Suttons'," broke in her sister.

Lady Barre nodded.

"And I intend to marry him."

"Good gracious, Julia——"

"Yes; he is looking for a wife—so Major Sutton told Maudie—and I am looking for a husband. He is middle-aged, wealthy, of good family—a colonel in the army—just retired—with enormous savings; he has a fine estate and castle in Ireland, and not one relation in the wide world!"

"My dear, it sounds too good to be true! Who is he?"

"His name is Doran; he is rather silent and a little shy. I've invited him to tea here on Tuesday. I hope you are not engaged?"

"But I am—yes, to the Lovells; however, I will certainly stay at home and see your—catch."

"Yes, it is time I was married; and I do honestly believe Colonel Doran has taken a fancy to me. He left when I did, and put me into a cab as if I were something precious and breakable. He has offered me tiger-claws."

"What on earth for?"

"To make a necklet, of course."

"You have fine claws of your own, Ju, if he only *knew*."

Julia, who had removed her cloak, now reclined in an arm-chair, as if reposing after some exhausting effort. "To think of it, Fan"—ignoring this scratch—"I am going to be off your hands—and my own hands—at last!"

"I know how clever you are, Ju; but there is many a slip. You remember Eddie Ellis——"

"There will be no slip this time if you will back me up properly. Get Tom to leave a card at his club; ask him to dinner once or twice, and be *nice* to him."

"Oh, I'll do all that, of course, with pleasure"—and her ladyship sincerely meant it. She would strain every nerve to get Julia settled—a homeless, impecunious sister, always clinging to her—a sister, too, with endless debts, quarrels, and flirtations. Of course she was fond of poor old Ju, but she would be truly grateful to the man who would marry her, and relieve her of an incubus.

Colonel Doran was not kept in the dark respecting Miss Barker's fine connections and amiable relations. He dined at Grosvenor Street; he had a seat in their box at the theatre. Indeed, Julia's family received him with open arms, as if he were a long-expected friend; being, indeed, an eagerly-looked-for, and well approved suitor. Julia's interest in sport was unquenchable; secretly she borrowed and read up books on Indian shikar, and was always radiantly pleased to see him—handsome, well dressed, and agreeable. In three weeks' time, Colonel Doran had spoken the fatal words. Sitting over the fire in the little drawing-room one dull afternoon Miss Julia described in pitiful tones her own sad and solitary life. Fanny had her family, who engrossed her. "And I," she added in a broken voice, "am really *alone* in the world. I shall be a forlorn old maid; no one cares for me."

And, emboldened by this splendid opening, Colonel Doran figuratively rushed upon his fate.

*   *   *   *   *   *   *

It was decided that the engagement was to be brief, as the lady frankly declared—

"We are neither of us young; there is nothing to wait for; and the wedding can take place before Fanny leaves town. She won't be back again till February."

To this arrangement the happy bridegroom readily agreed. When money matters came to be discussed, Colonel Doran's large estate dwindled down to £1,200 a year. This discovery proved a shock. It appeared that most of his surplus income had been lavished on his regiment; still, his pension was considerable, and living was cheap in Ireland. Fanny generously paid her sister's debts and presented the trousseau. The bride-elect talked continually of Kilmoran Castle, and distributed pressing invitations—among friends unlikely to accept. There was a brilliant wedding, and showers of presents descended on old Ju Barker, who had made an unexpectedly good match. After the ceremony the happy pair left, amid a buzz of congratulations and a shower of rice and slippers, for Colonel Doran's Irish seat.

Although he had repeatedly attempted to discount her expectations, Julia had turned a resolutely deaf ear to her fiancé.

"It is really nothing of a place," he protested; "the old family house was burnt down eighty years ago. My ancestors gambled, and raced through most of the property; and though once we owned miles of country, we have only about two thousand acres of land—some of it is bog—and I am the last twig on our family tree. The castle is merely a house tacked on to an ancient keep; there are no grounds or conservatories—it is just a gloomy old barrack. But you will brighten it. I've had some of the rooms papered, and sent over a little modern furniture."

"But your father and mother lived in it, as it was," she argued, in a querulous key.

"Yes, and my grandfather too. I remember him when Nora and I were small children."

"By the way, who is, or was, Nora?"

"Don't you remember? I told you about her. My only sister—such a pretty girl; but when she was eighteen, she ran away to America—with the postman."

"How awful! Has nothing been heard of her?"

"No, not for many years. I used to write to her, and send her money on the sly; my father would never allow her name to be mentioned."

"He was right, I think; she behaved disgracefully."

"My father married late in life, and had no sympathy with young people. Nora never had a moment's freedom, and she was a wild, gay sort of girl—poor Nora! I've lost sight of her this twenty years; she was five years younger than I."

In spite of her husband's warning, Kilmoran Castle proved a terrible disappointment to the bride. First of all a mean little hump-backed gate lodge, covered with ivy as with a cloak, and a common rusty iron gate, then a winding weedy drive, and finally, the Castle!—merely a square grey keep, against which a two-storeyed white house had propped itself. There were no towers or battlements, there was not even a pillared porch to hide the vulgarity of a grass-green hall door. The garden in front was a dreary wilderness of overgrown box and old fuchsias. In short, the Castle had nothing pretty, noble, or uncommon, to recommend it; it was not even dignified by a curse, or a ghost. Within were several large low sitting-rooms, antique furniture, family pictures, and a smell of soot and dry rot. The bride having ascended to her room, collapsed on the first chair in floods of tears—bitter, angry tears. However, Julia Doran was not the sort of woman to sit and weep, and she soon, to use an American term, "took hold." She explored the house, and cleverly appraised its mouldy contents, discovered the great stable-yard—capable of holding a troop of cavalry—and the huge garden, remnants of the glories of a former mansion; here, at least, was a sense of comfort and importance. The demesne was pretty, and the views lovely. After all, she was Mrs. Doran of Kilmoran Castle, and matters might be worse. For instance, she might still be Miss Barker—living on her friends, and her wits, in some cheap suburban boarding-house. To all important correspondents she despatched glowing accounts of her home, and on her cards and writing-paper was engraved "Kilmoran Castle" in clear large type; and as far as people in England could tell, it might be Chatsworth itself! Then the new lady (there had not been a Mrs. Doran for more than forty years) began to institute improvements. Trees were cut down, old lumber carted away, rooms were opened and aired; she set up a carriage, and taught the immediate neighbourhood to keep its distance. There was to be no running in and out of the Castle *now*. Next, she issued an edict, and dismissed several old servants. Dotards and blood-suckers, she termed them, and if they had been forty years at Kilmoran, it was twenty years too long. She set her face sternly against authorised beggars, and all pensioners; and oh, crowning enormity, she sold the skim milk, which for a century and more, had been a free gift. Alas, there was now no picking up of firewood in the plantations, no winking at stray cattle—or even goats; altogether it was a new régime.

Colonel Doran made a gallant struggle to stem the revolution, but found himself powerless. His wife had a strong and ruthless will. Remonstrances merely led to scenes: the lady, with a red face, stormed and scolded; she assured him that he was a fool, living in an old barrack, and being ruined by a pack of greedy parasites, and that she would never stand by and calmly witness such extravagance. So at last, for the sake of a quiet life, the unhappy gentleman succumbed; he was alive to the fact that his marriage had been a terrible mistake, but he bore his sufferings with a patience and resignation that was almost oriental in its character. He busied himself beyond the scope of Julia's operations, became a justice of the peace, farmed, hunted, and took up the broken links of ancient family friendships.

As far as lay in his power, the Colonel helped his poor dependents: in secret, and out of his own pocket he remitted rents, or bought on the sly a cow or an ass; for Mrs. Doran was a woman of business. Precisely like the model French wife, she kept the keys, the accounts, and all domestic power, in her own hands, and, but for her streak of hard greed, was an admirable manager.

The Dorans had two children, both boys—Barker, the elder, was stout, lumpish, black-eyed,—his mother's favourite, and a Barker, as she proudly proclaimed. Ulick, the second, was a slender, delicate child, with clear-cut features, and large grey eyes. As he resembled the Dorans, his mother did not care for him; he was strong-willed, undemonstrative, and passionately attached to his father.

When Ulick was seven years of age, and Barker nine, Colonel Doran caught a bad cold, which developed into pneumonia, and died suddenly. Being much respected, he was accorded that final tribute and compliment, a great funeral; it was more than two miles long, and the boast among his retainers for many years.

"A nice, quiet kind man. God rest him! A real gentleman," was his epitaph; and some went so far as to add—

"Faix, he has had a poor sort of life, and maybe he is glad to be out of it."

Ten years had elapsed since the great funeral. The boys were growing up. Ulick's godfather, Major Sutton, had sent him to Wellington, and occasionally invited him to London for a week, but Barker remained in Ireland, under his mother's supervision, qualifying for the position of Master of Kilmoran; he had been a short time at school, and then, in answer to his fervid representations, his devoted parent had installed him at home with a resident tutor, whilst Ulick went to Sandhurst; for Ulick had decided to follow the usual career of a younger son, and was resolved to be a soldier.

CHAPTER III

Mrs. Doran, generally called Mrs. "Colonel" Doran, and by her retainers "the ould wan," was well known to fame in the immediate region of her personal influence—that is to say, within a visiting distance of fifteen Irish miles from her own door. The lady cherished a delusion that she was one of the most prominent figures in the province, and if she had been persuaded to whisper her claims to this distinction, would have announced, "high birth, good breeding, and benevolence." But alas! how differently do others see us! The reputation she bore was in startling contradiction to her illusions. People talked openly of Mrs. Doran's arrogance, rudeness, and parsimony, and the lower orders boldly proclaimed her to be "a holy terror." Her blustering tyranny, her meanness, and inflexible resolve to get more than her money's worth, revolted the souls of her miserable retainers, whilst among the upper ten her systematic assumption of superiority, and barefaced endeavours to make use of every one, added to a malignant tongue, caused the lady to be not merely disliked, but feared. As for her benevolence, no one denied that she was a most indefatigable beggar. She begged boldly for money, blankets, and cast-off garments, and distributed the alms of other people; but she never contributed herself—indeed, the malicious went so far as to say that Mrs. Doran embezzled certain of these moneys, and put them in her pocket, believing that charity began in her *own* home; also, they declared that she gave the collected flannel, and blankets, to her servants, and wore the pick of the clothes herself! In fact, a certain class detested Mrs. Doran so intensely that they were ready to say or believe anything to her disadvantage.

Since the days when she came to Kilmoran, a showy and self-possessed bride, the lady was much changed, and was now a stout, red-faced matron, with a bustling gait, incredible energy, and a large balance at her banker's. To give her her due, she had worked hard, and nursed the estate for her beloved Barky, who loafed through life, whilst his active mother held the reins of government. But even her bitterest foe could not deny that the Englishwoman had wrought improvements. There was now an imposing entrance, with gilded gates; on either pier sat a great stone wolf-hound (the crest of the once noble Dorans); a pretty pleasure-ground lay before the Castle; and a smart man-servant (on board wages), opened the door; but unfortunately nothing could be done for the Castle itself!—nothing short of razing it to the ground, and rebuilding it. The rooms were all suitably furnished, with the most modern antique treasures, including tapestry. A flag waved languidly from the roof of the ancient tower. Certainly the place looked both prosperous and pretentious. Mrs. Doran, in a smart landau with a pair of fine bays, scoured the country, and established intimate relations with all the people of wealth and position. To these she was affectionate, sympathetic, and even confidential; but she was not given to hospitality, and preferred to see her friends in their own homes. Two garden-parties per summer, and a couple of hunting luncheons, were the limit of her efforts. With the professional class Mrs. Doran was stand-off, and "an Earl's grand-daughter" (unless she required a legal opinion, or a prescription), and she was a wonderful woman to borrow! The lower orders she simply looked upon as slaves. They were a race apart, and to these she was an autocrat, and a tyrant. Those who were unluckily her workmen, and born on the property, had to work longer than elsewhere. The bell clanged at six o'clock in the morning, and at six in the evening. The payment was one shilling a day—a penny an hour! And the active lady tramped round the fields herself, and saw that there was no idling. She did not trust her steward, in fact, she trusted no one, except Barky—it was for him she was toiling and saving; he should be a wealthy man yet, and marry into the peerage! Everything that made an outside show was properly maintained; but where matters were not open to the public eye, it was otherwise. There was a stinting in fires, in lamp-oil, in the servants' food, in matches, yea, and in washing! Time, which had wrought changes in the property, had not improved its future owner. Barky, as he was called, had been firmly secured to his mother's apron-strings and spoiled to his heart's content. He was naturally a lazy, self-indulgent boor, stupid and stubborn, with an enormous conception of his own importance. Much of this might have been eliminated at a good public school—where he would have been compelled to bestir himself, yield to others, and realise his own true value. In appearance he was thick-set, with short legs, and a long body: naturally no horseman. He had cunning little dark eyes, a high colour, a thick neck, and slouched as he walked. He spoke with a common accent, and rarely opened a book or wrote a letter; but he was fond of smoking, and as devoted to cards and gambling as his unworthy ancestors. He enjoyed low company, yet had a most exalted idea of his own status. Ulick, at the age of seventeen, presented a complete contrast to his brother; he was tall and slender, and spoke with an English accent, until he became roused or excited, which was seldom; like his father, he was a born horseman—in fact, he resembled him in many ways, and inherited his parent's popularity among the country people. Although Barker would unbend, and borrow sporting-papers from the coachman, and play "spoil fire" with stable-boys in the harness-room, yet for all this condescension his companions were never *sure* of him—he would "round on them" at a moment's notice, no longer the jovial comrade, but the blustering, cursing master; whilst Mr. Ulick, who made no freedom, was always the same, and a gentleman!

Mrs. Doran was a keen woman of business, and by no means a bad farmer, save that she grudged a proper supply of manure, got all that she could off the land, and put but little back. Young horses were one of her adventures, and as a rule, though they are considered a risky investment, they paid her well. In the first place, she had an invaluable head groom, an ancient retainer, who, for the sake of the old master, stayed on, receiving small wages and enduring many indignities; no better judge of a three-year-old long-tail than Peter Duffy ever stood in an Irish fair. These he brought home, handled, rode, and sold, with most satisfactory results.

Latterly, Peter was getting too heavy to ride to hounds, or school the young ones, and Master Ulick, when at home, took his place. All the world agreed that he was "the darling on a colt, with the loveliest hands in the world, and as bold as a young lion." It is unnecessary to mention that none of his admirers had ever seen a young lion following the foxhounds; but their praise, though ignorant, was heartfelt and sincere.

Ulick loved animals, especially horses; he was crazy about hunting, and when he was at Kilmoran spent most of his time in the saddle. His mother made no objection; she was alive to the pecuniary value of a light-weight rider, and knew that after a month or two of Ulick's training the young hunters' prices were sensibly increased.

Even from the time he was twelve years old, this light-weight boy, with light hands, a bold heart, and mounted on an animal as youthful and eager as himself, caused many a pang of envy, and memory of the "has-been days," to the veteran followers of the Harkaway hounds.

When Ulick was seventeen, and a cadet at Sandhurst, he met with an accident that nearly brought his career, and his neck, to an untimely end. One raw winter afternoon the hounds were running not far from Kilmoran. It had been a grand scenting day. Sport was good, and Ulick was out on a new investment—a fine upstanding four-year-old, with grand legs and quarters, but with an ugly fiddle-head and a small pig-like eye. He had, however, a famous pedigree—and with that same pedigree was allied a temper. At first he went kindly, taking all before him with extraordinary flippancy, sailing over places big or little, in a manner that it was a pleasure to witness. A hard-riding cavalry man had already bought him (mentally) and entered him for a couple of steeplechases at Punchestown and Sandown. Suddenly, something put the brown horse out—one never quite knows what upsets a hunter's temper. Leading the field, he came thundering down to a big boundary-fence, wheeled about sharp on the edge, as if on a pivot—in short, balked before the whole hunt, knocked fifty pounds off his price, and all but shot his rider into the next field. The thrusting followers of the Harkaways stormed the obstacle and galloped on, and Ulick made another effort, put the horse at the ditch, which he again refused; and he not only refused, but reared, and snorted. As the hounds were now far ahead, his rider was determined to get the horse over, so to speak, dead or alive; the brown colt was as positively resolved not to jump. Each, boy and beast, was furious with the other; their blood was up, and it was now a frantic personal affair between them. The beast stood planted, with tucked-in tail, ears laid back, in a lather of sweat and foam, the picture of stubborn strength; the boy, with set white face, was equally dogged, and used every means in his power to conquer the brute—whip, spurs, voice. These were answered by plunges, rearings, and loud snorts of angry defiance. Then Ulick Doran tried peaceful methods, soothing and coaxing, and gentle walkings to and fro. But all to no purpose. The contest had lasted for twenty minutes. The field was empty, save for an old white goat, who stared her astonishment at the proceedings, and a little girl of ten years old, who had been watching the hunt from the top of the boundary-fence, and was the only human witness of the struggle—rather a pretty, slender child, with an amazing quantity of bright red hair; she wore no cap or hat, and was out, so to speak, in her pinafore.

It was a raw December afternoon, and little Mary Foley, her bare arms wrapped in her bib, waited on the top of the big ditch with breathless interest to see which would win, man or horse; and if Master Ulick would get the better of the baste? Her curiosity and anxiety were equally kindled. All the country knew, to use a local expression, "that Master Ulick's riding bet all." But, on the other hand, the horse looked a real savage, and the poor young gentleman might be hurted or killed. Anyhow, the Gripe was a terrible big lep.

The Gripe was a huge, deep ditch at the taking-off side. The landing was on a big sound bank, the top of which was only a few feet above the level of the next field; it was a wide, but otherwise perfectly safe up-jump, and the brown horse had negotiated several others of the same description with ease; he could, and he would—and—he would *not.*

During his exertions Ulick became aware of a figure in a fluttering blue pinafore, who was the sole spectator—a little girl, with a pair of remarkably neat black legs, who capered about on the top of the bank at a safe and discreet distance. It was the Foley child; he recognised her carroty head; she was not in the way at all, but what was she waiting for? He hated to see her watching him; he wished to goodness she would go home—indeed, he would be thankful to go home himself. As a last desperate expedient, he struck spurs into the sulky colt, and sent him round the field full gallop; wheeled suddenly, and brought him down to the fence at a pace that was terrific. The horse was taken unawares. No time now for stopping or propping: it was a case of in, or over; his own impetus carried him sheer off his legs; he made a spring—landed on the bank——

The little girl's irrepressible yell of triumph died away on her lips when she beheld the hunter, after landing, stumble, lose his legs, and roll helplessly into the field, with his rider beneath him. At first she was too horrified to scream, or even stir. Surely to goodness they were both dead!

Presently the brown colt scrambled to his feet, shook himself, sniffed at his prostrate rider, then trotted off with high knee action, trailing reins, and proudly waving tail, as much as to say, "I think I got the best of *that*!"

Meanwhile, Ulick Doran lay in a motionless heap, precisely as if he were lifeless—in fact, as the child said to herself, "There was not a stir out of him! and what was to be done at all, at all?" Not a soul was likely to come near them; her father's cottage was four fields away, and he and her mother were out, it being market day, and there was not a creature within but the cat. She crept down from the bank, and cautiously approached the still form. Master Ulick was as white as a sheet; his eyes were closed, and from a deep cut in his forehead the blood was oozing. Mary Foley, an only child, was unusually sharp and self-confident for her age; her mother, a delicate woman, was given to "weak turns" and long faints, and on some of these occasions little Mary had tended her without assistance. Perhaps Master Ulick was only overcome with the same kind of strong weakness as her mother? She eyed him critically for a moment, then boldly filched his handkerchief from his pocket, and darted off to the Holy Well, which lay within a couple of hundred yards. Returning breathless, she dabbed his temples and forehead with ice-cold water; and still he never moved, but lay like a stone. Then she sat down on the grass and raised his head, and laid it on her small lap; and as she resumed her operations with the wet handkerchief, some salt tears became mingled with the water from St. Bridget's Well. In a short time she was weeping bitterly.

All at once Ulick Doran opened his eyes. Where was he? His head was reeling round, but he grasped that above him was a watery, wintry sky, beneath him the hard, damp earth, behind his head something small! What? He turned his glance upwards, and beheld a pair of streaming hazel eyes, and a mop of rough red hair. Was it a fairy? For a moment he lay motionless, and wondered; then, as his senses gradually returned to him, he recollected the child on the ditch. Yes, he had come a tremendous cropper! Was the horse killed? He struggled to a sitting posture. No, the brute was all right, grazing away in the corner of the field. The effort cost him agony, and he realised that he was badly hurt; his shoulder seemed twisted, and altogether he felt sick and faint, and as if he had been recently passed under a steam-roller.

"Holy Mary be praised! And ye are not killed all out, Mr. Ulick?" piped a small voice, and the child rose to her feet.

"No. Do I look like it?" he answered cheerily.

"And ye got the better of him after all!"

"I'm not so sure of that. Anyhow, he has the best of it *now*"; and his eyes wandered to the hunter, who was cropping grass along a headland with the zest of a gourmand.

"Are ye much hurted?" she asked. Generally, when her mother "came to," she was all right!

"My head feels a bit buzzy, and I believe I've put my shoulder out, and broken some bones."

"What's to be done?" she asked, wringing her little red hands. "What's to be done at all? Shall I run up to the Castle?"

"No, it's a good mile off, and I don't fancy sitting here; and besides, I don't want to frighten them." He was talking to this bare headed imp as if she were a grown-up woman. "If I could get on the horse—I know there's a lane hereabouts—I'd manage all right."

He made a violent effort and rose to his feet, but quickly collapsed again. "I can't walk, that's sure"; and he looked over at the brown colt.

"Shall I catch him for your honour?"

"You!" he repeated sarcastically. "What a chance you'd have!"

"Yes, faix, and I would," she rejoined stoutly.

"Are you not afraid?"

"Is it me! I'm afraid of no horse or man, or any sort of beast whatever. Wasn't it *me*, that bested Colgan's old savage sow! I'm not used to horses—but I'm fine and handy with cows."

"All right then, go and try your luck." And as young Doran sat on the ground endeavouring to stanch the blood which trickled into his eyes, he was amazed and amused at the manœuvres of the child in the blue pinafore. First she walked boldly forward, then she stood as if meaning nothing at all; next she stalked warily; finally she pounced almost imperceptibly on the reins, and before the big sixteen-hander could jerk back his head and snatch them and his liberty, she had him by the bit. Her very boldness and audacity astonished her captive as much as her captive's master. She soothed and patted the big, upstanding hunter, and he, being now full of grass, and also a little sobered and lamed by his recent fall, actually suffered himself to be led forward like the traditional lamb.

"Why, you are a regular horse-tamer!" cried Ulick, as she approached.

"I have a way with animals, they say," she replied; "they are tame enough with me."

"He has given himself a bad over-reach I see! Well, now little Foley, will you put your hand in my pocket—this one—and pull out a flask, and uncork it, as I've only one hand?"

She instantly did as requested, and with nimble, red fingers fished out a small silver flask.

"Whisky?" she suggested, as she unscrewed the stopper.

"No, sherry. I shall want some jumping powder to get on the fellow's back"; and he took a long draught. As he handed the flask to her to be replaced, he said, "Hullo! little Foley, what's this? You've been blubbering; there are two great dirty streaks down your cheeks! What were you crying for?"

"Well, then, Mr. Ulick," getting very red, "sure, didn't I think you were dead?"

"And so you were weeping over my remains? That was very kind of you, little Foley."

"And wouldn't any one cry after you, Master Ulick?" she demanded with an air of friendly wonder.

"Would they? Well I hope I shan't give them a chance for some years. Now, do you stand by his head, and I'll do my big best to get on his back."

Apparently the effort was not merely protracted, but agonising. When Mary looked up at the rider, she was startled at what she saw; his face seemed drawn and grey, like that of an old man; the skin looked clammy.

"Now run along"—he spoke between his shut teeth—"and try and break down the stone gap into the boreen."

This feat Mary accomplished without difficulty, and Ulick and his lame hunter passed through into the lane. All up the lane, they were closely attended by the child, who seemed to consider them both under her care. At last they reached a black wooden gate leading into the so-called demesne; as she opened it, she halted, and so did Ulick Doran.

"Well, little Foley, you are a queer little devil, and a real brick. I wish I'd something to give you, but I can't get at my pocket, as you know."

"Sure, I wouldn't take anything, thank your honour," she answered, with amusing hauteur, "not if it was gold itself."

He stared down hard into the serious, uplifted eyes, and asked—

"But are you not Pat Foley's girl; the one I see with the red head peeping through the gate at Foley's corner?"

"Yes, ye' honour, I am so."

"You have done a good job for me to-day: you know that I'd like to do something for you. What would you say to a nice big doll?"

"Is it a doll? No, no!" reddening, "nothing, nothing."

"Then I'm in your debt, and I hate to be in any one's debt. You've got my hat, I see; I can't put it on just now."

"No, sir, I'll take it up this evening; ye may be wanting it."

"Well, good-bye. I must try and get on home, before I fall off;" and as he gave the limping brown his head, the pair moved painfully away.

It was many a day before Ulick Doran wanted his hat. He had had a bad fall—broken his arm, and two of his ribs; it was a miracle how he had ever mounted his hunter and ridden home. The doctors agreed that he was a boy of incredible fortitude and resolution, and as a man, he would be bound to go far.

Ulick explained to his family the scene of the accident, and how Foley's little girl had come to his assistance.

"Only for her I suppose I might have lain there a week. She is a wonderful child, and has her head screwed on the right way. I daresay you know her?" he added, turning to his mother.

"Oh, yes, the little foxy thing," she rejoined indifferently.

"She's uncommonly plucky and handy," urged her son.

"I hope you did not praise her to her face! She is spoiled enough as it is," declared Mrs. Doran. "Being the only child Katty ever reared, they think the world does not hold her equal. Katty dresses her almost like a lady!—gets her shoes from Cork, and knits her long black stockings, just the same as the Rectory children wear. It's a sin to be giving the brat a taste for dress. For my part I think she is just a flighty, impudent little monkey, and whenever I come across her I take right good care to give her a setting down."

Little Mary often recalled the day of the hunt, and one event in her life. She had of course frequently related the incident to her mother and father, and even escorted them to the field, and shown them the very marks of the horse's hoofs on the bank, and explained how he fell, and where Mr. Ulick lay, as if stone dead.

"Faix, if it had been the other," muttered Pat to his wife, "he'd have been no great loss. But poor Mr. Ulick, thank God he was spared; he is the very spit of his father, the old Colonel."

As soon as he was convalescent, Ulick Doran joined the regiment to which he had been gazetted, and was not seen again at Kilmoran for some years.

CHAPTER IV

When Mary Foley was sixteen, she ceased to attend the local day school, being considered for her station a finished pupil. She wrote a good hand, was fairly well grounded in grammar and arithmetic, had acquired the Irish, and was an excellent needlewoman. Mary was no longer called "Foxy" or "Carrots," for she was bewitchingly pretty, and her clouds of auburn hair shaded a radiant face. She had also what was described as "a wonderful way with her" and an extraordinary fascination for most of the boys in the barony. John Foley had been dead for some years; his death was no pecuniary loss to his widow, who had him "well insured," but she gave up most of the land adjoining the farm, only keeping the house, garden, and the grass of a couple of cows, seeing there was, as she explained, "now but Mary and herself in it, and beasts were bothersome." To tell the truth, Mary was not particularly partial to farm labour; indeed, plain girls, her detractors, openly declared that "there was too much of the *lady* about Miss Foley"; but she did her share, as her fond parent bragged, if she was not over keen with regard to the wash-tub, or scouring. She was handy with her needle, and made quite a nice lot of money, sewing for Mrs. Hogan at the Glenveigh Arms. Also she looked after the fowls and eggs, the cows and calves. "Oh, she was," her mother declared, "a grand little girl for work." "Aye," agreed her enemies, "but it was all gentry's work. Who ever saw Mary on her knees scrubbing, or washing out the pots? Whilst as for pigs, she set her face entirely against them." She would neither be said nor led, and since poor Pat died, the stye was standing empty. Was ever the likes known?

There were two roads to the Castle from Foley's Corner; one lay across the fields, up the boreen, and through the iron gate—this was the fine-weather approach; the other, a long round by the high road, and imposing principal entrance.

One bright September afternoon Mary was returning from Kilmoran, swinging her empty egg-basket, when in the lane she descried a handsome young gentleman in a grey tweed suit and cap, and immediately recognised Mr. Ulick. This was no great feat; she had heard up above that "the Captain" had arrived home now for a good spell, and was a really splendid-looking young officer. But Mr. Doran lacked Mary's advantages; he had not the slightest suspicion of the identity of this pretty slim girl, in a well-fitting blue cotton dress, who was gradually approaching him from the demesne. He could not even place her. She was not the usual country type; her bones were small, her carriage erect, assured, graceful; and there was a finish about her dress that was unusual. He noticed the little bit of lace at the neck, the trim belt. However, she wore no hat, and was undoubtedly a peasant. As this girl was about to pass him, she dropped a hurried curtsey, and glanced at him timidly, with a pair of bewildering hazel eyes. Surely he had met those eyes somewhere? A sudden gleam of memory flashed into Ulick's brain. He halted and exclaimed—

"Is it possible that you are Mary Foley?"

"Yes, your honour." Another curtsey, and it was difficult to ignore her girlish flutter, her evident joy at seeing him again.

"I declare I scarcely recognised you. How you have grown!"

"Children mostly do," she rejoined with composure.

"I suppose you consider yourself grown up?"

"Yes, sir, I have left the schoolin'."

"And so your education is complete?"

"I would not say that, but," shifting her basket to her other arm, "I learnt all they taught, so I did."

"Reading, writing, arithmetic. The three R's."

"Yes, and grammar, history, and geography. I loved geography."

"Well, it is a harmless passion. Can you tell me where Malta is?"

"Faix, unless it's lost, sir, it should be in the Mediterranean Sea."

"Oh, I see you cannot be puzzled, can you?"

"Oh, then indeed I can, and am, often and many a time."

"Tell me what puzzles you."

"No, sir, I really couldn't make so free"; and she moved a step, as if to pass on.

Two long hours lay between him and dinner. Young Doran had nothing particular to do; his mother was irritable and continually scolding some one. It was rather pleasant, standing in this fragrant lane, talking to this pretty, shy, yet audacious colleen.

"You have been up at the Castle, I presume?" he continued.

"Yes, your honour, selling eggs to her ladyship."

"I hope you make a good thing out of it?"

"Well," a pause, "I just bid to take what her ladyship gives me—sixpence the dozen, and young chickens a shilling a couple."

"A shilling—a—a—couple!" he repeated; and he felt his face becoming warm.

"Well, of course I could get more in the market, or even from the hawkers," she continued, "but ye see we live on the land, and her ladyship has the first call, and—and—anyhow, though the price is not much, the Castle is convenient-like."

"Do you remember the last time I saw you?" inquired her ladyship's shamefaced son, "and the cropper I came, over in that field?" and he pointed in the direction.

"Aye, to be sure I do, sir! What would ail me that I'd forget it? Sure, weren't you nearly killed dead?"

"Nearly, I suppose. I have not forgotten what you did for me that day."

"Sure it was nothing, sir, I'd do as much for ye again."

"I hope you never may have the chance! You were a kind, active little helper. How you did run about, and how you mothered me! I've owed you a debt ever since; I'd like to give you a souvenir of some sort even now—better late than never."

"Thank your honour, but I have one already, and one is all I want."

"What may it be? Not my hat—you brought that after me!"

"No, I've no call for hats. 'Twas the horse's shoe I found, an elegant, bright new shoe; it was lying on the grass on the other side of the ditch. I have it nailed up, ever since, for luck."

"Has it brought you any?"

"Well, then, I can't say much for it so far, yer honour."

"It may do great things yet."

"Well, God send it. And now, if your honour pleases, I must be going on. I'm late as it is——"

"Why, where is your hurry?"

"Sure, hasn't the cows to be milked, and the calf fed?"

"I wish I could help you—for I'm out of a job to-day."

Mary suddenly broke into laughter and displayed a row of pretty little teeth. "You'd make a poor hand of the milking, I'm thinking," she said.

"Anyway, I'll walk back with you as far as the stone gap, if I may?"

"Sure, the boreen is your honour's own land, and what's to hinder you?"

"Old Crock na Bowl looks well this evening," suddenly remarked the young fellow, as they turned and faced a towering purple peak, on which lay the long afternoon shadows.

"Oh, he's there right enough," said Mary, with indifference.

"Now you'd like to see another mountain for a change?"

"Bedad, I would so. I'm always craving to visit the grand places I read about. It's your honour that has been round the world, and in fine countries, and foreign parts."

"Only in Spain and Malta so far; but we are going to India the next reliefs. Ah, here is the stone gap you once pulled down for me. Allow me to help you over——"

"Is it, help *me*?" and she laughed derisively. "Why there is not a wall or gap in the country to stop me."

"At least I may hold the basket?"

"No, no, sir," and she smiled, and stood irresolute, wondering how she was to bid farewell to the young master. Should she curtsey? or would she just take herself off anyhow?

"Before you go, Mary Foley, you might tell me at least one of the things that puzzles you. I've nothing to do. Maybe I can guess the riddle! I'm rather good at that sort of thing."

"Well, then, I just will, sir, since ye have axed me twice. There's a matter that sticks in my mind, and I cannot get shut of it."

"Yes, let us have it by all means."

"Can you tell me," and she paused, and looked at him steadily, "why some have every mortal blessed thing, and others—have nothing at all?"

"But how do you mean?" he asked, rather taken aback. This description of puzzle was far from what he had anticipated.

"Why look at Miss Cunninghams, and look at me!"

"Yes"; and he looked at her.

"They are ladies born, and live in a park, and wear beautiful dresses, and ride fine hunters, and eat with silver forks; they go away and see the world, with plenty of money in their pockets. And for me, I live in a little weenchie cottage, and work hard, and I will never lay an eye on any sight better than Crock na Bowl, or do anything but cook, and milk, as long as the breath is in me! And I'd just love to *see* life. Why were they born one way, and me another?"

"I'm sure I don't know," he replied.

"Well, ye see, I've asked ye my riddle, and ye cannot answer it," she said with a smile, "so now I'll be going"; and without another word, Mary Foley clambered lightly over the stone gap (she still wore black stockings, and had remarkably neat ankles), and presently disappeared.

CHAPTER V

And thus the young couple parted, going in opposite directions, each carrying in their thoughts a poignant memory of the other. Since Mary was a small child, "Master Ulick" had been secretly worshipped as her hero—the natural consequence of hearing on all sides praises of his feats of horsemanship, his courage, and his generosity. Little pitchers have long ears, and what they imbibe they remember. For a girl of her age, and class, Mary Foley was a widely-read young person. Mrs. Hogan at "The Arms" had a fancy for the child, and, knowing she was crazy after books, endowed her with various odds and ends that careless visitors or fishing folk, had left behind them. Mary had a wonderful imagination, and from the germs of her favourite characters, she composed a Paladin of her own. He was the embodiment of the Heir of Redcliff, Wilfred of Ivanhoe, the Black Knight, and Charles O'Malley, and his name she never whispered, but all the same it was some one resembling Master Ulick, whom she crowned with a choice selection of other men's laurels. It therefore will be seen that if Mary's little sixteen-year-old heart was free, it was not fancy free!

As soon as Mary reached home and opened the half-door, her mother cried out—

"Mary asthore! What in the living world kep' ye?"

"Sure I am afther meeting Masther Ulick," was the breathless reply. "There beyant, in the boreen."

"Did ye, agra; and what is he like now he's a grown man?"

"Faix I couldn't rightly explain, only he is tallish and upstanding, and I got a smell of tobacco off him!"

"Great fathers, child!"

"Yes; an' he has a small moustache on his upper lip, and a great big smile on him, and grey eyes—his eyes"—and she drew in her breath—"is real beautiful!"

"His eyes! God help us, Mary! that's the queer sort of chat for a slip of a girl. Sure ye have no call to be looking at the young gentleman's eyes."

"An' how can I help it, mammy, when I've eyes of me own! He is not a bit like her ladyship—no, nor Barky, with the great roasted face on him."

"God be thanked for that same," exclaimed Mrs. Foley piously. "He is the Colonel's own boy; but, Mary asthore, ye must know yer place, and not be making free, or be talking to the young Captain. Ye have such funny, queer ways of spaking up to high and low—I tell ye, sometimes ye have me paralysed with fright."

"Oh, make yer mind easy, mammy; I know me place. Augh! do ye hear the bawls of the calf? I must hurry up with the milking."

After her mother's word of warning, Mary Foley merely dropped a hasty curtsey when she encountered the Captain, and then hurried on; and he, manlike, was attracted by this avoidance; the less he saw of Mary, the more he thought of her. The unknown has a wonderful fascination.

Ulick was at present an idler. Cub-hunting had not yet commenced; his home was not particularly congenial. He and Barky had nothing in common; Barky was frankly jealous of his brother's smart soldier-like air, his knowledge of the world, his manner of speech, his well-cut clothes, and his popularity. Ulick contented himself with schooling young horses, reading, smoking, and making friends with the dogs, whom he overjoyed by taking out for many a long tramp.

One afternoon it came on to drizzle as he was approaching Foley's corner. He turned up his collar and pulled out his pipe. Alas! he had not a match left: there was nothing for it but to run into Katty's and ask for a sod of turf. He pushed open the half-door and entered, and found Katty, with horn spectacles on nose, hunched up by the window, patching an old sack.

"I just came in for a light, Katty," he explained. "I hope you won't mind the dogs," as two setters and a terrier followed him.

"Yer honour is welcome, and as many dogs as he likes."

"There are two more sitting outside, but these have no manners; I hope I see you well, Katty."

"Well, then, indeed I'm no great shakes, sir, and only among the middins; I'm gettin' into years, ye see."

"What nonsense!" stooping to pick up a live sod. "You can't be more than fifty, if you are that."

"I am fifty-seven, sir, and it's a long age for a working woman; still," and she sighed, "but God is good, and the devil himself not too bad entirely. And Mary is a grand help—and here she comes."

As the inner door opened, Mary, followed by the dogs with better manners, entered with a tin can on her arm.

"Now go out, every one of you!" shouted their master, authoritatively. "Good evening, Mary."

"Good evening, sir," she answered. "Sure, the poor dogs is doing no harm whatever. Me mother loves a dog, and so do I. 'Tis only the cat that's so particular."

"And there she is, on the top of the dresser, out of harm's way. I was sorry for poor John," he said, addressing himself to Katty; "you must miss him."

"In troth and I do, at every turn—a sore loss, both outside and in. Mary and me is not aqual to more than a couple of cows, and a few hens, and the potatoes."

"And who does the digging?" inquired the younger master, who stood with his back to the fire, for all the world as if he were at home—the dogs with manners lying near the door.

"Well, to tell yer honour no lie, Patsie Maguire does the heavy part. When his work is over, he comes and puts in an hour."

"I know Patsie Maguire—a smart, likely-looking lad"—here he addressed himself to Mary, who stood leaning carelessly against the dresser. "And what does he dig for, Mary—love, or money?"

"Oh, sir!" cried the girl, "now I declare to goodness ye make me laugh! For neither—but just his kindness."

"Mary is terribly clever with flowers," put in her mother irrelevantly. "'Tis she has the lucky hand; and as for eggs, hasn't the hens been laying the whole winter, and them mother naked, and not a feather on them. Winter does be awful lonesome for us now; not a living soul within half a mile. Sometimes, when I think of robbers and house-breakers, I am all of a tremble, and never close an eye."

"You ought to keep a dog," suggested the visitor; "he'd be company."

"He would so," agreed Mary. "I'd love to have one."

"Would you like this fellow?" asked Ulick, indicating a red terrier who had made his way to the fire; "he is only a pup, but he will grow!"

"Oh, sir! oh, yer honour! sure we would not expect the likes of him," protested Mrs. Foley. "Maybe Boland up at the Chapel has a pup he can spare."

"No, no, mother," broke in Mary, "I just hate that breed of Boland's—they are so long and black and deceiving, and, anyhow, are only good for poaching. They are quiet enough on a weekday, but all over the county of a Sunday. Oh——," and she paused, "Oh faix, I was forgetting Mr. Ulick!" and she laughed, and coloured vividly.

"I'm glad to hear you don't like poachers, Mary. This little chap here"—and he held him up—"kills rats already, and will keep off tramps. He is a gentleman."

"Sure," began Katty, with a wheezy laugh, "what would a gentleman be doing with the likes of us?"

"He will like you, and I know you will like him. See, Pap"—and he led him over to Mary—"this is your new mistress; and here is another"; and he pulled him towards Katty, who, however, held back, saying—

"Oh, sir, it's too great a condescension for us; entirely too much!"

"What do you say to him, Mary?" turning to her.

"If when you'll be going away ye would spare him sir, it would be a kindness and a consolation, for me mother is very wake in herself, and in dread of a night if she hears a sound, even of a mouse, let alone one of the cows stirring in the byre; she thinks it's some one coming to murder us, so she does. The little dog will be a grand watch, though of course he is above our station."

"Is any one within?" The voice came from the half-door, and the open space above was amply filled by a stout, elderly woman, wearing a jetted bonnet, a black front, and a blue waterproof.

"There is to be sure," replied Mary, who liked visitors, darting to the door. "There's no fear of the dogs, ma'am. I see it's spilling rain. Come in if ye plase and take a sate."

The tall, burly figure stalked forward, and shook out her wet umbrella; she stared very hard—first at Katty, then at Ulick—and sank heavily into the proffered chair.

"I am stopping at an hotel below," she began, with a strong American accent, "and I've lost my way. I am a pretty smart walker. Am I far out?"

"About a mile and a half," replied Mary. "It's the other side of the Castle-gates—ye know, the place with the two dogs. This is Mr. Ulick Doran, of Kilmoran Castle."

The woman looked up at him quickly, and said: "I'm in luck to chance on you, sir. I know your aunt, Mrs. Grogan, in Philadelphia; she lives not far from me, and is real well-to-do."

"There! to think of that now!" ejaculated Katty. "Oh, but Miss Nora was the splendid fine girl, and the grand horse-lady—and how is she, at all?"

"Not much of a horse-lady now, but she keeps her carriage."

"I am glad to meet any one who knows my father's sister," said Ulick. "Is there any chance of her coming over?"

"Well, not just at present; she heard I was to be a day or so in these parts—my people being buried hereabouts, you see—and I told her I'd go up and see the Castle, and bring her news right away; and she said she believed I'd be made welcome."

"And she was quite right, ma'am," replied Ulick. "I know my mother will be delighted to see you; will you come up with me now?"

"No, thank you, I'll wait till to-morrow; I'm all wet and muddy, and not just fit for Castle company, thanking you all the same."

The eagerness of Mrs. Doran to welcome the emissary of her sister-in-law requires some explanation. News had come, in the curious way in which it filters through other people's letters, that Tom Grogan was doing right well for himself in America. After a pause, there was whispered the magic word of "*wealth.*" When Colonel Doran died, his sister had written to his widow, a timid epistle, full of heartfelt condolence; this had received a most gracious answer, and a correspondence ensued. Mrs. Doran was always good at her pen; she wrote volumes respecting her want of capital, and the extraordinary attractions of her oldest son; the younger she rarely mentioned.

Mrs. Grogan despatched American apples, candies, beautiful books, and furs—undeniably money's worth; but no money. However, her sister-in-law built largely on Barky's expectations from his aunt Nora, and talked a good deal about the Colonel's sister, who was the wife of a millionaire; not a word of the mésalliance, much less of the postman!

"Then since you won't come with me," said young Doran, "I must be off. I'll let my mother know you are at the 'Glenveigh Arms,' and no doubt she will write to you. Good evening, everybody"; and he opened the half-door, and departed with his train of dogs.

"He is after offering us a pup," said Katty, with complacency; "we are so lonesome here, since I buried me poor husband."

"I know the names of the folk around from Mrs. Grogan," said the visitor; "she has the place still at her finger-ends."

"My name is Katty Foley, ma'am. I sure she will mind *me* well; we were the wan age, and she and I had some fine jokes, together; to tell the truth, I was a bit of a go-between. Well that's all past now. If the old gentleman had known, he'd have had me life! Aye, but he was the proud man. This girlie here is my daughter Mary, the only child I reared out of five, and all I have in the world, except a sister above at the junction!"

"Oh, indeed. Mr. Ulick seems a fine young man," remarked the stranger.

"That's true for ye, ma'am, as good as he looks, and the flower of the flock, the very twin of his father, the Colonel, so kind, and so feeling for the poor. Just a real decent clean-living boy!"

"That's fine news, Mrs. Foley; and what about the other?"

"Oh, bedad, ma'am, I'd like well to say a good word for him too, if I could; but silence is best."

"What ails him?" she asked peremptorily.

"Sure the mother has him ruinated since he could walk. He is just an eyesore to the township, and a scandal"; and Katty shook her head till the horn spectacles fell into her lap. "Av course, he is young, and may mend, but all I can tell you is, that if I see him coming into heaven, I'll say, thank God!"

The stranger did not pause to question Mrs. Foley's confidence in her own future state, but inquired, in a nasal key, "But what does he do, anyhow, my good woman?"

"Everything he ought to leave alone, ma'am. He is fond of low company, and cock-fighting, and betting, and all sorts of devilment. He gets in at night by the pantry window, and his mother thinks he is an archangel."

"It's a way mothers have. Poor woman!"

"Poor, is it! Faix, she's a real rich woman, and small blame, and has the place in tip-top style, and keeps terrible state; but her servants is just starved."

"Oh, mammy!" remonstrated Mary, "ye shouldn't be talking so free to strangers."

"A friend of Miss Nora's is no stranger to *me*, and since she wants news, I bid to give her the truth. I know I'm crabbed, but I was reared on the Dorans' land, and I'd put me hands under the Colonel's feet. Sure, all the world knows the bad wife he had, and how she scolded him, and shamed him, and sold the buttermilk, and sent the old servants to the poorhouse! Well, well, I'll say no more, I'll say no more. Don't mind me, ma'am. Mrs. Doran will be very sweet to *you*, and I'm only a bitter old woman. Oh, I wish ye could have seen the poor Colonel!—such a lovely, fine, tall gentleman, with a beautiful face, as if it was carved. Him and Miss Nora was always very thick!"

"Yes, so I've been told," said the stranger.

"And Tom? Tom Grogan—an' how is he? He was a fine, fresh-looking boy, and me own second cousin. Faix, if I was to say that to Mrs. Doran, she'd burn the house over me head."

"Mr. Grogan is well," replied the visitor; "a little stiff in the joints now; but he is a rich man, and rides in his carriage."

"Great fathers! to think of that now. Faix, 'tis no wonder as all the Grogans have gone afther him to America! And Miss Nora was the darlin' girl. Is she changed?"

"Yes. Who would not be in thirty years? She is grey and wrinkled, but I think her heart is young still. And now I see the rain has stopped, and I must be going."

"But won't ye condescend to a cup of tea, ma'am? Mary will wet it in a brace of shakes. It's good tay—Lynche's—and has a fine grip of the water. I'd like ye to tell Miss Nora ye had a cup of tay with old Katty. She will remember Katty, I'll go bail."

"I really must be moving, thank you—I'll maybe look in again; but if your gal here will set me on my road, I'll be obliged to her."

"To be sure, ma'am, with a heart and a half," said Mary, as she took a shawl and threw it over her head, and then led the way down the path to the gate, and into the main road.

Mary and her guide had a most interesting talk, so much so that they scarcely felt the time passing—the American putting clever questions to the girl, the girl, ever greedy of information, eagerly cross-examining her companion respecting "the sort of life over there"; and they were mutually astonished when they found themselves at the entrance of the "Glenveigh Arms."

Ulick Doran had lost no time in preparing his mother for a visit from his aunt's emissary; but Ulick's friends, or discoveries, were rarely appreciated at Kilmoran. Mrs. Doran was proud of her youngest son's good looks, good manners, and his horsemanship, precisely as she would be proud of a valuable piece of furniture which belonged to her exclusively. But the boy was too like his father; he reminded her at every look and turn of her life's—well, she would not go so far as to call it remorse; but at any rate, she was not fond of Ulick. Her share of maternal affection was expended on Barker, and she was ashamed to admit to herself, that her indifference to her second son almost amounted to dislike. However, he was home now for six months' leave, and she must just make the best of him.

"A woman who says she knows your aunt Nora," she exclaimed, as she set down her glass of cheap sherry. "That is strange. And coming to see *me*. How did you come across her?"

"At Foley's, at the corner."

"And may I ask what were you doing in there?"

"I just went in to light my pipe."

"So that's what he *calls* it, eh, mater?" broke in Barky, with a knowing chuckle. "Mary Foley is the prettiest girl in the whole side of the country, and the cockiest, most impudent little devil I ever came across. So *that's* your taste, is it, my boy!"

Ulick flung his brother an indignant glance, and went on. "The woman was there sheltering, and asking her way."

"What sort of a person is she?" inquired Mrs. Doran.

"It is not easy to describe her."

"No; it's easier to describe little Mary, with her red poll," interrupted Barky facetiously.

"But," resumed the narrator, "she is stout and elderly, talks with a strong American accent, and looks like a prosperous housekeeper."

"I suppose she has a letter of introduction from your aunt?"

"She did not say, and I did not ask her."

"No, so *like* you! But I shall ask her," announced Mrs. Doran, with an air of stern decision.

Mrs. Aron, as she was called, did not appear at the Castle for nearly a week. She had caught a wetting, and a cold, and remained at "The Arms" under the ministrations of Mrs. Hogan, imbibing gruel and a wonderful assortment of local gossip. At last, one afternoon, she presented herself at Kilmoran, but at an unfortunate moment: Mrs. Doran was in a bad temper; the cook and two other servants had given notice. Also she was momentarily expecting Lady Borrisokane, and various notables to tea. She sat enthroned in an arm-chair, pretending to read, clad in her best black satin. (Her toilettes now were rich satin, or silk for best, her everyday garment a black serge, with velveteen sleeves, which had long seen its best years.)

Suddenly the man-servant flung open the door, and announced "Mrs. Aron," and a tall, self-possessed, elderly woman stalked in.

Mrs. Doran sat still and stared; she never uttered a word, and looked really formidable, for she had been composing the character she was about to give her cook.

"I am speaking to Mrs. Doran, I believe," began the stranger.

Mrs. Doran nodded shortly; her expression was distinctly grim.

"I am a great friend of Mrs. Grogan—Miss Doran that was; she lives near me in Philadelphia, and as I was coming home to these parts she asked me to step in and see you, and bring her your news."

"Oh, indeed," drily. "I presume she sent a letter to introduce you?"

"No, ma'am, she did not."

"That was strange!"

"I don't believe she ever gave it a thought, nor that it would be expected or asked for."

"Why not? I might have half America giving me a call!"

"I'm sure I don't see *why* they should?" rejoined Mrs. Aron brusquely. "However, Mrs. Grogan, she told me that you'd be right glad to see me! In short, she said that most likely, for her sake, you'd give me house-room for a week or so." After a short pause she added, "My box is at the ho-tell."

"I'm positively certain Nora never said anything of the sort," burst out Mrs. Doran. "I prefer to invite my own guests. Surely you are not in her class of life?" looking her slowly up and down.

Mrs. Aron's clothes were cheap, and a little shabby: a long blue waterproof, a mock fur tie, black thread gloves, and a bonnet that had suffered from the weather.

"Yes I am, and just in her own class," she answered sharply.

"But Mrs. Grogan is a wealthy woman."

"Oh, is she?"

"I expect you were her—servant, were you not? Come now, tell me the truth."

Mrs. Aron, who had been standing all the time, looked about her—and coolly took a seat.

"Were you her servant?" repeated Mrs. Doran.

"Well, I won't deny that I *have* cooked for her; yes, and for Mr. Grogan, too; but it was many years ago."

"And you dare pretend to me that she told you to come here on a visit? My good woman, you are a humbug! Don't tell me that Nora Grogan associates with her servants; she is a Doran, and has the Doran pride in her blood—although she did disgrace herself. And you are an impostor."

"No, ma'am, I really am not: I am a respectable woman. Mrs. Grogan would tell you so——"

"But she has *not* told me so!" interrupted Mrs. Doran angrily. The Countess and party might enter at any moment and find her *tête-à-tête* with this person, who would probably disclose all manner of tales of Nora, and her husband, and disinter a buried and forgotten scandal!

"Mrs. Grogan told me a great deal about this beautiful place and her own country," continued the intruder, in a meeker key. "I seem to know it as well as if I had seen it before. I expect she would see wonderful changes——"

"No doubt," agreed Mrs. Doran, rising. Then she added with savage insolence: "Now I must really ask you to go. I am expecting friends. I firmly believe you are a fraud. There are too many frauds going"; and she rang the bell with energy.

"I'm not that, indeed!" protested Mrs. Aron, tremulously, also rising to her feet, "but I am in want—that is to say, I'd be thankful if you could spare me a little assistance to pay my way to Queenstown."

"Well, you will not get it here," replied Mrs. Doran with biting emphasis. "I've suspected what you wanted all along—money. You are a begging impostor. Thomson!"—to her man-servant—"show this person out, and do not admit her again on any consideration."

"And so, is this what I'm to tell your sister?" cried the American, suddenly confronting her hostess, "that you turned me out of the house!"

"You may, for all I care—I don't believe for a moment that you know her!"

"If I don't"—a pause, during which she seemed to struggle for an expression—"I know you—and well—for a hard, avaricious, cruel woman, that grinds the poor, and that drove your husband into his grave."

"There, that's enough!" interrupted Mrs. Doran, whose face had assumed the colour of beetroot. "Another word and I send for the police, you abusive old vagabond!"

A clang at the hall door announced the Countess, and Mrs. Aron was hurried into the hall. Thus the coming and the parting guest came face to face. The parting guest walked slowly down the avenue, every now and then pausing to look back. As she stood for a last glance, she was overtaken by Ulick Doran on a prancing bay filly.

"Hullo!" he said, "what's the matter?" He noticed that she had been crying. "Have you been up to see my mother?"

"Say!" she said in a choked voice, "I don't feel like talking to—to any one just now—" and she moved on, evidently struggling with some overpowering emotion.

"Oh, now," suddenly dismounting, "I'm not going to let you off like this! Won't you tell me what is the trouble? Come now."

"Well, your mother told me I was just an impostor and a fraud, and turned me out. Your aunt had certainly forgotten her people, for she assured me I'd have a warm welcome, and be asked to stay."

"My mother is a bit hasty sometimes," he murmured, "and as to visitors—she is dreadfully worried with servants; she never even asks over her own relations."

"Do you believe I'm telling truth or lies," demanded Mrs. Aron suddenly.

"The truth. Yes I do! I think you have it in your face. And it was kind of you to come and look us up. I'd like to know my aunt Nora. Mind you give her my love."

"Yes, I will. She has not many to love her."

"Why so?"

"Because she is so rich; now"—and she hesitated. "I am myself a bit pressed for money for the price of my hotel bill and a second-class ticket to Queenstown." She paused, and looked at him interrogatively, "and—you see for yourself I've no friends here!"

The young man reddened as he answered—

"I'm not to say flush just now, but I think I can scrape up ten pounds."

"That will be as much as I shall want; and you shall have it back on my word of honour. I suppose you have not got it about you?"

"No, but I will send or bring it over myself this evening."

"Is this your brother?" she inquired—"the stout young man with the gun coming in at the gate."

"Yes, my brother Barker—he has been out after hares."

"Hullo, Ulick!" he began, as he came within earshot. "I say, who is your lady friend?"

"Mrs. Aron, a friend of Mrs. Grogan in America—our aunt, you know."

"No, I don't know her, thank goodness, and don't want to. A lady who disgraced the family, and made a scandal and went off with a blackguard postman!"

"He was not a blackguard, sir," she broke in indignantly, "and he was the son of a respectable farmer. By all accounts, she was kept very strict, and had no young society of her own class."

"She doesn't seem to be keeping much society *now*, if you are a specimen of her acquaintances," scoffed Barky, with deliberate insolence, as he stared at her weather-beaten waterproof and old-fashioned bonnet. "*I* was always against my mother making it up with her, and you may tell her that if you like—from me. As to her money, I'll believe it when I see it! America is a queer sort of place!"

"Is it? And yet, by all accounts, some one sent off a girl there last month who was a *real* disgrace to her family."

Barky became crimson as she looked him steadily in the face, and added, "I see you are your mother's own son!"

"Well, so I have been given to understand."

"And she has a right to be proud of you!"

"I am glad you think so"; and Mr. Barker Doran turned on his heel and stalked away, carrying with him all the eclat which is supposed to be conferred by the last word.

CHAPTER VI

The conversation between his brother and Mrs. Aron was not overheard by Ulick. As the nervous young mare was cold and impatient, he had hastily mounted, and ridden away through the demesne. After an hour's exercise he returned home, hurried up to his room, hunted out his money, and, taking what was called "the dairy pony," galloped off to "The Arms." He told himself that he could just do it, and be back in time for dinner at eight o'clock, for Mrs. Doran kept fashionable hours. Fashionable hours cost nothing; a chop at six is the same price as a chop two hours later.

When Ulick arrived at "The Arms," a comfortable family hotel, the resort of tourists in search of fishing and scenery—the fishing a fiction, the scenery a delightful fact—he went to the bar and asked for Mrs. Aron. The landlady replied in person.

"Sure she is upstairs, after packing, and a bit tired, sir. If you will come along with me I will let her know"; and Mrs. Hogan conducted him into the best sitting-room.

In a few minutes Mrs. Aron entered, still wearing her bonnet and cloak.

"So you have brought it, I suppose?" she began abruptly.

"Yes. I'm awfully sorry: it's only nine pounds after all."

"Oh, I'll make it do, and I am ever so much obliged to you; you'll be no loser by me," she added with emphasis.

"I am sorry my people were—were—a bit rough, and I hope you won't tell my aunt more than you can possibly help. I know my mother has been bothered lately with several things, and I daresay my aunt would be vexed if she heard that she had not——well, you know what I mean: ignorance is bliss."

"Young man, you never said a truer word!" declared Mrs. Aron, with unexpected emphasis. As she spoke she rose and walked over to the glass above the chimney-piece, leaving the money on the table. Ulick sat for a moment buried in thought; then he turned about to look for his cap. It was on the floor. He stooped for it, and when he raised his head Mrs. Aron had disappeared. In her place stood a tall, rather elegant woman with a slight figure and quantities of grey hair.

Ulick Doran started to his feet, and stared at the lady in stupefied silence. The stranger was the first to speak.

"Come here and give me a kiss, Ulick; I am your aunt Nora."

"But why—and where?" he stammered, and held back.

"Oh, ever so many whys! As to where? Here is Mrs. Aron—my own name backwards;" and she lifted the wadded cloak from the sofa, then held up the bonnet and front. "It was a capital disguise, was it not?"

"Surely quite unnecessary—and why?"

"That is the second time you have asked *why*? Sit down there, and you shall hear all there is to it. I wished to see your mother, your brother, and yourself—what you called 'unknownst'—and find out what you were like."

"And, by Jove, you have been most unfortunately successful!"

"Not altogether unfortunate——"

"But I don't think it was fair, Aunt Nora," he protested; "I don't think it was playing the game!"

"Well, there we differ. I am a rich woman. Tom agreed that our money is to go to the Dorans, my brother's children, and I naturally wanted to discover what sort of people the Dorans were? As a girl, I was wild, and fond of fun and dancing; but my father, who was a very stern old man, kept me all but locked up. He had forgotten his own youth, poor man, and even his middle age. He married, you know, late in life. I was full of spirits, and daring, and once I got out and dressed up in Katty Foley's clothes and went to a wake as her cousin, a strange young woman from Dublin. I was glad to see Katty. That's a nice bright girl of hers; she has some notions, and is real well-looking. Well, to go on with my story, I had a great success. I could take off the brogue to the life, and at the wake I met Tom, and that was the beginning of the end."

"But did you never go out at all, in your own rank of life—meet people?"

"Never, except to church, and now and then after the hounds. The only pleasure I had at all, was through your father, and you see he went to India. Tom Grogan was handsome and steady, and well enough educated. He had a place offered him in the States. I was just crazy to see the world. I loved Tom, and I ran away with him, and never regretted it, which is more than some can say. He has always been just lovely to me. We have worked hard and done well, and out there we are as good as any—being respectable, self-respecting, and real rich. I often longed to come over and see the old place, but I was ashamed to face people and the *talk*. However, then Tom had a sudden call to London, and I came with him—almost at a moment's notice. The idea was his to start with: I got a hustle on, and felt I'd just got to do it, and that was all there was to it, and fixed myself up as you see, a week and more ago; and then I was laid up with a real bad cold. Mrs. Hogan herself nursed me. *She* knows—she actually knew me when the bonnet was off. But she can keep my secret, and she will. Of course, my dear boy, I'm not going to take your money. I was only trying and testing you, like an old witch in a fairy tale. I'm real glad I met you in the avenue this evening, for to tell you the truth I felt so discouraged I was going right away, never wishing to see a Doran again."

"I don't know what my mother will say, and Barky, when I tell them," said Ulick, after a pause.

"That is immaterial, Ulick. I wish you would come over to Queenstown with me to-morrow, and meet Tom; he would be real glad to know you."

Ulick shook his head.

"Thank you, Aunt Nora, but I could not get away now. I've ever so many young hunters on hand. Duffy is sick."

"Why, it sounds like old times to hear his name! Do you know that we once had a boy called Ulick; he was killed in a lift accident when he was eleven years of age, and now we have no one belonging to us whatever."

"I'm awfully sorry for you, Aunt Nora, and for your disappointment here. I am not much good at talking, but——"

"But better at doing."

"And I had better be going."

"No, no; here is Mrs. Hogan with the tray. You will just stay and keep your aunt Nora company, and let us get to know one another a bit, my dear boy."

So Ulick was persuaded, and he and his aunt made friends; he was so like her dear brother, not only in appearance, but ways, that she almost felt that it was she and the Ulick of her young days, once more *tête-à-tête*, and it was an easy matter to take his boy into her heart. The poor fellow, she knew, had a scanty allowance, and yet he had brought his little all, to his aunt's old begging friend; she secretly resolved that that kindly meant loan, should be repaid by a great fortune. Mrs. Grogan drew the lad out about his regiment, his comrades, his plans, and tastes. She made him promise to write her long letters, to keep her well posted in his affairs, and ultimately to go over, and visit them. At ten o'clock she rose, and said—

"Now I must turn you out, for I've an early start to-morrow."

"You won't think too badly of my mother and Barky, will you?" he pleaded.

"My dear, I am not going to think of *them*, one mite! At first I felt mad: now I'm as cool as a cucumber. *You* are enough for me. You may tell them it's no matter, and they have got no need to worry. Now, good-bye, my dear Ulick, and bless you. Keep a corner in your heart for your old American auntie"; and she kissed him affectionately on both cheeks.

Two or three minutes later the patient dairy pony was on his way home. It was considerably after ten o'clock when Ulick entered the dining-room and found his mother and Barky still sitting there. (For one thing it economised candle-light, and for another, Barky could smoke to his heart's content.)

"Ulick, this is a pretty hour for you to be coming home!" began his mother, in a high, excited key, "and you never told me you were dining out. I suppose these are military manners? Where have you been, pray?"

"At 'The Arms.' I've had my dinner. I did not intend to stay, and I had no way of letting you know. I am sorry you waited."

"Oh, oh! I expect you were hob-nobbing with some *lady*, if the truth were known, you sly fox," cried Barky.

"Well, yes, you've made a good shot. I was dining with a lady. Now for it," said Ulick to himself.

"I know! The old bag-woman! Ha, ha, ha!"

"Yes. And the old bag-woman turns out to be—who do you think? Our aunt Nora herself!"

"Ah, man alive, you're drunk," shouted Barky, pushing back his chair.

"Not I. I met her in the avenue this afternoon. I went down with a small loan I promised her, and after I got there, and saw her, she suddenly slipped off bonnet, wig, and cloak, and turned into a handsome, well-dressed, elderly lady!"

Mrs. Doran, for once in her life, was too horrified to speak; her feelings were beyond the power of expression. Words failed her, and she simply sat glaring at her youngest son, as if he were some horrible monster.

"She said she had long wished to come home and see us all, and what we were like?" he resumed, "but could not face the situation. At last, as her husband was over on business, she accompanied him, and explored about here, as you saw."

"Good-bye to her money!" roared Barky. "Mother, you've done me out of a million dollars, if all you told me that you said to her is true!"

Mrs. Doran's face had become mottled with red patches.

"Just what comes of associating with low company. A *lady* would never have played us such a trick," she said, when she had at last found her voice. "Is she going away early to-morrow?"

"Yes, to Queenstown, to catch the American boat."

"Then I'll write a line at once"—rising as she spoke.

"Mother," protested Barky, "*don't.*"

"Yes, I certainly will. I'll apologise, and explain. After all, she has only herself to thank for her cool reception. Your aunt had no business to come home as a masquerader, and she really got what she deserved; but I will send her a nice letter. Tom shall take the dairy pony and ride down."

Once again the dairy pony carried an errand to Mrs. Aron at "The Arms," but on the last occasion he had his journey for nothing—to Mrs. Doran's note there was no reply.

CHAPTER VII

As winter advanced, the outlook for hunting was excellent, but, on the other hand, the prospects of the poor were lamentable. It had been a miserably wet harvest; there was a blight on most of the potato crops. Altogether, times were bad, and many decent, respectable old people were just struggling to keep the workhouse at arm's length. The upper class in this part of the world were not wealthy; times were bad with them also, but they did what they could, and started a fund to provide firing, blankets, soup, and tea. In order to augment this subscription, Mrs. Doran, the ever bustling and benevolent, suggested holding a concert in the big drawing-room of the old part of the Castle, which, with one or two small passages, a cavernous kitchen, and pantries, was all of the dwelling that remained from the fire. This drawing-room lay at the opposite end of the yard from the present somewhat jerry-built mansion, and was utilised as a sort of general lumber- and store-room. It proved, when emptied, capable of holding three or four hundred people, and Mrs. Doran generously offered it free of charge. Decorations, she declared, were easy; chairs and forms could be borrowed; she would lend her piano—yes, and her youngest son should be one of the performers; for Ulick, as most people knew, had a delightful voice. The eager lady drove about the country and expounded her scheme to her neighbours with convincing eloquence. The concert, of course, to be undenominational: the schoolmistress could get up glees, Lady Tandragee would play the violin, Father Daly, the parish priest, should sing, and the rectory girls perform on the piano; kind friends must contribute their talents, and the public their money. Tickets were to be ten shillings, five shillings, and two shillings, and there were to be—oh, marvel!—refreshments, which would be served in the Castle dining-room and servants' hall, according to the rank of the ticket-holders. For, as Mrs. Doran declared, people could not be expected to come for miles and sit out two mortal hours and more, and then go away hungry. Her hearers listened and approved. But was this really Mrs. Doran who was setting forth such an innovation?—she, of all people, who suffered acquaintances to come and visit her from many miles distant, and rarely "put up" a horse, or offered the caller a cup of tea! What had come to her? Possibly now that her youngest son was at home, he had wisely prevailed on his mother to be less penurious, and more like other people. At any rate, Mrs. Doran was in her element; she was a born organiser; arranged a stage, wall-lamps, programmes, chairs, forms, and collected a really capital company. She borrowed far and she borrowed near; her pen, as she said herself, was never out of her hand! and, thanks to her exertions, which were prodigious, every ticket was sold. Lady Borrisokane was coming, weather permitting, with a large party, and General and Mrs. Haverstock were bringing a houseful of guests. For many days the grand concert and little but the concert was discussed in cabin, cottage, and Castle. The schoolmistress drilled a selection of girls to sing in the glees, and among the chosen was Mary Foley. The others were the daughters of strong farmers, or of people of the shopkeeping class; but Mary had a deliciously sweet treble, and could not well be overlooked; although her companions were a bit above her station, her voice soared above theirs, as a lark's above the twittering of finches. All were commanded to appear in white, and Mary's dress for her first communion came in nicely for the splendid occasion.

A full moon and a hard frost, made locomotion easy on the eventful evening, and by seven o'clock the yard of the Castle was packed with every description of vehicle, from an ass's car to a smart private omnibus, and a bicycle to a mourning coach; "the house," so to speak, was crammed to the door, the farmers and tradespeople gladly paid five shillings for a good charity, which combined songs, a supper, and a sight of all the quality in the country! The poorer folk expended two shillings, to show they could afford it, and were not coming on the parish; the boys also paid for the girls. There was much to see: the old drawing-room did not know itself; its walls were decorated with holly and pink paper, lit up by flaring wall-lamps. At the upper end was a platform (covered and draped in turkey red, rising from a forest of palms and exotic plants) on which stood a grand piano, chairs, and yet more palms. Behind this platform hung the doctor's best drawing-room curtains, concealing the exit and entrance to the green-room (down three rickety steps and into a mouldy pantry), where was a lamp and a couple of kitchen chairs. By the time the five- and two-shilling seats had digested all these splendid details, the ten-shilling places began to arrive. It was the first time that many of the simple crowd had seen a real diamond necklace, or a black velvet dress. Lady Borrisokane's head was covered with white plumes, "for all the world," as some one said, "like a child's hearse!" There was his lordship, bent in the shoulders, bald on the head, and furious in the face! Undoubtedly he was here against his will. Lady Tandragee, smart and showy in spangled pink satin, with a low body and pearls—the sight of her was worth at least one shilling. Next came Sir Thomas, in his pink coat, the honourable Mrs. Fagan and three daughters, all heiresses, but as plain as a heap of stones. The general, very gay-looking, with grand company; the rector of the parish; the parish priest. Each party or individual was loudly clapped as they entered; some were embarrassed, some laughed, others accepted the demonstration as their due, and indeed, Mrs. Fagan went so far as to scatter half a dozen stately bows! By the time they had all found seats, the doors were closed. The room was full—even the window-sills were occupied, and no less than five boys were seated (half-price) upon the chimney-piece.

It is perhaps scarcely necessary to mention that the concert opened with a duet—the Overture to *Zampa*! After this the comic man sang a capital song, "Lannigan's Ball." The next item was a solo on the violin by Lady Tandragee, much appreciated by the ten-shilling places, but the performance was rather over the heads of the others; she gave a concerto delightfully. The farmer folk thought it most amazing to see a lady playing the fiddle; the working of her arms was a real wonder, but she was not getting out much tune! However, when she concluded, they clapped and stamped from politeness, and a good-natured appreciation of her desperate exertions. After an encore, there was a humorous recitation by the rector; and the last item on the first part was a song by Ulick Doran, Esq. When he stepped forward in his evening-dress clothes, looking remarkably handsome and well groomed, there was a loud burst of applause, and a noisy shuffling of feet under the cheap forms. Mr. Doran was entirely at his ease, the result of a long apprenticeship to soldiers' sing-songs, and he sang in a fine, clear voice the well-known melody—

"Rich and rare were the gems she wore."

This being wildly encored, he gave them "Father O'Flynn," and subsequently, without waiting for an uproarious demonstration, descended headlong into the so-called green-room—which he had named "the black hole."

The interval lasted ten minutes only, and during the time people talked to one another, some even leaving their places, and visiting about; their voices sounded like the buzzing of a great swarm of bees; so far every one agreed that the concert was a wonderful success.

The second part of the entertainment opened with a glee. Ten young girls trooped up, and bashfully took their places on the stage, and sang "The Hunting Morn," no doubt in compliment to the members of the Harkaway pack, who were present. The glee went capitally, and was loudly encored; the ten maidens were duly prepared, and sang another with equal success.

Among the group, Mary Foley was supreme; she had a brilliant colour, her eyes shone with excitement, her voice was clear and high, she was not the least self-conscious, although the gaze of all her little world was concentrated on her, including the gaze of Mr. Ulick Doran—for, owing to the exigencies of space already indicated, performers who had played their parts, immediately resumed their seats among the audience. The girl created a sensation, not merely in the cheap, but the ten-shilling places. Her neighbours and friends asked one another if Mary didn't look for all the world like a lady born? as good as the best! and twice as natural as some that were there?

"An will ye luck at the turn of her neck," said Mrs. Hogan of "The Arms," "and the grand set of her head. She might well be somebody, instead of just a working girl, the daughter of John Foley."

Among the upper ten she was prodigiously admired; but Mrs. Doran did her utmost to damp all enthusiasm and extinguish curiosity, and was uncommonly sorry she had allowed the Foley girl to appear. She was far too conspicuous.

"Oh, she was just taken in to make up the dozen," she explained, "and is only the daughter of one of our cottagers; indeed, she lives in a humble way, and is not in the same class as the rest."

"Now, I should have said it was the other way about," exclaimed Lady Borrisokane. "It shows one should not judge by appearances. She really looks almost ladylike—have you noticed her hands?"

"No!" impatiently, "I never looked at them, though she is my egg-girl this six years. She is inclined to be a bit above her station, and I make a point of keeping her in her place. It is the really *truest* kindness."

"She is most awfully pretty and jolly-looking," put in a young man. "I only wish——"

"*Hussh!*" interrupted the presiding lady. "Father Daly is going to sing."

And the parish priest, who was a general favourite, emerged from the curtain, and gave them "Killarney" in a fine mellow voice, which was clapped to the echo by his parishioners. After a violin solo, and another glee, and a duet on the grand piano (Irish melodies and fireworks), there was a considerable delay. The lamp in the black hole had gone out, and an embarrassing collision occurred between coming and going performers. Then Ulick Doran stepped up on the platform; on this occasion carrying a much-beribboned guitar. He fetched a chair forward, sat down, deliberately tuned up the instrument, struck one or two rich chords, and then broke into "Torear por lo fino" ("The song of the Spanish bull-fighter").

"El tipo mas flamena que hayen

Espa-ña."

he sang—

"Es este cuerpecito con tanta

Gra-cia.

Con tanta gracia y este cuerpecito

Y este cuerpecito, Salero!

Con tanta gracia.

Olé con, olé ola, y olé, barbian de

Mas gracia no habra visto uste!"

Not one word could his audience understand; they could, however, realise that a remarkably good-looking young man, playing a guitar, decorated with beautiful crimson and yellow ribbons, was singing a catching and delightful melody with extraordinary spirit and expression; so much so, they felt fired with an almost irrepressible desire to join in the inspiriting refrain—

"Olé con, olé ola, y olé barbian de

Mas gracia no habra visto uste!"

Indeed, for many a day the boys in the neighbourhood might be heard whistling the air, or bursting suddenly into—

"Olé con, olé ola,"

for the Irish peasant is naturally musical, and has a true ear.

The audience, by the end of the third verse, were completely carried away. Something in the Toreador song stirred them. And if the general audience were thus touched, what of an impressionable girl? Something in the voice and the air seemed to call forth a sudden joy in the heart of Mary Foley—a joy, an ecstasy, that thrilled her. "Olé con, olé ola!" rang in her ears for months!

After the bull-fighter's song burst a wild hurricane of applause. Mrs. Doran trembled for the poor old cracked ceiling. And then with "God Save the Queen" the concert came to an end. People began to talk, to criticise, to collect wraps, and to wonder, "what sort of refreshments would be forthcoming?"

The light supper in the dining-room was excellent, as far as it went—hot soup, sandwiches, tea, coffee, claret-cup, jelly, cakes.

In the servants' hall were buns, bread and jam, tea, roasted potatoes, and cold corned beef. "A great spread entirely," agreed the company. Barky and

Ulick looked in, in order to see how the guests were looked after, Barky from curiosity and a profound sense of his own importance, Ulick carried there by an overwhelming desire to speak to Mary Foley. They found an immense crush, and a merry, noisy, hungry crew. People were standing, sitting, eating, drinking, and enjoying themselves just anyhow. At last he discovered Mary in a corner, hemmed in by a circle of admirers, which included Patsie Maguire. She seemed to stand out from her entourage in the most extraordinary way. Certainly Mary had a wonderful personality, and an intangible quality of refinement and piquancy. As her circle suddenly fell back, in order to make room for Mr. Ulick, she coloured vividly.

"Well, Mary, I congratulate you," he said. "You did splendidly."

"I—I," she stammered, "ah, sure it was nothing at all; but oh, sir"—and her eyes shone—"your song, although I did not know the language, it gave me a sort of wild feeling, a queer longing: I don't believe I'll ever get it out of my head"—here she caught Katty's eye, and added hastily, "humbly begging your honour's pardon for speaking so free."

"Not at all," he rejoined. "I'm only too flattered. I picked up some Spanish songs at Gib—Spanish music has a charm of its own, half Arab, half I don't know what. Don't you think the concert was a great success?"

"Yes, sir, I do, indeed. I wish we had one once a week."

"Ah!" he rejoined, "you'd soon get tired of it: the second of a thing is never the same as the first."

"I don't think I could give in to that, sir," and she smiled. "What about second thoughts?"

He was about to retort, "What about first love?" but prudently refrained, and said, "I suppose this is the first function of the sort you have ever been to?"

"Yes, sir, and I'm afraid it will be the last."

"No fear of that," he answered gaily.

As he looked at the girl in her dainty white muslin, with her delicate features and wonderful hair, he could have imagined he was addressing one of his own class; then he noticed the surrounding faces, the grooms, gardeners, and labouring men, and their families, and realised that Mary was one of *these.* She was unaccountably shy, and would only say yes or no, being aware that her mother was watching her keenly; so was Mrs. Hogan, and, to tell the truth, also the jealous eyes of a dozen other girls and young men were wondering to see Mr. Ulick making so much of little Mary Foley! Possibly the situation struck him as somewhat *prononcé*, and he hastened to distribute greetings and nods among a number of the crowd, in his pleasant off-hand manner; then he took himself away to his proper sphere, among the somewhat dull quality in the dining-room!

Mary walked home, one of a large and merry party that clear frosty night, silent herself, but listening to the "talk" about the gentry—their grand dress and looks—the quality of the refreshments, Father Daly's singing, and Mr. Ulick's, which "just beat all." "Begob, 'tis him could sing the heart out of a girl's breast," declared one admirer, and in this opinion Mary silently concurred; his song was still ringing in her ears. How different he was to the young men and boys, with his white glossy shirt-front, and beautiful little neat tie, the faint scent of cigars about him, and his nice clean hands—how superior to Patsie Maguire, with his coarse hair, broken nails, and atmosphere of turf and tallow. Even in his new tweeds, Patsie looked nothing at all, and had a great slouch on him. Undoubtedly it was hard on poor Patsie thus to draw comparisons between him and his master, who had the advantage of a drill-sergeant and a first-rate tailor; but at any rate Ulick Doran had unwittingly accomplished one feat.

He had "sung the heart out of Mary Foley's breast."

CHAPTER VIII

After the concert came a day of reckoning; that is to say, a winding up of the financial part of the performance. The parish complacently expected a substantial sum for coal and blankets, tea and sugar. Boots? Certainly there would be boots; and they were badly wanted. The simple folk had made their calculation something after this fashion: three hundred shillings was fifteen pounds, anyhow; the room was free. Take an average of five shillings all round, was not that seventy-five pounds? The neighbourhood nodded, and grinned, and figuratively rubbed its hands. But unfortunately the neighbourhood had reckoned without Mrs. Doran and her little bills for carting, hiring, lighting, decorations, printing, and refreshments—the amount came to £57 11*s.* 6*d.*—and when she handed the small balance to the Rector and the Rev. Father Daly, their countenances expressed the blankest dismay. The lady was in her own house, entrenched in a business-like attitude behind her writing-table, as she tendered the cheque with an air of bold assurance, not unflavoured with patronage. For a moment there was an awful silence. Mr. West took the bit of paper, stared at it as if he could not credit his faculties, cleared his throat, and passed it on to the priest.

Father Daly became red in the face (he was a man of full habit and of somewhat impetuous temper). He spoke at last, in his deep rich brogue.

"Goodness preserve us, Mrs. Doran! what does this mean? What has become of all the money for our poor people?"

"Become?" she repeated. "Some was spent in their interest; the balance is in your hand—a cheque on the Munster Bank."

"But surely to goodness——" he reiterated.

"There are my accounts," she interrupted angrily. The lady was not prepared for this inquisition, and believed that the two men would thankfully accept her largesse and so depart.

"I certainly understood that the refreshments were provided gratis," put in Mr. West, with unprecedented courage.

"Pray who said so? I'm sure *I* never did. See, it is merely stated," snatching up a programme, "*There will be refreshments.*"

A pause. Yes; the fact was patent; the statement had involved no promise; the matter had been understood, taken for granted, but Mrs. Doran never permitted anything to be *taken* from her.

"Surely you don't suppose for a moment," she resumed, with rising temper, "that *I* was to feed three hundred people, out of my own pocket, now do you?" and she threw herself back in her chair, and contemplated her visitors with her hard black eyes.

"Well, yes, ma'am," rejoined the priest, "I must declare that I was under that impression. After all, it was only once in a way."

"What nonsense!" she exclaimed. "Why, I was the only person who *gave* anything. The room, the piano, my servants' time, my own time and exertions, all the trouble. However"—and here she gave a sniff of definite resolve—"it will be a lesson to me not to put myself out another time."

"Well, I suppose there is no more to be said!" exclaimed Mr. West, turning to his companion with an expression of despair.

"Except, perhaps, the little word *thank* you?" sneered Mrs. Doran, who was trembling with suppressed rage.

"Well, I don't know about thanks," observed the priest, turning squarely on the lady, "but I'll just say the *little word*"; and he paused. "God forgive me if I am wrong, but I believe, woman, you have cheated the poor! Yes"—with uplifted hand—"you got up this concert for them, and have put the earnings into your own hungry pocket. I am not a fool. You need not tell me that a few gallons of tea, and soup, and a couple of tins of kerosene oil, would cost nearly sixty pounds! And see, now I'll punish you."

"What? You will punish me!" she screamed hysterically. "I'd like to see you attempt it."

"Yes, I'll publish an account of the grand concert, and its takings, and all your little bills"—here he stretched out his big hand and gathered them up—"in the Cork paper and the *Irish Times*. This I will do at my own expense, and so let the world know what you are made of. If the Colonel were alive, I would never do it, nor shame him, good, innocent man; but as for you, you avaricious cormorant, you have no shame whatever—you do not know the name. Come away, West; this is no place for the servants of God!" and before Mrs. Doran could recover her senses and speech she was alone.

When the amount of the balance became known, naturally there was a terrible outcry. "The old wan" had surpassed herself this time! The lady had beaten every record. Some people laughed, others were furious, and as for the poor, they said, "Arrah! what could ye expect from Mrs. Doran? When did she give away bite or sup? She only gives trouble. Faix, the ould wan has it in for her."

The particulars of the great scene in the study were imparted to Barky and Ulick. Barky, who was, of course, on his mother's side, swore a terrible vengeance on Father Daly, but his brother was overwhelmed with shame. He wrote to his banker's, and he rode down to Mr. West and had a good square talk with him; and the result of the conversation was that Father Daly withdrew his threatened exposure when he received an anonymous contribution of sixty pounds. Well, he knew where the money came from—generous young Ulick was his father's own son; and accordingly, the scandal respecting "refreshments" was quickly hushed up, and not suffered to spread, though in the immediate neighbourhood of the Castle "Mrs. Doran's concert" is talked of to the present day!

* * * * *

The frost did not last long. Hunting was speedily resumed, and Ulick was in his element. He had three capital horses, and rode them in the first flight. As the meets were early, and at a distance, and it was dark when he jogged home, he had not much chance of prosecuting his acquaintance with Mary Foley; now and then he came across her; once he met her on Sunday, just outside the Castle gates, coming from mass, with her prayer-book neatly wrapped in a clean handkerchief, and accosted her.

"So you've been saying your prayers?" he began.

"Yes, yer honour"—a curtsey—"but there was a sermon too."

"Was it a good one?"

"It was so, sir."

"Tell me what is your idea of a good sermon, Mary?"

"Oh, well, one that makes yer blood creep. Father Dunne is a nice quiet man, but he never frightens ye, or puts the fear of death in ye, not like Father Daly. 'Twas him as preached to-day."

"Yes. Tell me all about it?"

"Then, sir, I declare ye might have heard the people breathing! They were just paralysed!"

"Ah! And were you frightened?"

"I cannot say I was all out—just a bit disheartened with myself. I know I'm a black sinner."

"I wish to God my soul was as white as yours, Mary!"

"O Lord, sir!" she ejaculated, aghast, "you must not say the like of these things to *me*, and—and——" Colouring up, and taking a firm hold of her resolution, she curtseyed herself off.

One afternoon, some weeks later, Ulick Doran overtook the pretty egg-girl on her way from market. Her mother was beginning to feel the distance long, unless she could get a lift, and Mary was alone.

The young man dismounted from his weary horse, and walked beside her with the bridle over his arm for three whole happy miles. The afternoon was clear; there was a slim young moon. A red coat is somewhat conspicuous, and the couple were passed by one or two of the neighbours, and descried from a distance by Father Daly himself! All the same, their conversation was absolutely harmless—it was even stupid (but they could subsequently recall each precious syllable); and yet, with every step they took, they fell deeper and deeper into love (but with a frightened consciousness, like—as R. L. Stevenson says—a pair of children venturing together into a dark room). Sixteen and twenty-three—how could they help it?

They were both sensible of an indescribable something that drew them irresistibly towards one another. He appealed to her, because he was just Mr. Ulick—and a gentleman. She to him by her strange magnetic personality; she was totally different to any girl he had ever seen—coarsely clad yet dainty, bold yet shy; as for her face, it recalled the exquisite miniature of some piquante beauty at the court of Louis XIV., and Ulick Doran was poignantly aware of her soft low voice, her sweet eyes, her hair, and her upturned, questioning gaze.

But Mary was Mary, a peasant's daughter, and, being a girl of the people, his lips were locked. Nevertheless, he adored her.

By-and-by, with the spring weather, a little "talk" began to circulate. It was whispered that Mr. Ulick had given Mary Foley his red pup, and that more than once he had been seen walking out with her! The news came to the ears of Father Daly, who had indeed beheld the couple with his own two eyes, and promptly descended upon Mrs. Foley and Mary, and gave them an impressive, never-to-be-forgotten lecture. The gossip also reached Mrs. Doran, who was furious. She made no remark to her son, but she went to Foley's corner, and enacted a great scene with Katty, having discovered that unhappy woman alone. The lady strode into the cottage, and began without any preamble, such as "How are you?" or "A fine day!" "Katty Foley, only you have a lease here, do you know that I'd throw you into the road!" Long residence in Ireland had infected the matron's vocabulary.

"Ah, for why, me lady?" rising stiffly as she spoke.

"Why? Because of your daughter's brazen behaviour with my son, Mr. Ulick. It's the scandal of the county."

"Mary is a good girl," responded Katty, in a tremulous voice. "God knows there's no harm in her, whativer."

"Is there not? She is going the right way about losing her character, walking the roads with a gentleman."

"She never did no such thing! Once I'll allow he overtook her; on another time she overtook him—it was a pure accident."

"An accident on purpose!" said Mrs. Doran venomously. "She waylaid him. And I suppose he has not lent her books; that's not his dog lying there?"

"Sure, Mr. Ulick gave him to me, because the house is so lonesome, me lady," she answered, with submissive deprecation. "No one in the house since I buried poor John, so Mr. Ulick, he says, 'Would you like a dog, Katty?' and there he is."

"There he is, indeed! Love me, love my dog. You could have got one anywhere; pups are as common as kittens. He gave that terrier to Mary—a prize one, that cost him three guineas."

As Mrs. Foley could not combat this statement, her visitor resumed: "I've just come to say one word, and it is my last. If you encourage my son here, and he ever darkens your door, you never enter my gates, and I will make it very unpleasant for you, Mrs. Foley. Look after your daughter, forbid her to speak to him, or you will be sorry yet. You don't suppose that he would marry her, do you?"

"God knows I never thought of such a thing, my lady; I'd never wish my girl to be looked down on. I would not let him put a ring on her; I have my pride."

"*Your* pride!" cried Mrs. Doran. "Well, that is a good joke. Your pride!" she repeated hysterically, as she swept out of the kitchen, like a tornado in black petticoats.

Not long after this raid, the lady of the castle came suddenly on the culprit herself. It was a fine March afternoon, and, wearing her best merino frock and her Sunday shoes, Mary was on her way to drink a cup of tea with her friend Bridget Curran, and show her the elegant fine-drawn work she was after doing for Mrs. Hogan. Suddenly, at a corner, she found herself face to face with the person she most dreaded in the whole world, who deliberately halted, stared hard, and then burst out, "Where did you get that gold locket and chain? But I need not ask; you have a bold face to be going about the country, wearing my son's presents"; and before the girl was aware Mrs. Doran suddenly stretched out her hand, broke the chain with a violent snap, and flung it and the little locket, into the middle of the road.

"What are ye doing, ma'am?" cried the girl, roused to passion.

"I'm tearing my son's presents off you, you wicked, scheming little hussy!"

"'Tis none of your son's presents," rejoined Mary, with her face aflame. "I'm not that sort; I take nothing from a gentleman."

"You took his dog!" retorted the other triumphantly.

"I did not," replied Mary, quivering with antagonism; "and I bought the locket with my own money"; and she held up her head and surveyed Mrs. Doran with fierce, if unspoken defiance.

"You're a liar! a liar! a liar!" screamed her enemy, now abandoning all self-control.

"I am not, and it's as true as if I was to be judged, that I bought it with my egg money; and God knows it took me long enough to gather—six mortal years; but it came out of his mother's meanness, and not out of Mr. Ulick's purse." And when she concluded, Mary stooped and picked up the battered little gewgaw, which had cost her three pounds.

"As for being a liar," she resumed, "them's queer sort of words for a lady to use—but then *you* are no lady."

"If you don't take care, I'll box your ears!" screamed the matron. Father Daly had called her "shameless." This chit of an egg-girl declared she was no "lady." Was the world coming to an end? "Mind"—and she seized the girl's arm in a grip of passion—"if ever you dare to speak to my son again, it will be worse for you."

"I see ye have a poor opinion of Mr. Ulick, ma'am," she answered, wrenching herself out of Mrs. Doran's grasp.

"No, but of you, you double-faced schemer—you odious little red-haired flirt. You will come to a bad end!" and Mrs. Doran passed on, now breathless, and completely exhausted by the violence of her own emotions.

Mary had solemnly promised her mother and the priest that she would never speak again with Mr. Ulick, and somehow the little scandal (and it was a small one) was scotched and smothered. The girl kept out of her lover's way with conscientious avoidance; once, indeed, she met him riding with a beautiful young lady on a grey horse, and he had nodded gaily to her; but when they were out of sight, the miserable girl had crept into a field close by, pulled her shawl over her head, and wept, oh! such hot, painful, jealous tears. Shortly afterwards Mr. Ulick went away to England, and his admiration for Mary Foley was forgotten; the little Foley girl now took her eggs to market town—she never went near the Castle. This stubborn defection was a disagreeable experience to Mrs. Doran, who drove a thriving trade with a considerable egg connection—friends to whom she offered the surplus of her hen-house, posting many boxes at a clear profit of sixpence a dozen. Mary's supply was regular—such nice, large brown eggs! Unfortunately the recent scene on the road had actually cost poor Mrs. Doran several shillings a week!

It was noticed that Mary had grown rather white and "dawnchie" looking; some people said the poor angashore was losing her good looks, whilst others declared she was going into a decline, same as Kathleen Kelly when her boy died in America, and eagerly recommended a strong infusion of cat-nip tea.

One evening late, Katty was in bed; Mary still sat up working—what was the use of lying down, she asked herself, when she could not sleep? She was knitting close to the kitchen window, by the light of a fine April moon; outside it was nearly as bright as day. She intended to finish the stocking that night; she liked knitting, for she could both knit and—think.

All at once something interposed between the moon and herself—a face, a man's face, was pressed against the window. Mary rose with a half-stifled scream, and then recognised, with a violent thrill and shock of joy, the well-cut features of Mr. Ulick.

"Mary!" he said, "Mary! Come quite close to the window, will you?"

"Whist," she answered sharply. "I must not speak to you; I've promised my mother and the priest." But she approached nearer to the window all the same.

"You may speak to me this once, Mary, for I've come to bid you good-bye. I am off to India to-morrow."

"Is it to India?" she repeated mechanically.

"Yes, and I ran across the mountains just to try and catch a sight of you before I start, for the chances are——" He stopped, and his lips twitched.

"Yes?" she asked.

"That we shall never see one another again."

"Oh, Mr. Ulick! Oh, Mr. Ulick!" She broke down, her thoughts filled with the terror of separation, and tears ran from her eyes. "Don't say that. Don't."

"Yes. There is nothing half so sweet in life as love's young dream, and it has been very sweet. Mary, although I've never said one word to you that I might not have addressed to your mother, I'm sure you have *guessed.* Now I came here to tell you the truth; I felt that before I went away, I must speak. I love you, Mary, and I know my own mind. I shall never forget you to my dying day. Yet we can never be anything to one another."

Mary gazed at his face—white in the moonlight—and made a sudden shivering gesture, pierced with a sense of something tragic and irreparable. She moaned, "Oh, I wish I was dead, that I do."

"Oh, no, don't say that. You will have many happy years before you. Why, you are only sixteen. You will soon forget me, and it will be better for you."

"If you can remember, so can I," she answered proudly.

"It is hard lines, Mary. I wish I was just a labouring boy for your sake; but you know that unequal matches bring no luck. There is a barrier between us, like this pane of glass."

"Yes, that's true," she murmured.

"Open the window, Mary," he urged. "Just an inch."

"Sure I can't; it's nailed fast! Are ye up at the Castle?"

"Up at the Castle they think I am in Queenstown. My mother was very rude to you, I'm afraid; she has a hot temper, poor woman, and she believes the Dorans are next door to royalty. She would like me to marry an earl's daughter. I'll never marry now, and I must go. God bless you. I wish I could shake you by the hand, but I won't ask to come in——" He paused, and stared hard at her. "Mary, look here. Will you kiss me through the window? It won't be a *real* kiss, you know, but it will be something for me to carry away, and a sign you cared for me—here, just on this little star."

As she nodded quickly, he bent his head, removed his cap, and pressed his lips on the pane. Mary too leant forward, and deliberately laid hers on the self-same spot. Then he stepped back and looked at her with misty eyes that said farewell. Suddenly he, with a vehement and pathetic gesture, waved his hand, and vanished.

Mary Foley spent the remainder of that unhappy night rocking to and fro and sobbing in a chair. Her heart was broken, she told herself—broken, broken, broken! What was the good of living at all, when she could never again lay an eye on Mr. Ulick, and Mr. Ulick loved her! Struggling through the eclipse of grief, that truth shone like a fixed star.

Meanwhile a light, active figure might be seen, running or walking by turns along a short cut which led to a junction over the hills nine miles away. Ulick Doran had to catch a mail train at one o'clock. If he missed it, he would forfeit his passage in the trooper lying at Queenstown, and be reported absent without leave.

He had dallied too long with his love, and now it became a race for his commission, and his career. In the still cool night he fancied he heard the train approaching miles away, the faint, muffled rumble becoming more and more distinct. He ran the last mile downhill at extraordinary speed, and dashed into the junction just as the signal was lowered, and the night mail to Cork came thundering over the points.

"It had been a narrow shave, and he had only just done it," Ulick said to himself, as he sat in a corner of an empty smoking carriage. When the express moved on, he seemed every now and then to see Mary Foley's beautiful wistful face gazing at him from the other side of the glass.

But no; it was a mirage—a mere mocking fancy! All that was visible through the clear pane, was the flying landscape, the high full moon, and the melancholy dark mountains of his native land.

END OF PART I

PART II
CHAPTER IX

A brisk little gentleman, with a sharp profile and a slight stoop, was walking along a road in the south of Kerry. He had a somewhat lost, undecided air as he halted now and then, and vaguely stared about him. He was, in fact, a total stranger to the locality, being a certain Mr. Bence Usher, head of a well-known firm of London solicitors, who was spending his vacation for the first time in Ireland, and Ireland's beauty had decoyed him far astray; the active, enterprising tourist was a good five miles from his hotel and his dinner—he was exploring alone, for Emily Usher, his housekeeper and sister, preferred to sit in the shady garden at the "Glenveigh Arms," in company with the hotel tortoise and a new novel. As he moved onwards, sheer above him rose the purple Reeks; low on the right hand glittered a silver lake, of which each bend in the way, or break among the trees, revealed an enchanting vista of wooded islands, bays, or promontories. By degrees the prospect became lost to sight, and at length a high, dilapidated wall screened it completely—a wall bulging out dangerously here and there, but held together with ropes of ancient ivy. An equally dilapidated entrance presently came into view, and perched on one of the tumbledown gate piers sat an old man in his Sunday clothes, smoking a short black dhudeen. This he removed from his mouth in order to say, "A fine evening, yer honour"—for the southern-born peasant is always gracious, and never meets a stranger without some civil salute.

"Can you tell me whereabouts I am?" inquired the Englishman, in his thin, polite voice.

"And to be sure I can! An' why wouldn't I?" he returned, with unexpected emphasis. "This place," indicating a grass-grown avenue which wound away vaguely among the trees, "is called Lota, but sure, 'tis in ruins. An empty house hereabouts falls to pieces in ten years' time. 'Tis the soft climate as does it."

"How far am I from the 'Glenveigh Hotel'?"

"Faix, it depends on the road ye go—by wan way it's in or about six miles, and the other it's three—though it's all the same distance. Ye understand me?"

"I cannot say that I exactly apprehend you, but if you would put me on the shortest route, I shall be greatly obliged——"

"Then the shortest root, as ye call it, is through here, and I'll put ye on it in a brace of shakes an' kindly welcome."

"Thank you, I should be glad of your guidance," replied the stranger, as he proceeded to clamber over the broken stile.

Meanwhile, Mike Mahon, having knocked the ashes out of his pipe, deliberately descended from his roost, and led the way between an overgrowth of trees and shrubs, down a back avenue into a yard, entirely surrounded by large roofless outhouses.

"Now, did ye ever see the like of that?" he demanded, with a dramatic wave of his horny hand.

No. His companion never had, and he shook his head in solemn commiseration. Rank grass a foot high covered the stones, the pump was a wreck, the stables lairs of nettles and old iron.

"This place has not been occupied for a long time, I take it."

"There hasn't been a fire in the chimney, a soul inside its doors, for twenty-one years. Ah, when the ould master, General Macarthy, lived here, there wasn't as much as a straw astray, no, nor a leaf itself. He was a great soldier, who had lived mostly in the Indies, and was a wonderful man for flowers."

Then they passed through a gap in a wall, and came on traces of the front avenue winding out of a forest of trees. There were trees on all sides, and on a sort of wide plateau stood the house. At the first glance its appearance administered a shock. The house was but a cottage. From the dimensions of the yard, the entrance, the imposing stretch of lawns and timber, one had naturally expected to see a mansion, or at least the ruins of a mansion. The grounds sloped gradually to the water's edge, which was almost entirely hidden by a dense growth of shrubberies, and scattered over the wilderness to the left were marvellously luxuriant flowering plants, pampas grass, arbutus, rhododendrons, giant fuchsias, and at a little distance, a high and hoary garden wall, through its gates a vista of a wild jungle of high bushes and aged fruit-trees gone mad.

The little spare lawyer absorbed each item of the scene with his quick, professional eye, and then turned to his guide with an air of mute interrogation.

"Yes, 'tis a mortial pity," he exclaimed, "for 'twas once the loveliest spot in the wide world."

The stranger made no reply, but gazed at the lake and the woods, and mentally admitted that the situation and view were not to be surpassed.

"And so you say it has been empty this twenty-one years," he remarked at last.

"Yes, sir, 'tis twenty-one years last September since they left it. I worked here, man and boy, for the General, and the garden over there was just a wonder. When he died, it was let for a short term, and after that it went to rack and ruin as ye see."

"And does no one ever come near it?"

"Only the caretaker, once a week," he replied. "It is rented to graziers for dry heifers, and that's all. Oh, 'tis a mortial pity."

Mr. Usher turned about as he concluded, and looked into the empty shell of a dwelling. It had originally been a glorified cottage with four spacious rooms and a wide hall; kitchen and servants' quarters were at the back. The roof was intact; remnants of rich carving, and scraps of expensive wall-paper, still streaked the walls—and bore the signatures of half the country! In the drawing-room was a boat, whilst the dining-room served as a byre for the dry heifers.

"Of course when a house is left empty for years 'tis a sore temptation," resumed the Irishman, in an apologetic key. "The poor people around has made away with the grates and doors and window-sashes. Faix, the old General spared no money on it, and if he was to see it now, he'd haunt the place."

"It looks as if it had a history, or a law-suit," remarked Mr. Usher, as he settled himself on a low window-sill, and produced his pipe.

"Well, then, no, yer honour, God be praised, it has not either wan or the other; but I could tell you—if yer in no hurry—a mighty queer tale of a child that was born there."

"Oh, I'm in no hurry. It is not more than four o'clock," said Mr. Usher, "and I'd like to hear the story," offering his tobacco-pouch as he spoke.

"Well, then, hear it you shall, and so here goes!" rejoined the other, stuffing, as he spoke, a generous supply of tobacco into the bowl of his pipe, and thrusting it down with a horny thumb.

"'Tis more nor twenty years ago, when there were no gentlemen's lodges round the lake, nor no railroad or telegraphs, nor tourists, but terrible long journeys and great hardships on cars, and the *best* of shooting and fishing; now we have a power of quality coming to and fro, and admiring all this"—waving his hand,—"and bringing good money into the country. God knows it's badly wanted; but when I was a young gossoon, a stranger hereabouts was as much of a curiosity as an elephant; so it made a notorious stir when this very place was took by the Earl of Mulgrave and his Countess."

Mr. Usher started, and hastily pulled his pipe out of his mouth. "Mulgrave," he repeated, "*Mulgrave*, did you say?"

"Yes, Mulgrave, sir. I learnt off the name by thinking of graves. They was not too long married, and come on a spree like, and without hardly any servants."

"Yes, yes, yes," assented Mr. Usher, "but how did they discover it?"

"I don't rightly know," he replied, "but they were highly delighted, I can tell ye—his lordship with the sport; for in those days ye couldn't put down yer foot on the mountain without standing on a bird. The woodcock was just dying of old age; and as for the fish, they were waiting on ye."

"More than they do now!" grunted Mr. Usher.

"Himself liked the sport, and her ladyship the place. It was soon after the old master dying, and was just pure fairyland. The fuchsia hedges were a sight, the palms a wonder, the magnolia-trees the size of a cabin; and as for passion-flowers, the house was smothered between them and roses, and the carnations scented half the lake!" He paused to draw breath after this burst of eloquence, struck a match, and then resumed: "Ye may see the terrace here. I keep it still weeded. 'Twas here the old master took his stroll; 'twas here *she* used to walk." He heaved a profound sigh, then proceeded in a brisker key.

"Yes; his lordship and her ladyship was well content, though maybe it was a bit lonesome for her. Many an evening I've seen her pacing up and down this same terrace, watching for the boat. Oh, she was a picture, I declare! like an angel on the chapel window."

"Then you remember her?"

"Ah, who wouldn't? Bedad I do! If I was to shut me eyes, I could see her standing there still; her hair (and she had crowds of it, enough to stuff a pillow) was dark red, like a copper beech; a small lily face, set on a long, white throat, a pair of wonderful dark eyes, and wee hands, like a child's; just a blaze of stones; her voice was as sweet as a song, and when she smiled, ochone! ochone! it gave yer heart a squeeze. I never saw anything like it before."

"Or since," suggested Mr. Usher.

"Oh, then, bedad, sir, I won't give in to that! I've seen the very comrade of it, an' I'll tell ye no lie! Well, her ladyship was mad on flowers, and she used to come and talk to me when I was weeding and working, asking questions about the country folk, and their matches and queer ways, and the old master—God rest him; and she said how sad it was to see his beautiful place let to strangers. 'It's a paradise,' says she—'the loveliest spot I've ever seen. You ought to be proud of your country, Mike Mahon!' I told her I was so—and prouder again that it was plaisin' to *her*."

"Now that was a fine piece of blarney," exclaimed his companion.

"'Twas not, sorr. 'Twas her due!" he retorted with vehemence. "Well, one night there was a terrible whirra loo—her ladyship had a baby unexpected! No doctor, nor nurse, nor clothes ready. Old 'Betty the brag' was called in, for the French maid was no good at all, only for screeching. Well, the baby was a girl, and a cruel disappointment, as a boy was wanted; however, av coorse she had to be reared all the same, and there was no means of feeding the crature, till Betty bethought her of Katty Foley. She had a young infant. Katty was about forty, a big, strong major of a woman. She'd been terribly unlucky, and had lost four children—some was born dead, some had just breath in them. People gave out it was a fairy blast. Howsomever, she had a living child at long last, four weeks old, and she took on the other poor little crawneen, and it throve elegantly. Well, when everything was going fair and aisy, her ladyship all of a sudden took and died. Just went out like a candle, and wid no more warning nor a snow-flake. And oh, but she made the beautiful corpse!"

"Why, you did not see her, surely?" said Mr. Usher, in a key of startled protest.

"No; but I heard tell the like was never beheld. Just the same as a dead angel! And I tell ye more: his lordship was all as wan as a mad man, and out of himself wid grief. The windows used to be open—it was summer—and I weeding and working hard by, and I heard him calling on her, and crying to her to come back—to come back. I declare to ye, sir, it was enough to melt the rock of Cashel; but sure, she was gone." Here he gave a profound sigh. "They took her to England along with a great train of black mourners, and left the place just as it stood, and the child wid Katty. She had a bit of a farm and cows, and a nice decent slated house of her own; and his lordship would not so much as *look* at the baby, and was terribly bitter against it. Bedad, there seemed a sort of blight on the family, for in about two months' time the child pined off and died, and was packed in a grand little white coffin, and sent away to the family burying-ground, and laid alongside the mother."

"And so that was an end of the whole affair?"

"It was, sor. His lordship sent Katty fifty pounds to bank for her little Mary, and a long while after news came as he had married again—a widow lady. Little Mary throve well. Begorra, she was a rale beauty, and just the core of John Foley's heart, and the apple of his eye. She was that clever and quick, wid such taking ways, but awful dainty about her food, and wid a terribly high sperrit. Learning was no trouble to *her*, and she has grown up a lovely girl, and it isn't alone the golden sovereigns she has to her fortune, that makes all the boys crazy to marry her, 'tis her pretty face, and quare manners—not bold at all, but imperious and commanding. She could marry any wan she pleased; there is a strong farmer from this side of Kenmare, crazy about her, and I know a police-sergeant that is *clean* out of his mind."

"And which is she going to take?" inquired Mr. Usher, who had finished his pipe, and stowed it carefully in its case, and began to think this story was rather long-winded, and that he would now cut it short, in favour of the short cut home.

"Neither wan or the other," was the solemn response, "and she won't have no match drawn down for her; she's all for pickin' and choosin', the same as a lady. They do say she favours a car-driver at the Glenveigh Hotel, Pat Maguire, my own cousin's son, a good-looking boy, as wild for fun and dancin' as herself. He has sorra a penny or a penny's worth but his two bare hands, a beautiful voice, and a concertina; but she is as hard to catch as a sunbeam, and all for play and joking. She'll spend half her time standing at the gate at Foley's corner, colloguing and laughing wid the neighbours, or running off fishing, or picking flowers, and she's at every dance and wake in the barony. Oh, she's a rare one to sing, aye, and to talk, and has always a word with the men, and a pick and a bit out of them; and yet no one could ever say that Mary Foley was bould, though they do give out she's a terror for spending."

Mr. Usher had heard more than enough of this little peasant and her attractions. He was beginning to feel a bit chilly, and he rose stiffly from the window-ledge, stamped down his trousers, yawned and said—

"Well, thank you, my good fellow, I've enjoyed my smoke and chat here, and your interesting story, but——"

"Story!" echoed Mike Mahon, hastily rising to his feet. "Sure, I haven't told it to you yit."

Mr. Usher turned about, and contemplated the speaker with an air of dignified surprise.

"Faix, it's a true word, sor! All the talk I'm after pointing out was only the fringe, or the outside. I'm coming to the kernel now, and if your honour will just hold on a few minutes I'll maybe surprise ye!"

"Oh, no doubt you will do that; but you see, I must be getting on now. Another time, perhaps, my good man, another time."

"No, sir, but *now*. Since you've been so kind as to give me your company and the best of tobacco, I'd like just to finish off my bit of history like. I cannot tell what's got at me this blessed day, but it drives me to speak, and to talk. Maybe it's the place itself that edges me on! I ax yer pardon for making so free as to bother ye wid an old man's chat."

"As for that," responded Mr. Usher, "I'm an idle man at present. At home all my time means money, and I forget that here I have no occasion to hurry myself. The day is long, and besides—this is rather a curious coincidence, but I've heard part of your tale before. The name of Mulgrave is familiar, and I am interested in seeing the spot where the first Lady Mulgrave died. It is extraordinary that I should, in the course of a casual afternoon ramble, come upon it just by accident."

"Do ye think it was an accident, sir? I'd call it a queer chance. Anyhow, 'tis many a Sunday afternoon I put in here, and you're one of the few visitors I've seen. If ye like, I'll be setting ye on your road home, for I can walk and talk, and I would not be wishful to be a torment and a hindrance to yer honour; but when I've put the story off me mind, ye, being English and a gentleman, well up in years and experience, might give me your opinion and advice."

"It is my rule to charge for both," rejoined Mr. Usher, with a grim smile. "That is how I make my living. I'm a lawyer."

"God help us!" ejaculated Mike under his breath, and then, in a louder key, "Meaning no offence, but ye don't look like one. I'd take ye for a blooded gentleman!"

"Thank you. And now perhaps you will take me out of this delightful wilderness, and put me on the road to Glenveigh. If you will tell me your story, you shall have my best advice gratis—that means, without a fee."

CHAPTER X

Within the next five minutes the man in the frieze coat was pioneering the man in the grey tweed through the jungle of fuchsias and arbutus which smothered the steep footpath leading down to the lake. A broken gate lying on the ground marked the extreme limit of Lota. Presently the lawyer and labourer were striding by the water's edge side by side, and Mike resumed the relation of his story, precisely as if the thread had never been snapped.

"Ye see, old John Foley, who was terribly proud of Mary, was took off of a sudden in a fit, and of late his wife got queer in her head. They do say her mother was the same, though some made out it was tay-drinking; sure enough, she never had the taypot out of her hand. Whatever it was, she turned so mortal strange that Mary had to get her aunt Bridgie, Katty's sister, to come over and help mind her; but it wasn't better, but worse, she got-shockingly unaisy and restless and worrying in herself, or else sitting and never speaking, all as wan as some stone image. At long last she bid them send for the priest, as she had something on her soul. And when he come, she ups and she told him, and she told Mary, and she told any one that would listen, what I'm about to tell *you.*"

Here Mike cleared his throat energetically, and continued—

"And *what* do ye think Katty giv' out? That her child died; it was always droopy, and she could not bear to part wid the other. She loved it as her own. Its father hated it, and would marry again, and rear a family, and never grudge *her* the pretty little girlie at all! And so she sent off her own dead baby to the grand place in England, and she kept the stranger, who has grown up fine and strong and clever, and everything that is surprising for quickness and talk."

As Mike related this audacious case of child stealing, his companion's expression changed from the countenance of the tolerant, easily amused listener, to that of a keen man of business, who is suddenly made acquainted with a most serious piece of intelligence. He removed his pipe, his lips set in one grim line, and his face was slightly flushed, as he glanced at his guide with a penetrating sidelong look.

No, the man was no garrulous "Ananias," but an Irish peasant of a faithful and romantic nature, who still, year after year, week after week, haunted the place which had once held his ideal. To the best of his ability he was telling what he believed to be the truth.

"Katty took great pride out of the child, and soon forgot as she wasn't her own flesh and blood; and as for John, he never knew, and he just lived for his daughter. Well, now Katty was growing old, and her sin rose up and faced her, her conscience tormented her, and she said she must ease her mind before she died. She made out she felt awful bad, and when Mary looked in her face with her ladyship's own two eyes, when she smiled at her the same as her mother, she just stiffened in the bed!"

"And how did every one receive this amazing news? What did they say to it?" demanded Mr. Usher, in a sharp legal key.

"Oh, bedad, Mary laughed at it for pure nonsense. She was a country girl born and bred. To be an English countess with a castle and servants, and to wear a gold crown on her head, would just kill her, if it was true; but it was only a fairy tale, and she was her mammy's daughter, and no one else——"

"What did the priest say?"

"Faix, his reverence give it against Mrs. Foley, too! Anyhow, she was too late; twenty-wan years had passed, and there was no call to go and upset a grand English family, and maybe for nothing. Katty, ye see, had no proof beyond her bare word; no papers, no witnesses. Every one jeered at Mrs. Foley's queer notion, and treated the story as an elegant fine joke. Mary is no Englisher, and there's not a lighter foot to dance a jig, or a better warrant to sing an old Irish lament, in all the country."

"And is that the end of it? Eh?" said the lawyer briskly.

"'Tis in a way; howsomever, Katty still whinges and whimpers and moans, begging and praying them to make restitution—sometimes beating on the walls with her two bare hands, and crying by the hour; she can't stir now, having lost the use of herself; and her legs being crippled with rheumatism, she sits in her chair all day. Whiles, she's reasonable enough; but about Mary she is properly mad. She says she's no child of hers—and calls her *Lady* Mary. Ye see the head of Katty is not right, and her own mother went the same way, so people just humours her; they are all very good to the poor crazy creature, she being a sort of 'innocent' in her old age."

"I suppose they never imagine there is any foundation for her delusion," inquired Mr. Usher.

"No; and if there was they'd hold Mary Foley hard and fast, and keep her, I believe, against all the lords in England; for she is one of themselves."

"And what do you think yourself?"

Mike made no immediate reply, but took one or two loud sucks at his pipe. At last he said: "I believe, on me solemn oath, that there *is* something in the story all the same."

"You do!" cried Mr. Usher, coming to an abrupt halt, and fixing his sharp eyes on his companion.

"In troth I do," rejoined the old man doggedly.

"What grounds have you to go upon for supposing there is something in it?" asked the lawyer.

"Faix, it's no sacret," he answered, with an air of sullen resolution; "any one would see it that had eyes in their head. John and Katty was as black as two crows. Mary has hair like a copper kettle, a white swan throat, a dancing eye, and a little weenchie hand. Oh, I declare she's the born image of her ladyship. Now, is not that strange?" and he turned and looked fixedly at his companion's hard-set, wizened face.

"Not if she is her daughter!"

"Whisht!" he cried, turning about, as if he feared that the very trees had ears. "Never let *that* pass yer lips; I only whisper it in my heart, when I go there alone, and sit on the terrace of a Sunday—and to you, a black stranger, it makes no matter what I say; and somehow it's a relief to give out me thoughts to another creature, whether a gentleman or a man."

"Has this strange likeness struck other people?" inquired Mr. Usher, in his cool, judicial tone.

"No, sir!"—now drawing up his bent back, and speaking with overwhelming dignity. "You see none of the neighbours had much chance of seeing the Countess. She was mostly out boating, or staying at home. It's twenty-wan years ago, ye know, and not a sowl remembers whether her hair was black or yellow. Now, *I* saw her every day, and I can never forget her, for I never saw any wan like her, and never will again."

"Except Mary Foley," amended his listener. "Is she not admired, and remarked all over the country?"

"No, I can't say rightly that she is, though the young men does be wild about her; the old people and the women says she's no great shakes; she's too slim and small-made for the Kerry folk, and has no colour; they talk of her sperrit, and her singing and dancing, and her clever, smart chat, within three parishes: but they don't say much of Mary's *looks*, bekase, sir, they are a rough sort of ignorant people, and she's out of the common."

"I must confess I should like to see her!" exclaimed Mr. Usher.

"An', sure, what's to hinder ye? That's aisy enough, if ye will give yerself the trouble to walk up some afternoon to Foley's farm; there ye will see Mary herself standing in the doorway, ready for a word and a joke, and the house behind her just anyhow! She has no great heart for work, though she has a kind heart for the poor, and all the dumb creatures."

"Well, you have told me a most interesting story," said Mr. Usher, as he came to a halt, "and I shall do my best to make the acquaintance of Mary Foley. Look here!" he added, as if struck by a sudden thought, "don't say a word of what you've been telling me, to your wife. Women talk."

"Sure, man alive, don't I know that, when I've buried three!"

"Three wives?" repeated the old bachelor incredulously. "Three?"

"Yes, faix—and all had a bit in the bank."

"Then you must be what they call a warm man."

"Augh, not at all"—with a gesture of repudiation—"what with bringing them home, and putting them out, they cost me a sight of money! As for what I'm after telling ye, sir, 'tis Bible truth, and here our roads goes different ways. Augh, not at all!" he exclaimed. "Sure, I would not be taking your silver, sor—it was a relief to me to spake. Well, well, then, I'll not say agin the tobacco! I'm thankful fer your company and yer kindness to a bothered old man, listening to his quare, foolish talk"; and, with a hasty nod, Mike turned his back on Mr. Usher and hobbled away.

"But was it all quare, foolish talk?" the lawyer asked himself, as he stood gazing after the retreating figure. "Was it one of two things: a mere 'mare's nest,' or 'a pretty kettle of fish'?"

He was, by one of the strange coincidences (which really occur more frequently than is supposed), Lord Mulgrave's solicitor, agent, and man of business. Five-and-twenty years previously he had succeeded his father in the same responsible and lucrative billet. Mr. Usher remembered perfectly, and with a poignant regret, the first Lady Mulgrave, a truly exquisite creature. Her reception by the family had been cool and suspicious; she brought but a small fortune, and she was half French: a member of a great race (ruined and scattered by the Terror), the head of which, on small means, and in a contracted circle, still endeavoured to maintain their ancient pride and traditions.

The Duc de Hernoncourt, with much-reduced rental, clung to the home of his ancestors. (The Château de Verbèrie, a famous gem of French architecture, lying remote from cities, and surrounded by a moat, the two wings flanked by turrets, with pointed roofs, is a well-known picture on the local post-card.) He married an English lady, mother of the future Countess Mulgrave. During a tour through the valley of the Oise, Lord Mulgrave had been entertained by the de Hernoncourts—his distant connections—and later, when Madame La Duchesse and Mademoiselle Joseline came to

London, he had persuaded the young lady to remain in England, as his wife. Mademoiselle de Hernoncourt had hair the colour of a copper kettle, a mignonne face, a wonderful personal charm, precisely as described by her former gardener. She was a lady of a distinctive appearance—once seen, never forgotten. Even the bloodless little lawyer recalled her with an emotion that he was unable to classify or explain. If this girl Mary Foley was her image, she was undeniably her daughter, and Katty's ravings were no ravings, but embodied the painful truth.

Oh, yes, the painful truth! Lord Mulgrave was childless; his present wife had been a fascinating little widow with one girl, when he married her, fifteen years previously. Her ladyship was smart, ambitious, devoted to society, dress, and social diplomacy; her daughter was also smart and up-to-date, who shot and danced, acted and smoked; she and her mother managed his lordship, who was a tall, taciturn man of fifty, fond of fishing and of peace—proud, reserved, and ceremonious. What would be the effect of introducing an uneducated Irish peasant girl—a girl celebrated for "sperrits" and "chat" into this aristocratic and exclusive circle? Mary was, of course, a Catholic. She had never been in a carriage, or seen a silver fork, in her life. Yet if all this circumstantial evidence went for anything—not to speak of Katty's confession—she was Lord Mulgrave's only child and heiress. It was in a highly perturbed frame of mind that Mr. Usher pursued his way to the hotel. He had so much food for meditation that he made a very poor dinner, and was unusually silent. Questioned by his sister with respect to his excursion, his replies were brief and unsatisfactory. "He had walked about eight miles. Yes, it was a pretty country. No, he had not met any motors."

Subsequently, as he sat out in the garden after dinner, smoking cigarette after cigarette, his sister, Miss Usher, who knew his moods, came over and took a seat beside him and said—

"Bence, I see you are getting your old London expression, and thinking of some business."

He nodded assent.

"Can't you leave it behind even for six weeks, and enjoy yourself like every one else? You know you promised me you would."

"Yes, Emily, I know I did. It is all very well to say I'll leave business behind me; but what can I do when it *follows* me here?"

"What do you mean?" she demanded. "There were no letters for you to-day."

"Never mind, my dear, I've got some hard thinking to do. A most serious case has recently come to my notice."

"Well, I suppose"—rising as she spoke—"I'd better leave you to do your thinking alone. I can be no help, can I?"

"No—or—By the way! You poke about the neighbourhood a good deal, and are in and out of the houses, looking for bits of china, and studying the people, as you call it. Have you ever come across a place called Foley's farm?"

"Foley's farm," she repeated. "Yes, at Foley's Corner. Quite a small farmer lives in it, I believe. I stopped there the other day to ask the way, and saw a beautiful girl."

"Oh, that's a common sight in these parts."

"Yes, I know—of a certain style; black hair and grey eyes put in with a dirty finger. But this one is of another type. Chestnut locks, a graceful figure; she carries her head like royalty, and Vandyck would have been proud to have painted her hands, though they *are* rather red I must confess. I have promised to lend her some magazines, and will take them up to her one of these days."

"Take me, too—will you?"

"But, Bence, you are not in earnest? Why, you grudge every hour you have not a rod in your hands."

"I'll give the fish a holiday. I should like to see something of the natives—the Irish at home, and that sort of thing."

"All right, then, I will escort you up to 'Foley's' as they call it; only too happy to have your company. Well, good night."

As she moved off, her brother remained immovable, buried in thought and tobacco-smoke.

"No harm in going to see the young woman, at any rate," he reflected. It committed him to nothing. After all, perhaps he ought to leave well alone. Apparently the girl was happy; her present home was her natural sphere. She was but a peasant. Why upset her life and the lives of others who were all content with their lot? Yes, to stir in the business would be a grave and responsible action. "Better let sleeping dogs lie"; and having arrived at this conviction, Mr. Usher sought his couch.

CHAPTER XI

Although it was a nice, cloudy day, and the wind perfect for fishing, Mr. Usher sacrificed himself the following afternoon upon the altar of duty. He had slept on his discovery, and had come to the conclusion that it was his office, as Lord Mulgrave's man of business, to interview this girl, whom fate had, so to speak, flung at his head; and four o'clock found him escorting his sister, Emily Usher (aged fifty, a good soul, and a bit of a blue-stocking), along a high, breezy road which ran above the lake, and at a certain sharp angle plunged into, and was lost among, dense woods which crowned the hill, and spread to the water's edge. Clouds had gathered, a thin, cold drizzle was descending, when the couple came to the elbow or joint where the long, bluish-white road turned abruptly in order to accompany the lake; they arrived at the same time at a comfortable slated cottage, with geraniums in the windows, and a crimson rambler trained over its walls. The cottage stood back in a little field, and was flanked by several outhouses. At one side was a garden full of straggling hollyhocks, currant bushes, and poultry; at the other the usual substantial turf rick. A heavy wooden gate opened directly from the field into the road—a most excellent talking trap for passers-by, and doubtless the identical gate referred to by Mike Mahon. The general appearance of the place was well-to-do, but thriftless. A couple of pigs were rooting and grunting in the short grass; a speckled hen was perched at her ease upon the half-door; the currant bushes and apple trees exhibited a family washing;—conspicuous among the items were pink petticoats, and black stockings.

The nice soft afternoon and the drizzle was developing into steady rain, and Mr. Usher was by no means sorry to hear his sister exclaim—

"Here it is! This is Foley's—Foley's Corner, as they call it. I hope we shall find the girl at home." And as her brother shoved back the gate she added, "I'll go in first. Shall I?"

The pigs and geese pressed hospitably round the visitors as they walked up the path, and when they reached the half-door the hen flew off with a loud skwawk of expostulation. Miss Usher gave a genteel little cough—an ineffectual signal, for the room within seemed dim and empty. Presently she supplemented the cough with a timid "Ahem! Is *any* one at home?"

No reply. Brother and sister then with one consent peered into the big flagged kitchen. Bacon in solid flitches hung from the rafters. On the well-varnished dresser a lean white cat sat comfortably lapping from a large pan of new milk. The fire was low, but on a girdle on the embers a large soda cake was baking—and burning. Crouched over the fire on a three-legged stool sat a slender, auburn-haired young woman, deeply engrossed in a somewhat tattered volume. Cough and speech, cat or hens, were alike indifferent to her, for at the moment she was living in another world, far away from this gloomy kitchen and this burning cake. In short, the auburn head was buried in *Monte Cristo*.

As Miss Usher and her brother boldly entered (immediately attended by two geese), Mary Foley started, came back to her own everyday life, and sprang to her feet, greeting Miss Usher with a radiant glance.

"And so," said her brother to himself, "this was Mary Foley!"

Yes, though not locally credited with "looks," she was undeniably pretty—nay, even beautiful—with clear-cut, high-bred features, and, for all her peasant's clothes, an *aristocrat* to the tips of her little pink fingers.

"Ah, sure then, miss, it's entirely too kind of you to come and bring me the books." As she spoke her eyes fell on the parcel, and a wonderful smile—her ladyship's smile—lit up her whole face.

"This is my brother," explained Miss Usher, introducing him with a gesture.

"I am glad to see your honour"—dropping a curtsey—"and hope your honour has had good sport."

"Pretty well, I thank you," he faltered, for he was gazing at the living image of the late Countess of Mulgrave—supposing the countess to be dressed in a short blue calico gown and coarse white apron.

"And how is your mother to-day?" resumed Miss Usher.

"Oh, indeed, she's only among the middlings, miss, and she's keeping her bed. Me aunt is gone to the town for some medicine."

"And you are minding the house?" suggested Mr. Usher.

"And doing it badly, too, sir. Shoo! ye greedy divil!" and she made a dart at the cat. "Out of this wid ye!" and she drove off the geese. "But the truth is I've got stuck in a book, and when I do that I clean forget everything—more shame for me." She still held the book between her fingers, and from the bottom of her heart wished herself alone.

"May I see what it is?" said Miss Usher. Then, as she glanced at it—"oh, *Monte Cristo*! No wonder you were enthralled!"

"Isn't it splendid!" she exclaimed. "Oh, it beats Banagher! I've just got to where they are dragging him into the boat. Isn't it grand!"

As she and Miss Usher stood talking, it never seemed to have occurred to Mary Foley, that she was lacking in hospitality or good manners. As she remained discussing the engrossing romance with his sister, it struck Mr. Usher that Mary preferred to lounge against the table descanting and listening, and lacked the true Irish instinct, which instantly offers a welcome, a seat, and, if possible, refreshment. His quick, grey eyes wandered round the room, and noted its contents. It was of a good size; the furniture was strong and useful, but a tub with a half-washed gown stood near the window; the floor was littered with sticks and cabbage leaves. It was plain that Mary's little hands were incapable of rough work! But he noticed some pathetic attempts at decoration: the dresser exhibited a large bunch of wild flowers; on the walls was a considerable gallery of coloured pictures, cut from the illustrated papers; the window curtains were white, and looped back with strips of pink calico. As the visitor stood staring about the half-door was thrown back with a kick, and a thin, tall, peevish-looking woman, with a basket on her arm and a shawl over her frilled cap, entered, immediately followed by a red terrier. For a moment she stood aghast, then recovered and said, "Yer servant, ma'am—yer servant, sir," as she dropped two curtseys, and deposited her load with an air of relief.

"Mary, me girl," turning to her niece, "where's yer manners? Won't the lady take a sate?"

Mary coloured guiltily as she dusted and offered a chair. "Faix, I'm forgetting myself. Rap"—aside to the dog, who was sniffing the visitors—"behave yerself! Ma'am, I beg your pardon, but the house is all upset, and through other, it being washing day."

"Lord save us! the cakes is a cinder!" cried the new arrival, hurrying to the fire. "Mary, girl, I lay my life you've been reading a book. Bedad, ma'am"—turning to Miss Usher—"if she was as good a hand at rearing pigs and calves as she is for reading and rearing flowers, we'd all be in clover. Oh, but she's the terrible girl for a story——"

As she spoke Mrs. Grogan made a desperate attempt to tidy up the place, carried away the tub, and endeavoured with all the strength of her lungs to rekindle a few sods.

All this time Mary, her niece, with true patrician unconcern, stood knitting and talking to Miss Usher, precisely as if she were receiving her amidst the most luxurious surroundings, and absolutely unconscious of any shortcomings. If she had been a true-born Irishwoman she would have been pouring forth an irrepressible torrent of excellent and plausible excuses. And here, to Mr. Usher, was yet another incontrovertible proof that in Mary's veins ran no Foley blood, but that she was the descendant of a colder race, the daughter of a hundred earls. Whilst Miss Usher made use of her tongue, her brother continued to make use of his eyes. The young woman, leaning against the dresser, with the dog at her feet, was plainly not in keeping with her background; her pose was grace itself, unconscious and unstudied—possibly the heritage of centuries of court life. The short blue cotton skirt revealed a pair of black woollen stockings and cobbler's shoes; but even these failed to conceal a high-arched instep and slim little feet, and the hands that twinkled among the flying knitting needles might have been painted by Vandyck or Lely, so delicate, taper, and absolutely useless did they look.

Mary Foley had a sweet voice and a pleasant and melodious brogue; she and her visitor had much to say to one another on the subject of books, and the English lady was secretly amazed at the extent and variety of the Irish girl's reading.

"Father Daly lends me the *Times Weekly*, and Mrs. Hogan at the hotel gives me all the stray old books and magazines, and I keep her in stockings; then I buy books myself in Cork."

"You don't get much of a selection do you?"

"Oh, ma'am, sixpenny reprints is not too bad—I wish I knew French!"

"I suppose you only know your language?" put in Mr. Usher.

"The Irish, sir? Yes, I can speak that well, and read it too, they teach it in the schools now, but it is not much use if one went travelling—not like French."

"Do you wish to travel?"

"Sometimes I do. I get a queer roving feeling,—a sort of longing comes over me; but mostly I am very well content here, and I've a notion that if I ever left this part of the world it would be like tearing the heart out of me, same as you see the poor people going to America."

"Well, Mary, me girl, aren't you going to ask the lady if she has a mouth on her?" put in the shrill, whining voice of Mrs. Grogan, who had been busy with a kettle and some cups and saucers.

The hot soda cake, retrieved from the cinders, sent forth an appetising invitation. Mrs. Grogan had cut it into large chunks, which she split and buttered with a generous hand.

"Emily, I really think we ought to be going," protested Mr. Usher, who hated and despised afternoon tea, and would as soon partake of rhinoceros as hot buttered soda cake!

"Oh, but, sir," pleaded Mary, turning her battery of smiles on him, "my aunt Bridgie would be shockingly disappointed if you won't honour her, after making the tay and all; she's the real manager and mistress since me poor mother took bad, and I'm only good, as she'll tell you, for a little nursing, and minding the hens and the flowers. I hope you will stay?"

Bence Usher was astonished to find himself presently drawn up at a table, spread with a clean coarse cloth, and seated before a steaming slice and a steaming cup, *tête-à-tête* with the two peasant women.

"No milk," he cried, remembering the scene on the dresser.

"No milk," echoed his sister.

"So it goes in families, misliking milk," remarked Mrs. Grogan gravely. "I hope the tay is to your taste? I get the best, like me poor sister, four shillings and sixpence the pound. None of yer cheap mixtures!"

(There is no one in the world so particular respecting her tea, as the Irishwoman of the lower middle class.)

Mary, he noticed, was exceedingly dainty about her food, and reduced her share of cake to a mere slice, half of which she shared with the dog.

"That's a handsome terrier," he remarked; "he looks thoroughbred. Where did you get him?"

"He was given to me mother as a house watch, when he was a pup."

"Your people are not from this part of the world?" remarked Miss Usher. "Any one can see that, Mary!"

"Deed then they are, ma'am," she replied emphatically; "and where else? Why wouldn't I be Kerry born and bred?"

"Because you are so unlike the other people, who have dark hair and blue or grey eyes, and are more strongly built; and you——"

"Oh, yes," she interrupted, "I'm aware I'm altogether different—very small-boned, wid red hair and brown eyes, and no colour to spake of, but it's just a chancey thing, like a piebald horse—or a blue-eyed cat; we can't all be cut out on the same pattern."

Mary was doing the honours of the feast; her aunt had undertaken the part of servant, and she now stepped gracefully into the rôle of hostess. Her manners were charming and fascinating; even Mr. Usher, laden as he was with care and apprehension, fell under their spell. In a kind of dream he ate a dangerous supply of soda bread, and disposed of two cups of strong tea; for as this most fascinating creature chattered away to him, he forgot both his digestion and his duties.

"Oh, faix, it's not every day we have a gentleman to tay, I tell ye! If me poor mother was stirring, she'd be a proud and happy woman to see yer honour sitting here," declared Mary.

"And how is she?"

"Just dozing now within in the room. She's had one of her bad turns, but I nursed her out of it. Oh, she's awfully changed since her mind gave way."

"And do you think she really is—peculiar?"

"*Think!* Sure, don't we know it? She, that used to be the sensiblest woman in the parish, and every one running to her for advice, is now, God help her, teetotally moidered, and wake in herself." After a pause, "I see you looking at me very constant, sir. May I make so free as to ask if ye get a likeness of any one out of me?"

"Oh, I—I—beg pardon," stammered Mr. Usher. "I'm a bit near-sighted. I hope you don't mind. I see you have splendid potatoes," he remarked suddenly, pointing to a basketful. "I suppose you like them?"

"Is it me? Augh, no!" with a gesture of abhorrence. "I hate potatoes; they just choke me. And when our bag of flour went astray on the train 'ere last week, I was daggin round for something to keep me alive, so I was. I'd die on potatoes."

"And what did you find?"

"Ned Macarthy gave me a couple of salmon trout and a pigeon." "Oh, he's a great poacher!" and she laughed. "So I did finely. I think I hear me mother calling me, if you'll pardon me"; and she rose and hurried into an adjoining room.

"She keeps you all alive, I am sure," observed Miss Usher, "so full of life."

"Aye, you'd never be wanting to go to a theatre or a pantomime as long as ye have Mary in the house," assented Mrs. Grogan. "The chat out of her is wonderful, and she can talk to any one, as ye may judge! I can't think how she comes by her freedom, for John and me sister was not a bit gabby themselves; but every one likes Mary, though she's a poor worker. Half the boys are ready to put their hands under her feet. It's not the looks, but what ye may call the cleverality of her!"

"Is her mother really no better?" inquired Miss Usher.

"Yes; she's in her senses—no more foolish rambling, and rousing the priest with mad tales. But the head of her is full of pains. Oh, she's greatly failed! She's been lying a good while, and I'm thinking she won't be long in it."

"I suppose you don't remember Lord Mulgrave coming here?" ventured Mr. Usher, who had risen, and, with his back to Mrs. Grogan, was searching for his stick.

"And troth an' I do, and why wouldn't I? I remember him well," she rejoined, in her whinging voice. "I met him in the woods one day, and he gave me a great salute. Such a lovely, tall, fine gentleman! I never seen her ladyship; she never stirred out much. It was at Lota she died. Oh, but she made the lovely corpse!"

"Indeed!" said Miss Usher.

"Yes, that was an awful affair, and unexpected. They do say"—lowering her voice almost to a whisper—"she *walks*! Anyway, no one will go near the place after dark."

"Surely you don't believe that?" protested the lady.

"Well, ma'am, I've seen and heard many a quare tale in me time, and I don't rightly know what to believe and what not to believe; but it would be more reasonable-like if she'd stop with her own folk, and haunt them, instead of scaring poor Irish people, as are black strangers."

"Really, Emily, it's six o'clock," said her brother, suddenly looking at his watch. "We must not intrude on Mrs. Grogan any longer. You see it has quite cleared up now"; and he made for the door.

Miss Usher, an intelligent woman, who wrote a little, and was particularly anxious to study the Irish peasant, and interiors, would gladly have thrashed out with Mrs. Grogan the subject of ghosts, warnings, and Banshees; but her brother was already at the gate. Should she offer payment? She put her hand to her steel bag, and looked interrogatively at her hostess, but read an invincible "no" in those little twinkling greenish eyes.

"Thank you very much. Please say good-bye to your niece for us."

"Aye, she'll be sorry to miss ye; but she is mighty taken up with her mother. She's a real, good decent girl, for all her funny ways—wan that always satisfies ye, and me sister cannot spare her out of her sight—that is when she's in her right senses. Well, good-bye, my lady, good-bye. Mind the gander; he's a bit wicked to strangers"; and she curtseyed her out.

"Well, Bence!" said Miss Usher, as she came up with her brother, "tell me frankly what you think of that girl? Is she not beautiful, and has she not an extraordinary air of refinement and distinction?"

"Oh, yes, she's uncommon-looking," he muttered, in a peevish tone.

"Did you notice her slow smile? A family smile, I should imagine; and yet, of course, I am talking the most arrant nonsense! Can you believe that her grandmother was some old Kerry woman, who dug potatoes and smoked a pipe! Now, *can* you?" she repeated impressively.

"No, I cannot," he answered doggedly. All the time he was mentally making a draft of a letter.

"And yet there is her aunt, a common, ignorant person, as you see. I rather wanted to give her half a crown as a return for the tea; but Irish hospitality is a thing by itself. As for Mary, the day I lost my way I offered her a shilling, and you should have seen how she coloured up and refused it. I almost felt as if I had offered it to an *equal.* Really, one would take her for a lady if she were dressed up—a somebody, in fact!"

"In fact, Lady Joseline Dene," her listener mentally added, as they walked on for some time in silence. The Mulgraves were a notoriously proud family; ancient, exclusive, wealthy, now dwindled down to one last branch. What would Owen, Earl of Mulgrave, say to this Irish heiress who fed pigs, washed and cooked (very badly), and had adopted the religion, language, prejudices, and accomplishments of a Kerry peasant? Could she ever be educated, transformed, and fitted for her high degree?

"Come, come, Bence, you have not opened your lips for half a mile," remonstrated his sister. "A penny for your thoughts. What are you thinking about?"

"That I hope we may have cranberry tart for dinner," was the mendacious reply.

"Oh, you greedy person. I fancied you might be puzzling out the enigma of that red-haired girl. I must confess that she baffles *me.* She's a physiological freak; she's a white crow. What business has she to feed pigs with those little taper hands? Tell me that?"

But her cautious companion was not prepared to tell her anything as yet; he would keep his discovery to himself. Emily had an active mind, a healthy curiosity, a world-wide correspondence, and in answer to her question, "Tell me that?" he merely shook his head, in token of hopeless ignorance.

Personally, he had no shadow of doubt as to the girl's identity, and as he strolled up and down the road in front of the hotel after dinner, he held a long debate as to what he ought to do. Should he hold his peace, leave Lady Mary to her wash-tub and her gate, or should he write the wonderful news to the earl, her father?

CHAPTER XII

From the slated cottage at the corner of a country lane it is a long step to an historical castle in Perthshire. Here the Marquis of Maxwelton is entertaining a large party for the twelfth. His moors are as celebrated as his gaunt old fortress, built after the French fashion, in the time when the Guise family held sway in Scotland. The château has been modernised, and the gardens and grounds are unsurpassed for beauty and originality.

Among the guests are the Earl and Countess of Mulgrave and Miss Tito Dawson—the Countess's daughter by a former alliance. The ladies are lounging in the gardens, the earl is on the moor with the guns. He is a fine shot and a keen sportsman. A tall, slim man of fifty with clearly cut profile, grizzly hair, and a pair of deep-set, melancholy eyes. He has a polished manner, a pleasant voice, is an agreeable acquaintance and popular landlord; but the real Earl of Mulgrave lives far behind those melancholy eyes, entrenched in an impenetrable reserve. Thus far and no further his guests can go. He is ready to entertain them, to shoot, play billiards, talk politics, and subscribe money; lavish with time and with his fortune, he is niggardly of himself. His life—how little people guess!—has for years been one long disappointment.

After his young wife's death he became a rover—driven from country to country by his own despair.

One autumn afternoon at Granada he came upon a party of tourists, or rather they came upon him, and among these was a lady who, to his starved heart, brought dim memories of Joseline, his lost idol. Mrs. Dawson was slim and animated. She had brown eyes and mahogany-coloured hair. A free lance, with great ambitions and small possessions, she set herself to lay siege to the handsome, heart-broken *parti.* Her cue was "sympathy." Each had known losses—irreparable losses. The departure of Captain Dawson had been hastened by drink. Oh what profanation to bracket *him* with Joseline Mulgrave!

Mrs. Dawson admired, in a really genuine fashion, the handsome, desolate widower, and he, knowing that he must once more accept the burden of his position, and imagining her to be a sweet, tender-hearted woman, energetic as wise, invited her to be the partner of his sorrows.

The likeness to Joseline had become indistinct and faded, save for the hair-tint (which was duly revived at necessary intervals); but he believed that they would make the best of two sad lives, and face the future sustained by mutual experience, and mutual sympathy. The Countess of

Mulgrave, with her carriages, diamonds, town-house, and country-seats, was an entirely different individual to the pretty, pathetic widow his lordship had known in Spain. They were not the same. People talk of children being changed at nurse; it seemed as if Lottie Dawson had been changed at the altar!

She was ambitious, agreeable, and selfish. A luxurious home, crowds of servants, quantities of money, a great name, and a connection, were all delightful in their way, and she was fairly well satisfied with her lot. Certainly Owen was peculiar; she managed him beautifully—yet she stood a little in awe of him, although he had never uttered a sharp word, or denied her any reasonable request. He attended her to functions, he submitted to her friends, he made Tito a generous allowance; and yet somehow they remained strangers.

Of course, they had not identical tastes. A country life, sport, books, and peace, were all he cared for; she enjoyed the racket of town—six engagements of an evening, with races, the opera, Hurlingham wedged in between visiting, charity concerts, and milliners. She had acquired the great art of dress, and was still a pretty woman, with auburn hair, and a brilliant colour, a wonderful faculty of making conversation, a fair amount of tact, and a reputation at bridge.

Her daughter Tito, who was small and dark, with a *nez retroussé,* found it necessary to live up to her profile, and was as jaunty and impudent as her nose—extravagant in dress and conversation. Tito Dawson had a reputation for being clever, and making the most daring and original remarks.

As a rule, women and girls liked her, and men considered her "good sport." She had a sharp, amusing tongue, and a capital seat on a horse.

The marquis and his guests were lunching in a glen after a first-rate drive. Long rows of dead grouse were spread in lines near where the beaters were eating their dinner. The guns, twelve in number, reclined under the lee of a rock, discussing cold grouse, cold pie, sandwiches, and cake, when a gillie arrived with the letters. These were those which had come from the south by a second post, and, being the most important of the day, were invariably sent out to the guns, as among Lord Maxwelton's guests were men high in the political and diplomatic world and the services, to whom the delay of a few hours, meant much in these hurried times. Letters and telegrams were handed about to where their recipients sat lounging or cross-legged, enjoying a pipe or cigar.

"Two for you, Owen," said his host and brother-in-law, and he handed him a couple of missives in the long, narrow envelopes dedicated to business.

Lord Mulgrave glanced at them indifferently. The post had no surprises or pleasures for him. One was from his farm bailiff, no doubt about wire fencing; the other was from Usher, his man of business. Could anything be more prosaic or commonplace?

An interesting young colonel, his next-hand neighbour—a keen soldier and a keen shot—was immersed in a woman's letter, written in an enormous hand, with violet ink. As he turned the page, the words "My own darling boy" were as plain as a sign-post. Those who sat must read; but the lady's "darling" was blissfully unconscious.

Lord Mulgrave, about to consign his letters to his pockets, paused. He might as well see what Brown and Usher had to say. He cut the envelopes carefully with a pocket-knife, being the most methodical of men, and drew out first of all Brown's estimate for so many yards of netting.

Then he examined the other. At the first glance, at the words "astonishing discovery," he simply lifted his eyebrows. At the second glance, he read on with colourless face to the bottom of the page; he turned it with a trembling hand—he finished the letter, three sides of a sheet—crushed it up, rose abruptly to his feet, and walked away.

"Hullo!" exclaimed the little colonel, looking up suddenly, "I am afraid his lordship has had bad news?" and he turned his head, and watched the tall, active, tweed-clad form, striding towards the banks of a foaming mountain torrent, where the figure seated itself in an attitude which implied, "Leave me alone. I wish for my own company!"

"Perhaps something has disagreed with him," muttered a man who did not like Lord Mulgrave's cold and courteous manners.

"Perhaps so," assented the little colonel; "*you* have never agreed with him, and I heard you just now abusing his pet scheme for compulsory service."

"And he jumped down my throat, spurs and all."

"Well, it must come to that, sooner or later. The world's conditions are changing. Can a half-armed people survive, when the whole of the rest of the world is trained to arms? The growth of immense foreign armies is introducing new problems into British national life, whilst all the omens point to the probability that England's position will be challenged in the near future! Diplomacy may do much, but, as Napoleon said, diplomacy without an armed force behind it, is like music without instruments!"

"My dear chap," sneered the other, "you talk like a newspaper correspondent."

"I do. I am actually quoting the Press."

"Oh, I bar these big questions. Sufficient to the day is the evil thereof. I suppose we are going to the west beat after this?"

"Yes."

"I hope to goodness they won't put *me* in a butt next old Sir Timothy Quayle. He's dangerous. Talk of being under fire! He blazed right into me—cannot see a yard. No business on a moor. Never was so frightened in my life! I threw clods at him and yelled, and he thought it was something to do with the coveys. There'll be an accident some day. I say, why aren't we moving? Where's the marquis?"

"Down there by the waterfall, talking to Lord Mulgrave."

"Well, I'm here to shoot my twenty to forty brace, not to talk"—rising to his feet and stretching himself. "I wish—— Oh, I see, it's all right. There go the beaters."

"I say, Owen," said the marquis, as he joined him, "I hope you have not had bad news, old boy?"

"No," replied the other, raising a colourless face, "but news that, if it is *true*, is the best that has come to me for more than twenty years. Here"—and he thrust the letter into his friend's hand. "You had better read it yourself. To tell you the truth, I'm a bit knocked out of time. Of course, I'm going to Ireland to-night."

"Ireland!" echoed his companion. "What in the world would take you there?"

"Read that, and you will understand."

The marquis, who was near-sighted, deliberately fumbled for his pince-nez, stuck it on his nose, and read with provoking leisure.

"GLENVEIGH HOTEL,
"CO. KERRY.

"MY LORD,

"I have recently come upon an astonishing discovery, and beg to acquaint you with my experience. I must ask you to prepare yourself for a piece of intelligence which must naturally be to you of the nature of a shock.

"By accident I rambled into a ruined place called Lota, of which, many years ago, your lordship was the tenant, where, in short, her ladyship the first Lady Mulgrave died, after having given birth to a little girl. I there met an old man, once your gardener, who disclosed to me the amazing news that your daughter did not, as was supposed, die in infancy, but was kept in place of her dead child by the foster-mother, Katherine Foley, and reared as her own.

"Recently remorse, illness, and age, have overtaken Mrs. Foley, now a widow, and she has made the extraordinary confession that Mary Foley, a girl of one-and-twenty, is no child of hers, but the child of the Earl of Mulgrave. Of course, no one credits this statement, for Mary is a Kerry girl, with all a Kerry girl's tastes. Every one, including the priest and doctor, believe the poor old woman to be suffering from a delusion, and crazy. Mary herself has no doubt whatever of her antecedents. Hearing from the old gardener that her appearance was remarkable, I made my way to Foley's farm and interviewed the young woman, and I have come to the conclusion that the ravings of old Katty are the *truth*. The girl's likeness to the late Countess of Mulgrave is so extraordinary, that for my own part I believe the relationship to be undeniable, and I am confident that this girl is your lordship's daughter and heiress.

"I am afraid my information may be unwelcome, for several reasons: the girl has been brought up as an Irish peasant; she has had but little education, and is, of course, a Roman Catholic. On the other hand, she is remarkably intelligent, has read all the books that she could lay hands on, and has a natural grace and charm of manner, that is lacking in many young ladies that have had ten times her advantages. If I might venture to make a suggestion, I think your lordship should come over and *see* the girl and judge for yourself. I have not breathed my conviction to a soul, and, should I be mistaken, at least no harm is done. I am staying at the Glenveigh Hotel, where fairly comfortable quarters are available. It is within an easy distance of Foley's farm, and five miles from a station. I have debated with myself whether to disturb your lordship with my discovery or to pass over the event in silence. I am aware what a change in the girl's circumstances, and in other people's expectations, such a revelation will occasion. At present Mary Foley is happy, satisfied with her lot in life, devoted to her mother, and full of high spirits, vivacity, and contentment. It will be for *you* to judge, for you to speak the word, and to break the spell.

"Awaiting instructions, I remain,
"Your lordship's obedient servant,
"BENCE USHER."

"Well," exclaimed the marquis, as he deliberately folded the letter, "this is a nice thing to spring on a man after twenty-one years!"

"Nice! Yes. Oh, Max,"—and his voice shook—"I hope to God it is no mirage, and that it may be true."

"Then you are glad?" he asked sharply.

"Yes, I should think so. Why not?"

"But it is such an outrageous event—so unnatural and impossible. Of course, I'm aware that you and poor Joseline were all in all to one another—a sort of fairy tale, your marriage; but that is over. You are no longer a young man; you have other ties."

"But no child?"

"No; and this one, if she is your own flesh and blood, will be an alien, a stranger in ideas, prejudices, and religion—nothing more or less than a pretty Irish peasant, eh?"

"He said she was the image of her mother."

Lord Maxwelton looked incredulous. Then he resumed—

"The likeness may be accidental. Such things do happen. Just think of the horror of the present Lady Mulgrave to have a girl less refined than her own kitchen-maid thrust into her intimate society—in fact, bound to accept and chaperone the stranger as her daughter! And as to that story of a baby changed at nurse, I don't quite believe that; it sounds too much like a shilling shocker. Your man Usher is, no doubt, a romantic old bachelor; he has been captivated by a pretty girl—I can *see* he has—and found a mare's nest. If I were you, I should do nothing hastily; in fact, I'm not sure that *I* should do anything at all."

"Max, I'm amazed to hear you talk in this cold-blooded fashion."

"Cold-blooded! No, but prudent and far-seeing, my dear fellow. Do you realise the results of bringing over this Irish girl? She will be Baroness of

Marchlyde in her own right. She will inherit a certain amount of the family property—she, an uncouth, raw, country girl! You could do nothing with her. Of course her character is formed by now. She will probably make your present quiet life most sensational and wretched. She is happy where she is—*you* are happy where you are."

"No, Max, you know very well that I have never been happy since her mother left me. But oh! if fortune were to give me back Joseline in our daughter, I'd ask no more."

"Then what do you propose to do?" inquired his listener, in a sharper key.

"Return at once to the castle, get a few things put together, and leave by the six o'clock from the junction. I'll go alone, and not take my man, and you will make my excuses to every one, and say that I was called away by important business."

"All right—though in my opinion it's all wrong. Shall you tell Lady Mulgrave and Elgitha?"

"Only my wife just yet."

"If you are wise, you will wait."

"Wait! For what? If this girl is my daughter, I shall bring her back with me."

"And if it is a wild-goose chase, how foolish you will look!"

"Yes; one has to take risks, and I'm ready to chance that. Now I see all the others anxious to start and I must not detain you. Good-bye, old man"—wringing his hand—"I leave you to explain everything. Wish me luck."

"I wish you *luck*," rejoined the other, putting his own construction on the word; and in another minute the two had separated.

CHAPTER XIII

Lord Mulgrave, having given directions to his man to immediately pack a portmanteau and order a dog-cart, set out in search of his wife. The quest proved long. She was not in the boudoir, the hall, the drawing-room; she was not even playing bridge or croquet. At last he discovered her in the garden—a most sequestered spot, some distance from the castle. Two ancient fishponds, surrounded by terraces and broad grass walks, were its principal features. On an island in one of the ponds was a pretty clump of trees, in that clump a hammock, in the hammock a smart lady with a novel, a cigarette, and a tiny "sleeve" dog.

"My dear O," she cried, as he crossed a footbridge, "what brings you back? Not an accident! Has anything happened? Any one blown off anyone's head?"

"No, not quite; but something has happened. I've had a letter."

"From the duke?"—struggling to sit up. "So he is coming for the pheasants after all?" Her face was radiant.

"No, I've not heard from him"—and he put his hand in his pocket and drew out the letter.

Lady Mulgrave's expression changed, as she said, "I really do think there ought to be a law against all the men going out together. Half should remain to amuse *us*. It is ghastly dull. Tito and Griselda are going to walk with the guns this afternoon, but I hate that sort of thing. Lady Madge and the marchioness, and a whole pack have driven to see a ruin. They couldn't see a more splendid ruin than Lady Madge herself! Some are playing croquet; some are asleep, and I was nearly off. Oh, you abominable little dog!" suddenly addressing the mite, who had been chewing her book. "Oh, you little horror!"—and she gave it several hard cuffs.

"Look here, I want you to read this, Charlotte. I've had a most startling piece of news. I am going to Ireland to-night."

"Ireland?"—carelessly taking the letter. "Ireland, of all places! But *why*? It's not even the horse-show week, and that's its only inducement!"

"You will see the why, when you read what Usher has to say."

Lady Mulgrave glanced over the pages with a puckered, frowning face.

"My dear, what nonsense!" she exclaimed at last. "Surely you don't believe such utter rubbish. A common country girl your daughter?"—and with an impatient jerk she threw away the cigarette which had been suspended in her fingers.

"I cannot tell you until I've seen her. Seeing will be believing, or disbelieving."

"My dear man, I can tell you one thing. You will have your journey for nothing."

"I sincerely hope not," he answered gravely.

"If there is anything in it, it will really be awful, Owen. No, I'm not meaning anything nasty! Awful for the girl, and also for us. I expect she wears no stockings, and says 'bedad' and 'begorra.'"

"These matters can easily be remedied. You will be good to her, won't you, Lottie?"

"Of course. I will be good to any one belonging to you," she answered. Then, suddenly getting out of the hammock, with a great display of orange silk petticoat, and standing before him, she added, "But I feel confident it is some mistake. And if not, do think of the feelings of Dudley Deverill, brought up to be your heir."

"Well, he will have the title and a good share of the property. But we are travelling a little too fast. I must first go over to Glenveigh. I might have kept my own counsel till I returned; but I thought you'd like to know."

"*Like* to know!" she repeated, under her breath.

"Pray don't let it go any further. I've not told even Elgitha. Say I'm called away on urgent business."

"And the word 'business,' like charity, covers a multitude of sins and secrets!" Lady Mulgrave looked at her husband with an odd smile; but he was grave—he was even agitated. She could read the signs. He had been besotted about his first wife, so people declared, though it seemed incredible, for he was always so cool, self-possessed, and undemonstrative. Was he going to be as idiotic with respect to his daughter?

But of course half the evils in the world are those which never happen. No doubt this creature was a myth.

"At least it will be an adventure," she exclaimed. "And think of the scare lines in the morning papers: 'Long-lost heiress discovered in Irish cabin.' 'Peasant girl, aged twenty, a peer's daughter.'"

"Well, Charlotte, if any unexpected good luck had fallen to *you*, I think I'd not have jeered and laughed."

"Dear old Owen!"—and she patted his arm—"did I jeer and laugh? I beg your pardon, but the idea is so grotesque I cannot get to face it, and it all seems so *funny*. You know I've an extraordinary sense of humour; it bubbles up in spite of me, like a kettle on the boil! In my mind's eye, when I see you so tall, erect, and dignified, with a wild and tattered Irish colleen hanging to your arm, I really cannot feel serious; but you know very well, dear, that my heart is in the right place! I suppose"—and she paused and looked up in his face—"you would not like me to go with you?"

This was, as she was well aware, a perfectly safe offer.

"No, no, I must be off. No time to lose. Pray do not mention the matter to a soul. I'll write and wire. Good-bye"; and despite her protestations that she would come with him and help him to pack, he waved her a denial and a valediction.

As she heard the garden gate click her ladyship scrambled once more into the hammock, lit a cigarette, and abandoned herself to contemplation.

No, no; if it really came to anything, if the story were true, if this journey provided her with a stepdaughter, it would be too detestable. How she would hate the commotion, the gossip, and—the *girl*!

CHAPTER XIV

It was a soft and exquisite autumn afternoon. A delicate blue haze lay over the hills; the dense, dark woods were steeped in breathless silence, and the only sound that caught the ear, was the rattle of a reaping machine. As Lord Mulgrave and Mr. Usher turned down the long, straight road leading to Foley's Corner, the earl was livid, his expression was set; evidently he was struggling in the grip of some vehement emotion, and the name of this disturbing element was "suspense." Would it be true? or false? Would it be Joseline's daughter? or some raw, uncouth stranger? Was it the wild-goose chase his wife had predicted, or the pursuit and capture of happiness? Oh, these next ten minutes would mean so much to him; he almost felt, this self-contained man, as if he were treading on the very boundaries of life and death.

"Joseline's daughter," he was saying to himself. "Joseline's daughter."

Mr. Usher, instinctively aware that his companion was in a highly strung and nervous condition, like the wise little man he was, held his peace; yes, even when they came within full view of the slated house, with its commonplace white face half hidden by a veil of crimson roses.

"There she is!" he exclaimed abruptly.

Yes; standing at the farthest side from them, attended by a terrier, feeding a multitude of bold and presumptuous poultry, stood Mary herself.

"See, now! that's all I have for ye," she declared, as she tossed the last crumbs away, and a race ensued between a strong-limbed cochin and a dissipated-looking hen turkey. The bang of the gate caused her to turn her head, and she beheld, to her surprise, the "little grey man," as she called him, and a fine, tall gentleman; and little did she guess how deeply he was agitated.

"Here I am again, Mary!" announced Mr. Usher, with an off-hand air. "I thought, as we were just passing, we would look in and bid you the time of the day!"

"And kindly welcome." As she spoke she glanced up at the stranger; he was awfully white, and his eyes, as he looked into hers, seemed to pierce down to her very heart. "What ailed the poor gentleman?" she wondered; "was he taken bad?" Yes; he suddenly sat down on a bench outside the door, and, in a husky tone, asked for a "glass of water."

He really seemed faint and come over, and Mary hastened into the house, and presently returned with a brimming tin porringer.

As he sipped it, the hand which held the porringer shook visibly, and Mr. Usher, in order to make a diversion, inquired—

"How is your mother to-day, Mary?"

Lord Mulgrave started violently.

"Deed then, your honour," she replied, "she is in a way better. She is sitting up, and the pains are gone, but her head is bothersome."

From within a shrill old voice called out querulously:

"What are you after? Who is it that's talking to your ladyship?"

"There it is!" she ejaculated. "The head of the poor thing is not right. Maybe"—hesitating—"you'll come inside? or will the other gentleman?"

"Thank you," he interrupted, "yes—yes, if you will permit me, I should like to see your—Mrs. Foley."

Mary instantly pushed back the half-door, and ushered in the visitors.

Old Katty was seated in a comfortable chair near the window. On her lap lay a peculiarly complacent white cat, whose loud purrings testified to its supreme satisfaction, although she had the fur half singed off one side, and was in appearance the very lowest of the lower order of the great tribe, with a thin, pointed head, and a disgracefully dirty face.

Mrs. Foley, on the other hand, presented the remains of remarkably good breeding and good looks—slender and erect, with well-cut features, wavy black hair, but slightly powdered with grey, and dark, deep-set, tragic eyes. She bore but scant resemblance to her half-sister—the sandy, mealy-skinned, peevish Mrs. Grogan—and had made the more successful match of the two sisters.

"Here's two gentlemen, mother!" was Mary's somewhat vague introduction.

Mrs. Foley slowly turned her great melancholy eyes, first on Mr. Usher and then on his companion. As she gazed she suddenly seized the arms of her chair, rose to her feet and cried, "God help me! 'tis the earl himself!" and she trembled violently from head to foot.

"Now, can't ye sit down, mother," protested Mary, "and don't be exciting yourself. Sure, 'tis only a chance friend of the visitors from the 'Glenveigh' as has looked in."

Mrs. Foley threw herself back in her chair, and, rocking to and fro, began to wail and sob.

“Oh, my sin has found me out. Wirrah, wirrah, asthue! My sin has found me out! You’ve come to put me in jail and take her away at last.”

“Katty Foley,” he replied, “I will do you no injury in any way, you may be certain of that”—and his voice was strong and encouraging. “But I implore you to tell me the truth.”

“Aye, your honour,” she moaned, “I will so, and sure, haven’t I been telling it this twelvemonth, and not a soul will believe me!”

“I will believe you, I promise you on my honour.”

“Ye may think I am mad, but it was only *bad* I was; yer lordship will remember when I was sent for to take the poor little motherless babe?”

He nodded his head gravely.

“Oh, it was a fair and lovely darlin’, and so fine and healthy; but my own little girl grew droopy and pined—I’ve had four, and I never reared one. It killed me to see them just fading off and my heart withering along with them. When my little Mary—God rest her!—died, quite sudden, I was nearly crazy, but that other little one was a consolation, and as I lay in the bed I made up my mind I’d keep her for my own. Oh, wasn’t I the wicked woman? I had no scruple. Oh, may the saints pity me! But the little live warm child just caught me by the heart”—her voice rose to a wail of agony; “*how* could I send her away, and sit again by the empty cradle?”

She came to a pause, fighting for breath and overcome by the violence of her emotion.

“And how did you do it?” he inquired in a low voice.

“I kep’ my own baby well covered up, and the room within dark; and John telegraphed over, and there was a great stir, and a mighty gay little funeral; and no one knew—for young babies is so similar—that it was my own little girlie, I laid in the beautiful white and silver coffin under the flowers.”

“Tell me”—leaning forward as he spoke—“did no one ever suspect you?”

“Sorra a wan, but Mike over beyant at Lota. When he saw the child growing up he would come to the gate there and just stand and look over at her and then at *me*, in a way that put the fear of death in me. You see, he had worked for her ladyship; he saw the *likeness*; he saw her walking, living, talking image. Sure, don’t you see it, sir, yourself?”

“Yes, I do,” he asserted gravely.

"And what are you going to do with me and her?" she asked, in a broken voice.

"I intend to take her home," he said quietly.

"Sir, if I'd suspicioned you'd have cared, I'd never have kep her from ye all these years. I surely believed ye thought yerself well shut of her. For you will remember as you were terribly bitter against her, and wouldn't so much as lay an eye on her."

"That is true, Katty; but if I had known, she would have been a wonderful comfort to me."

As these two talked together, Mary herself listened in white-faced, petrified silence. Surely she was dreaming! Either that or going out of her mind! During a sudden pause in the conversation there was not a sound to be heard, but the distant reaping machine, and the immediate purring of the white cat.

"Mary," said the earl, suddenly turning to her, and speaking in a husky voice, as he took her hand in his. "Do you understand that all your foster-mother tells us is true, and that you are *my* daughter?"

Here he looked hard at the little fingers which lay so limply in his grasp, and Mary, having thrown her apron over her head, burst into a violent storm of sobbings.

"Oh, no! Faix, I couldn't face it! No, no, I'm not going out of this," she stammered in gasps behind the apron. "Sure, sir, I was born and reared here; my life is here—not among grand folks."

"They are your own folks, Mary," he said gently.

"Well, anyhow"—and she flung down her screen, and flashed upon him a pair of challenging wet eyes—"I'm no lady, and I'm dog ignorant; so what can you do with me?"

"Love you, my dear," he answered, in a low voice.

"Arrah, how could you? and you and me strangers—you a grand lord, and me just a common girl with no manners, and very foolish and unhandy in myself? I can't even do a day's washing; and the bread I bake turns out like leather! I'm no good whatever here, and sure I'd be a million times worse in a strange country!"

"You're making an awful poor mouth about yourself, Mary asthore," put in the high, complaining treble of Mrs. Grogan. "Why don't ye up and tell his lordship how good ye are at learning—how ye were in the sixth book, and if there'd have been a seventh, you'd be in *that* too?—and that learning and reading and singing and dancing comes as easy to you as kiss me hand?"

"Sir," said Mary, suddenly drawing herself up and confronting him—did she but know it, with the very face and form of her mother—"I'm no credit to ye. For God's sake leave me here, where you found me. It will be better for both you and me. Think of the awful scandal and talk it will raise in this parish" (and what of the great Mulgrave connection?), "and my mother always so respected—when people thought it was only raving and wake in the head she was. Now, if it is *true* what she's after telling us, they will be saying she'd a right to be jailed up in Tralee!"

"My dear girl," he said, "since Mrs. Foley has declared before witnesses and a lawyer, that you are no relation to her, but a very near relation to *me*, do you suppose I will leave you among people to whom you have no ties whatever? No; I am much too thankful to have found a daughter."

"O God! What ails Katty?" screamed Mrs. Grogan. "Glory! she's come over, and she's going off in a faint and a wakeness!"

This was true. The recent scene and excitement had been too much for the poor frail woman, and after a few weak gasps she fell back in her chair insensible.

Cold water was procured immediately, also whisky (Mr. Usher, who looked the last man in the world to carry a flask, produced one), and then he and his employer went out of the cottage, leaving the women to attend on the invalid.

As Lord Mulgrave's eyes met those of his companion, he said—

"Yes, Usher, she is my child, and her mother's daughter. Oh, what a blessing and happiness to come so suddenly, when I thought that life held no more—that nothing lay before me but the long, monotonous road that leads to the gate of death. Now I have something to——" He paused abruptly, and remembered himself. "You see how it is. The discovery of an unexpected treasure has been a shock, and I'm rambling, from sheer happiness. I will never forget, Usher, that I owe it chiefly to *you*."

A frightened face now appeared at the half-door, and Mary said—

"Oh, sir, me mother is took awful bad in her breathing. Will ye go and send some one for Doctor Manns? I've no red ticket,—but we can pay him."

The two visitors set off at once, and despatched a doctor post-haste from Glenveigh, with instructions that no exertions or expense were to be spared on behalf of Mrs. Foley.

The sick woman remained unconscious for twenty-four hours, and then rallied; but on the morning of the third day, when Lord Mulgrave walked over early in order to make his usual inquiries, he was met by Mary at the gate. Her eyes were red, and her face was sodden with crying.

"Oh, sir," she began, "sure I see you can guess!" She sobbed aloud, and the tears poured down her pale cheeks. "She was took off in her sleep about sunrise. Me mother is dead!"

CHAPTER XV

The letter (for it was altogether too serious and strange a story to telegraph) which reached Lady Mulgrave, relating the fact that Mary Foley was Joseline Dene, disturbed her to such a degree that she was compelled to plead a shocking headache, and lunch as well as breakfast, in her own apartments.

It took her some time to attempt to realise a stepdaughter, aged twenty-one, Irish, uneducated, vulgar, and tawdry. *What* could she do with the creature? A social atrocity, a well-born deformity! A girl with the best blood of France and England in her veins, and the ideas, aspirations, and deportment of a kitchen-maid! Oh, she felt as if the foundations of her position, were being upheaved.

If it were only possible to marry the creature, and get her out of the way! But who would care to be the husband of a horror who spoke with a common brogue, probably took sevens in gloves, dressed in emerald green, and had a passion for turf and potatoes?

This discovery was crushing. It seemed to threaten a hopeless state of affairs—a lifelong incubus! Yes, and an incubus who would take the precedence of Tito, and perhaps engage the somewhat flickering attentions of Tito's cavaliers!—not because of what she was, but of what she would ultimately be—Baroness Marchlyde in her own right, and heiress of many thousands per annum. Apparently there was no mistake about the matter. A sworn information, a legal witness! Alas! there was no escape in that direction. If the girl had been brought up under her father's roof it would have been a different affair; but twenty-one years in a dirty Irish mud cabin (impossible to dissociate the idea of mud and dirt from anything Irish)—it was too awful to contemplate. The abominable old foster-mother deserved to be hanged; but hanging and capital punishment she had cleverly evaded by death!

There was one small consolation: this new, uneducated person would be easily kept in the background; she resembled the horse and elephant, and was entirely ignorant of her own power, and ignorant she should remain. Lady Mulgrave was a woman who had acquired a special gift for repressing people. In the sweetest and most charming and smiling fashion she could administer the cruellest snubs; her rudeness of speech and manner at times bordered on brutality. To those whom she wished to "put down" or cast out from her circle, to any pushing nouveau riche, or dangerous rival, her affronts were as terrible and as ferocious, in their way, as if she were an East End virago, battering an enemy with a chair or a saucepan.

Lady Mulgrave sent off a charming, sympathetic letter to her husband, declaring that she was longing to welcome the dear child (lies are *so* easy on paper!), and that in a day or two she would move south and prepare to receive her at Westlands. She wrote the news to intimate friends as a dead secret, and would leave it to them to break it to all their acquaintance. "The old stock plot of a child changed at nurse has actually been flung as a bombshell into our quiet and everyday little family." (This is how she began her epistle.) "Imagine poor dear Owen, most conventional and practical of men, having a strange grown-up daughter, Irish and uneducated, suddenly thrust into his arms! Of course he has recognised her, claimed her, and brings her to England very shortly; but please, dear, keep this to yourself. We don't want any *talk*." When her ladyship had despatched her correspondence and her lunch, she summoned Miss Tito to her presence. Tito came in with a dishevelled appearance and a flushed face. She had been disturbed in a game of tennis—a match but half decided.

"Well, mum," she began, "are you better? What is it? Please don't keep me; I'm having such a ripping game, and they are waiting—Lord Bobby, Mr. Beaufort, Julia Legge, two sets all."

"I must detain you a few minutes to tell you a piece of family news"—and she took up her husband's letter, two sheets closely written. "What do you say to a sister?"—and she looked over at Tito.

"A sister!" repeated the girl, with a laugh, "a sister-in-law you mean; I suppose she will be a necessary evil?"

"No, but 'necessary evil' is a capital name for the new addition to our family"—and in a few pungent and rapid sentences, Miss Dawson was made acquainted with the facts.

First she opened her eyes, and then her mouth, and stood staring dumbfounded, and totally unable to speak. Next she tore off her hat, flung it on a table, and cast herself into a chair.

"It's not a joke, is it, mummy?"

"No indeed, but deadly earnest. Could anything be more unexpected, inconvenient and *odious*? Is not it too awful?"

"Yes; but I cannot get it into my head. What shall you do?"

"Make the best of it, of course."

"Fancy a common, low, Irish creature! Oh, I hope she won't expect me to kiss her, or to be seen about with her!"

"You had better be civil to her, Tito, though I grant you it is hard to have an interloper forced on one. She will make us three women—such an uncomfortable number in the carriage and at the opera; and, of course, she takes precedence of you."

"Well, anyway, she won't take any pals from me, or any partners. I should think she cannot come out, or be in the least presentable, until she has learnt how to dress and behave herself. I suppose she has never owned a pocket-handkerchief or a tooth-brush. Can she read and write?"

"Of course. Your father is delighted. Well, it is only natural. But——"

"But we are *not*. And it's only natural, eh, mum? There! they are calling me. I must fly. Shall I tell them?"

"No-o; only Lady Maxwelton and the girls privately. She is her aunt! It will ooze out presently. There will be the usual nine days' wonder. We must put up with that."

Tito picked up her hat and went over to a glass, settled her ruffled hair with both hands, and pinned on the picturesque pink muslin headgear, and stared at herself with a critical expression.

No—although her eyes were good and her dark hair thick, and curly, her nose, as she said herself, was all wrong—she was not pretty, only fascinating and fetching. She had no fear that the coming companion would supplant her. She felt serenely confident that no one would compare her with an awkward, ignorant country girl, even although she *was* an earl's daughter.

"I suppose I shall have to sit with my back to the horses in future," she exclaimed, "and walk behind her ladyship into a room! But I haven't got to share my allowance, or my maid, or partners. After all, perhaps I may like her very much; there's nothing bad that might not be worse. Yes," to a servant who had entered, "I'm coming—coming this moment."

Meanwhile, Mary—she could not get accustomed to her new name—had left Foley's farm the evening of Katty's death, and had been carried off to the "Glenveigh Arms" by her father. Here Miss Usher had been her true and kind friend, and endeavoured to comfort and console her, in what, in the lady's experience, was an unparalleled situation.

The girl was heart-broken at the death of a woman who was no relation, who had actually stolen her and brought her up in a station different to the one in which she was born; who had robbed her for years of her patrimony and her parent, as well as her position and wealth; yet Mary had no desire to be claimed. She shrank from "his lordship," as she called him, and earnestly pleaded to be permitted "to live for the rest of her life, according," as the Prayer-book says, "to its beginning." Her bewildered father was at his wits' end. All his newly-found daughter did, when in his society, was to weep, and weep, and weep! She most urgently desired to attend the wake, and passionately protested that if she were not present, people would "talk," and it would raise a terrible scandal in the county!

But no. Lord Mulgrave, although exceedingly anxious to please her in every way, was firm. It was not befitting that his daughter should be present at a wake. In every possible manner Mrs. Foley's funeral would be conducted with respect—the Foley family should be benefited; but Mary must endeavour to remember that she had no real connection with them—and was Lady Joseline Dene.

"Lady Joseline Dene!" cried she. "I just *hate* the likes of her!"—and she got up precipitately! and rushed away to her own room, where she buried her head in the bedclothes.

"There, you see. And what can I do?" he cried, appealing to Miss Usher; and his tone expressed despair.

"Leave her to Mrs. Hogan of the hotel," replied the lady; "she will talk to her in her own fashion, and by-and-by, when she has had a good rest—you know she has been sitting up nursing Katty for three whole nights—she will be different. At present she is overwrought and out of herself. It is a startling change for a girl—much less one of her impulsive and passionate nature—to lose an identity and a mother, and to find a father, all within the same week. Give her time, a good sleep, and some nourishing food. I should certainly permit her to attend the funeral, and I would arrange for her to have a long interview with Mike Mahon; he has been haunting the hotel. By-and-by he will turn her thoughts to her own mother in a manner, and in speech, we could never emulate."

"That is an excellent idea. Yes, she must then begin to realise things a little. At present, of course, she is suffering from want of rest, from grief, and from the first sad wrench. At present——"

"At present she is like some newly-caught bird," continued Miss Usher, "most miserably unhappy."

"I suppose every bliss has its drawback. This, which has been a supreme joy to me, is agony to her!"

"Leave her to herself for two or three days, and you will see a difference; her own friends will be your strongest allies. They will be so proud of her rank and uplifting that no matter *how* she desired it, they would never suffer her to return to Foley's Corner, and live among them as Mary of the gate."

"Thank you, Miss Usher; you give me wonderful comfort and encouragement, and I will take your advice—do all you say: go with her to the funeral, and allow her to remain here for a time. I *had* hoped to carry her off to-morrow. Of course, I have a great deal to do, as your brother points out. I must immediately make a new will, and I have to prepare my friends, and——"

"Would you permit me to offer yet another piece of advice?"

"Certainly. I shall be only too glad to accept it."

"Leave Mary here with me for, say, a fortnight, or even a month, and then return and fetch her. Yes, it may be terribly against the grain, but it will well repay you in the long run."

"How?" and he looked at her sharply.

"You see, if you take the girl away now, a grief-stricken, reluctant captive, who has not had time to realise herself and her new position, she will fret and pine—she will receive, and give, a wrong impression."

"But she is beautiful—you admit that?"

"Yes, but she is Mary Foley; she does not know how to dress, or enter a room, or arrange her hair, or even behave at table. She drinks out of a saucer; she uses her own knife for butter and salt."

"May I ask how you know?"

"I had tea with her once," replied Miss Usher drily. "Besides this, I would help her to weed the too forcible expressions out of her vocabulary—expressions such as 'For the love of God,' 'The saints protect me,' 'Faix,' 'Bedad,' 'Musha,' and 'Begorra.' Of course, a month is not long enough to supply the necessary instruction, but it will clip off the sharp corners and give her a little polish before she faces the severe ordeal of being presented to Lady Mulgrave and your relations. To leave her for a short time among her old surroundings would be a true kindness to her. She will have by that time become accustomed to her new character, and may have attained a certain amount of self-possession and confidence."

"All right then, Miss Usher; but the kindness is entirely yours. If you will continue to be her guide, counsellor, and friend, you lay me under a lifelong obligation. I will return home the day after the funeral and will leave you in sole charge. Shall you remain here?"

"Yes, that Mary may presently see herself as others—her old associates—see her."

"Miss Usher, you are a clever woman."

"No, no, only sensible. Bence has our brains."

"Of course you will have a private sitting-room, a carriage, and a maid?"

"Oh, no maid yet," she protested—"we are not quite ready for that; but we will be glad of this sitting-room and an outside car. And now I'm going to suggest something funny. Please send her a gold watch and chain. I gather that to an Irish peasant—and she is that—a gold watch and a long chain represent the visible sign of a great rise in life. It will come home to her as a most tangible proof that she is a girl of some position. Every time she looks at the watch she will be reminded of this fact. The watch and chain will give her proper pride and consequence."

"I cannot imagine it; but you know women, and I do not."

"You see, you must approach your daughter through the *Mary Foley* side of her character—touch her sensibilities as the peasant girl. There is one thing for which you have to be devoutly thankful."

"Yes, and what is that?" he asked gravely.

"She has no lover."

"Good heavens!"—and he grew suddenly white. "What an awful idea!"

"But surely a very commonplace idea. She is the beauty, or, at any rate, the *boast* of the county. She is twenty-one; she might have been married. Think of that!"

"Oh, I could not entertain such a horrible notion. Yes, I own I have much to be thankful for."

"Her inherited disposition, the race in her veins, has undoubtedly been her safeguard. She, as old Mike declared, was always for 'picking and choosing like a born lady.' Her suitors were beneath her standard; she is too fastidious."

"Thank God for that!" he exclaimed, with pious emphasis.

The following afternoon, the funeral of Katty Foley took place. It was an immense affair, for not only was the whole neighbourhood represented, but cars, asses' cars, and even turf cars, came laden for miles and miles—not so much to see the last of Katty Foley as the first of Lady Joseline! And Lady Joseline was present—accompanied by her father. Here she would have her own way, being dressed, or rather draped, in black—yes, and in the crêpe so dear to the heart of the Irish lower classes. Her gown was of heavy material that broiling August afternoon; but then, she had not been obliged to walk; she came in a carriage, it was noted, like the real lady she was—now. All eyes were concentrated on the girl as she stepped out and followed her father into the wild, overgrown graveyard which surrounded an old ruined church. She wore a hat, and a long crêpe veil with a deep border, and a pair of loose black kid gloves. Yes, they were proud of her!

She looked a lady, every inch. She was crying too, as any one could see, and not a bit uplifted, for all the neighbours could hear her sobbing and sniffing behind the crêpe fall. His lordship was a fine-looking, upstanding man, grave and erect, as became a lord. It was a terrible pity he wasn't Irish; but anyhow, his daughter was Irish born, and a credit to him, and the country.

Taking it all in all, he had behaved handsomely to Katty Foley, and the burying, which was of the best—a hearse and plumes, a beautiful coffin, and two coaches—was at his expense.

There was a good deal of whispering and nudging when the ceremony had concluded. Mary threw back the long veil, looked about her, and exhibited to the hundreds of watching eyes, a tear-stained and utterly miserable countenance.

In spite of her father's overawing presence, she was immediately encompassed by a crowd of friends. They swarmed round her, shook her by the hand, looked hard into her eyes to see if they were proud? No; only very sad, and wet with tears. More fluent than sympathy and regret for Katty, came warm expressions of amazement, and congratulation; but these were somewhat jarring, and found no echo in Mary's heart. Tom Kelly looked sheepish, and hung back. To think of his having made up to a lady born! When he glanced at his lordship he felt half inclined to run and hide behind one of the tombstones. Old Betty the Brag was present; she was getting on for eighty, but still wonderfully active. "Oh, me own little darlin' fair creature," she screeched, in her shrill old voice, "and hadn't she the great nerve to steal ye, and keep ye out of your own?"

Mike Mahon, the author and originator of the great discovery, remained aloof, gazing with melancholy pride upon her mother's daughter.

At last the earl, who had been surprisingly long-suffering, made a move to depart, and the crowd wrung Mary by the hand, with every description of English and Irish benediction. Hitherto she had been their own, and now she was leaving them—leaving them in tears. All the same, no bride in the country had ever received such a grand "send off" from her home, as did Mary Foley from the old Clonlara churchyard. The crowd streamed down *en masse* to the gate and lined the road three deep. "The place was black with them," as a man subsequently described it; "and such a commotion over a young girl was never, never seen." There was no thought of the poor corpse who had just been laid to rest. Every interest was centred on the young woman who was about to enter another state of life.

All her friends and acquaintances realised that Mary had taken leave of her former station, when she drove away in the pair-horse brougham, now rapidly passing out of sight.

The occasion was unprecedented. The crowd felt inclined to shout and to cheer, but a glance at the hearse, and the near sound of falling earth, restrained their enthusiasm. Presently, they scattered each to their place, or their own little shebeen, there to marvel, to discourse, and to prophesy, concerning Mary Foley's future.

CHAPTER XVI

It was wonderful how an old maid like Miss Usher had developed such a motherly heart, as well as so much worldly wisdom. She prudently abstained from intruding on her companion's grief, and left her to enjoy several good comfortable cries, and talks with Mrs. Hogan. She accompanied Mary on a car to see Lota one Sunday, and left her in the hands of old Mike, who proudly escorted her round the place, and pointed out the terrace, the room where she was born, and gave her the first and, needless to say, most eloquent, description of her own mother; and the disconsolate girl began at last to realise, as she stood listening to him, this mother whom she had never seen.

"An' sure ye have the hair and eyes and hands, aye, and the very walk of her," declared Mike. "Though Katty brought ye up on a flagged floor, ye see these things come out in the appearance."

"And so you have guessed it all the time?"

"Is it guess?" he repeated indignantly. "Sure, haven't I *known* it."

"And that was why you used to come and stare at me in that strange way?"

"To be sure it was. And what else?"

"And I have never seen her!"

"It would be hard for ye, seein' she giv' her life for yours. But when ye look in the glass ye see her. I'm told when his lordship first laid eyes on ye he got a terrible turn. He's gone home for the present, and left ye with the ould wan over there," indicating Miss Usher, who, under a distant tree, was happy with a book. "An' for why?"

"Because I didn't want to stir, I think, and I made so strange——"

"Now what balderdash is that, yer telling me?" cried Mike.

"Man alive, isn't he a stranger? Ye'll not deny that. If he'd let me, I'd go back and live in Foley's Corner, this very blessed hour."

"Would ye now!" he rejoined, with an expression of sovereign contempt. "And all by yerself, too! Bridgie Grogan is going home at wance, wid her pocket well lined. Faix, that was the easily earned money! His lordship also giv' her all the furniture and stock, you having no call for it. The place is to be shut up, and not a hate left in it. Bridgie says it's entirely too lonely for her, is Foley's Corner."

"But suppose I *chose* to stay on?—then what would ye say?"

"That you had a right to be taken out of it, and put in the county lunatic asylum."

"But surely the lease, and the cows and pigs, were coming to me?"

"An' for why? Ye were no relation to Katty whatever, and isn't Bridgie her own sister?"

Mary stared at him in silence. Yes, he was right; the house was Mrs. Grogan's, and the door of that home was closed to her. She was shut out from her old life in the cottage, and must accept her new quarters in the castle. For the first time since Katty's death she began to catch a faint glimpse of herself, as "Lady Joseline."

"I expect you'll have Bridgie coming round to see yer ladyship this evening. She might bring you a few bits of things and your duds. I know she's aching to get off home."

"Who is going to have the cat?"

"The white cat, ye mane? 'Tis no bargain for any one; an ugly blackguard of a thing. I'm thinking the lake will take him, as it has done his betters."

"No, no, Mike, I'll have him! the poor angashore."

"What's that yer saying?"

"Yes, and give him whatever home I have, as long as he lives."

"Faix, it's well known he has nine lives! You and the white cat! Well, to be sure. A nice ornament he is to be transported over to England. I'm thinking they'll get a cruel bad notion of the breed of Irish cats. But maybe he's dead by now."

"No. And I want you to go up to Biddy Grogan's and tell her to bring him this evening in a basket, will ye?"

"'Tis a quare fancy ye have! But I'll do yer commands. I wish it was meself yer ladyship was taking along wid her instead of an ould scorched tom-cat, wid a bad character."

"Do not call me yer ladyship!"

"Arrah! an' what else am I to call ye?"

"Mary."

"Sure, how can I put such a lie in me mouth as *that*?—yer name being Joseline, and a quare one, too, and it was given ye within there in the drawing-room"—pointing to the apartment which harboured the boat—

"and you were christened by the Reverend William Scott, in a great hurry, and out of the General's old china punch-bowl."

"How do you know all that?"

"Because the windows, as ye see, are big, and I was working round the flower-beds. And sure, didn't all the world know ye were baptised that day; her ladyship, your mother, wished it. I saw ye; we all did, for his lordship was the proud man. Ye were wrapped up in a white shawl, and had a head on you as red as a carrot, and a screech out of ye like a peacock. More betoken, there was a peacock sitting on the roof; it came over from Lord Warner's place. When I saw it, the heart crossed in me, for them's, as ye know, the *unlucky* birds. Sure enough that night her ladyship took bad. Oh, it would have made a great differ to you, aye and to every one, if she had lived; and by all accounts she found it terribly hard to go and leave ye all."

"Who told you?" inquired the girl under her breath.

"Oh, I heard it. When she knew she had but a couple of hours to spare, she sent for his lordship and talked, talked, talked, striving her best to comfort him, and telling him to be brave, with her very last breath. Oh, 'twas she had a spirit, and when she went it made small differ to her—sure, she was always an angel."

"She was buried over in England?"

"Yes, and with Katty Foley's three-months baby lying alongside of her."

"Well, I'm glad I've come here, Mike, and seen this place and had a talk with you—you who found it all out. Somehow it makes things seem more *real.* But I'll never get used to it—never; and that's as true as I am standing here."

"Oh, yes, ye will; only take your time. When you get fine dresses, and learn talk and manners, it will be as easy to you as eating your dinner."

"But sure, I've no talk, and no manners, Mike."

"You'll soon learn them, me dear, for ye see it's not as if you were a real common country girl; ye have her ladyship's manners and talk *in* ye somewhere, and they are bound somehow or other to come out! I tell ye this, that in a year's time you won't know yourself, and I won't know you."

"But I will always know *you*, Mike; and you must come over to England, and see me, if I am to have any say."

"I think you'll find you'll have a good say."

"Perhaps with his lordship, for—for"—with an effort—"my mother's sake; but the ladies."

"Sure, aren't you a lady, me darlin?"

"No, no! I feel so frightened of all that's before me."

"And what would frighten ye? Keep a stout heart—be a good girl; what harm can come to you? One would think they'd ate yer!"

"People have a way of doing that, sometimes."

"I know what ye mane—some bad ones, that never has a good word for a crature, and are always chewing up others and passing remarks; but the likes of them are not among the gentry!" (Poor simple Mike!) "All your friends is proud for ye, but sorry for themselves, ye being taken up out of their station. There's one, howsomever, that will be glad of yer uprise, when he hears it." Here Mike paused, and his expression became shrewd and personal.

Mary stared at him interrogatively, and then a sudden tinge of pink, flooded her pale face.

"Ye mane Mr. Ulick," she said boldly. "I'd just hate——Whist!" for here Miss Usher broke in upon the *tête-à-tête*, which had lasted more than an hour. It seemed to her, that the time had been well employed. Mary's expression was not quite so dismal; there was a little colour in her face, a spark of animation in her glance. She accepted a bunch of flowers from Mike, and as Mike and Miss Usher moved away together, talking, they suddenly noticed that the girl lagged behind.

"Take no notice," he muttered; "she's coming to herself nicely. I think she's picking a pebble off the terrace where her mother used to walk, aye, and a bit of a rose from the house. Pass no remark whatever, but ye may take it from me, that it's a good sign. The lady bred in her bones is bound to come out *yet*——"

CHAPTER XVII

As they swung along homewards, one on each side of a well-hung jaunting-car, with a slashing four-year-old between the shafts, Miss Usher and her companion never exchanged a single remark. The elder lady was reflecting that she had done a capital afternoon's work in introducing Mary to her birthplace, and she felt confident that the words she had heard from old Mike had sunk down into her heart, and brought the girl to realise what had never yet dawned upon her: that only by birth—the mere accident of birth—did she belong to this beautiful, romantic, green and blue country—for if the trees and pastures were emerald, the mountains were royal blue, the skies cobalt.

The crafty lady determined that she would not break the spell, but give Mary ample time to meditate on these matters, and presently adjust herself to her strange circumstances; she must now begin to see about some suitable clothes for the girl, and to offer, cautiously and by degrees, a few lessons on manners and deportment. After all, it would not be an onerous task; in fact, to an old maid with a warm heart, hitherto centred on her brother and a white cockatoo—it was a pleasure to interest herself in this young life, for the time entrusted to her care. Indeed she felt her own youth renewed as an eagle's! Lord Mulgrave had left them but one week, and already Mary was a little less Mary Foley than formerly. She drove out in a hat (swathed in crêpe), no longer in her "hair." She had cast off with joy her aprons and cobbler's shoes, and taken quite meekly to black thread stockings, a black silk parasol, and kid gloves; also she often closed the door when she entered a room, and did not now peel her potato on the table-cloth, or drink tea out of her saucer. Yes, already there was an improvement, the girl was adaptable and quick to learn—she never required to be told anything twice; her personal tastes were curiously and unexpectedly refined; her petticoats and stockings were certainly coarse, but as neat and trim as those of any fine lady; and as to pocket-handkerchiefs, they were almost as fine as Miss Usher's own.

Whilst the good, kind woman was occupied with these reflections, Mary was engaged in a similar manner. Her active, imaginative brain was filled with the picture of the beautiful lady who had died at Lota. Could she really be *her* mother? Was it true that she was like her? She pulled off her glove and gravely considered her hand. Certainly it was small—too small for dairy work—and the fact had been cast up to her! If that marvellous beauty were her mother, oh! she was a shocking falling off; a common, ignorant, low creature, who did not know how to talk, or walk, or sit, or eat, like the quality—and who was too old to learn. But if she was this other girl (even to herself, she would not say "Joseline Dene")—and people seemed to believe it, and Father Daly had been very eager about her taking up her birthright, and her duties—she must learn. With the help of God she was bound to do her best, not forgetting her old friends, as he had said, nor disgracing the beautiful lady that had brought her into the world, and whose place, late as it was, she must endeavour to fill. Oh, but what was the use of talking or thinking. She never could be anything but Mary Foley. The driver of the car happened to be a certain Patsie Maguire, Mary's former partner, friend, declared (and declined) lover. He too had his private meditations, which now and then stung him so sharply that he laid the unnecessary whip, on the sleek and thin-skinned flanks of the flying chestnut, and almost invited a catastrophe. Here was he, by the stress of circumstances, actually driving for hire her ladyship, no less! Mary Foley—the great lord's daughter, who was soon quitting Ireland and him. She, his partner, his girl, his intended wife—for of course if let alone, she'd have come round, and married him. And what would hinder him now, to let the young red mare run away, accidentally on purpose, and break their three necks? The present situation was enough to make a man mad. Was he not attending in the capacity of a servant, a girl whom hitherto he had considered a little beneath him in position? His mother, the daughter of a well-to-do publican, rented a small farm, had been brought up on a carpeted floor, and kept even now her own cover car. And Mary Foley, was just a good-looking, gay little creature, with fifty pounds fortune. Of course, every one knew he could have done far better, but *she* had such pretty, joking ways with her; she had made a fool of him, and faix, by all accounts he was in good company! Then before anything was fixed comes this sort of fairy tale, and "Mary at the corner" is turned at one stroke into her ladyship, and he himself driving her like any hired boy. When she got up on the car she had just nodded at him, her face as long as a ha'porth of bacon, and said— "Is that yer self, Pat? How are ye?"

And not another word; and coming home she had never opened her mouth once. He'd make her do that, if it was only screaming—for a pin's head, he'd upset the machine.

Pat—"handsome Pat" as he was called—was about seven-and-twenty, and certainly as good-looking a fellow as could be met with in a day's walk—and not indifferent to the fact. His was the real type of Celtic face—dark blue eyes, dark hair and brows, well-shaped, somewhat refined features, white teeth, and eyelashes so long and so effective, that to a London débutante they might have proved an asset of extraordinary value.

Pat was capable and active when he chose, but innately lazy and self-indulgent. He liked dancing, he liked horses, and porter, and singing, and girls. The girls liked him—indeed so did many people, for when Pat was in the humour, his manner was irresistible. His mother and eldest sister kept the farm, where at present he was out of favour, and had taken on a job at the hotel. His mother adored her handsome Pat—so clever, so well schooled, and so smart! His shirts were invariably white as snow, his clothes well mended. Once he had taken it into his head to go to America, where he remained one year, and then returned, because, as he said, "His mother was dying after him"; also because (though this he did not divulge) the country did not suit him. It was true that good money was to be earned, but the work was hard and continuous, and the price of everything was so high, that it swallowed up the dollars. It suited him better to have smaller earnings and easier labour; to live at home, and be a comfort to his mother. Pat and his sister, an industrious, strong-willed, hot-tempered woman, did not always agree. Now and then a domestic storm arose. Occasionally Lizzie's tongue drove Pat abroad, and he went off and took service. He enjoyed the bit of change for one thing, and for another, he was pleasantly alive to the fact that, during his absence, his mother was leading Lizzie a devil of a life, and paying off his score with interest.

Having arrived safely at the "Glenveigh Arms," Miss Usher descended in a gingerly manner from the car, and walked straight into the hall in search of letters.

Here was Pat's opportunity, and leaning over to Mary, he thus addressed her in a low voice.

"Am I never to have a word with you again, asthore, and you going off for ever and ever, and taking the heart out of my body along with you?"

"I'm not going yet—no, nor soon. But sure, what's the good of talking nonsense about yer heart? To me own knowledge, you've given it away twenty times."

"It will be a relief to me to spake, anyhow. Are ye going up to the corner again?"

"Of course I am—to see my aunt Bridgie and the place, and to fetch away the cat."

"I'll bring him down to-night for you. You have only to say the word."

"Well, then, maybe you might as well, Pat; and you must mind and butter his feet, and put him in one of the old egg-baskets. I'm taking him to England."

"Faix, he'll be an elegant souvenir! But every one to his taste, as the monkey said, when he kissed the parrot! Whist now, there's Bridgie Grogan sitting within the hall a-waiting to see ye. I believe she has all cleared out at the house above already. She's mad to be off home wid her takings. That wan will talk ye out of yer shoes! Mind, you and me must have a few words together before ye go—for the sake of old times."

Mary nodded her head in assent, and the frantic chestnut, who had been champing, jumping, and tearing up the ground, was at last suffered to fling herself into the stable yard.

The news of Mary Foley's sudden transformation flew round the county like wild-fire. Barky heard it in the stables, and brought it to his mother at dinner.

"Now Barky," she cried, "you've been drinking again! and you know you promised me on your honour, not to touch whisky between meals."

"I'm as sober as a judge, so don't be flying into one of your tantrums for nothing; it's the solid truth I'm telling you."

"What, Mary below, the daughter of Lord Mulgrave! And Kitty bringing her up as her own! Well"—and she gasped—"I don't believe it."

"You can please yourself about that, but it's true."

"I remember them at the cottage," she returned, "and I went and called, but they just left cards here. They wanted no visitors. She was a pretty, Frenchy-looking young woman and—yes—Mary has a look of her. I wonder I never noticed it. But who would dream of looking for *her* child in Katty Foley's smoky cabin?"

"If for it's smoky, 'tis your own fault. You never will do a thing to the chimneys—often as you are asked."

"Yes, I see the likeness. And there was always something queer and independent about Mary, that I could never quite make out; she was never shy, or embarrassed."

"Now you have it. She's an aristocrat."

"And what a match for some one!"

"It's a pity you snuffed out that affair with Ulick, or she might be your daughter-in-law this day."

"Of course she is impossible-a mere ignorant peasant. What an awful situation for the poor Mulgraves!"

"Oh, she's a bright enough girl. I daresay she can write, and speak, as well as any—and hold her own too."

"Who told you this story?"

"Tom Whelan; he had it from Mrs. Hogan at the 'Arms'; the lawyer and his sister are there, and his lordship too."

"Really! Oh, then, you must leave a card on him to-morrow."

"You and your card-leaving, mother! Maybe you will go and leave one on Mary."

"Of course; as soon as she is established in her new position I shall certainly call; it will be my duty to do so, considering that she was reared here, and lived on our land for twenty-one years."

"And has kept you going in your trade of eggs and chickens. This is no doubt one of her chickens I'm eating this minute."

"I wish you would marry her, Barky."

"And I don't. In the first place, she wouldn't look at me; she is accustomed to refusing; and in the second, she's too much coxy and fiery. I tried to kiss her once, and she left the print of her five fingers on my face."

"You ought to be ashamed of yourself, Barky."

"Why? I'd kiss any girl that would let me. Now if I'd been Ulick, it would have been *all right*".

"Maybe it will be Ulick—yet."

"No, mammy. Use your common sense. She's as much above him now, as he was above her before; it's like a see-saw. Now I'm up, now you are down."

"Ulick is good enough for any one!"

"Faith! you don't think so when he is here; he is not nearly good enough for you. You have always a pick out of him!"

"I mean as a match!"

"Such as an earl's only daughter, with, say, ten thousand a year—oh, stop coddin, now!"

"Barky, where *do* you get hold of such horrible expressions?"

"Anyhow, Ulick is in India," he continued. "Shall I telegraph out to him, 'Come home at once—Mary Foley is a peeress'?"

"No, she is not a peeress—and you're an unmannerly boor!" As she spoke, Mrs. Doran got up and pushed back her chair; and as she walked to the door, Barky gave a loud, unfilial laugh,—

"If ye were more civil to common folk, mammy, and less civil to the big ones, it would be better for us. Look at Aunt Nora, and the fine fortune you lost *me*! And now Mary Foley, and the great match you lost *Ulick*!"

"How was I to know that the old bagwoman was your aunt herself, coming to spy on me?" she demanded passionately. "And would *any* mother, in her senses, allow her son to marry a common country girl off the side of the road? Tell me that? When you talk such nonsense you drive me mad!" and she went out and slammed the door with violence.

Mrs. Doran called in due state on Mary and Miss Usher. She sent up her cards in proper form.

"Oh, it's Mrs. Doran," cried Mary. "Oh, miss, I don't want to see her. I can't *bear* her; she makes me tingle all over, ever since I was a young one. 'Tis she is the hard bitter woman."

"Still, she is coming to start a fresh acquaintance, with a new Mary Foley, and you must receive her as one lady receives another."

"She's no lady! and I told her so to her face!"

The door opened as she spoke, and Mrs. Doran, in her best beaded mantle and feathered toque, sailed in, now all smiles and affability.

"Well, Mary"—offering two hands—"this is indeed *great* news. I am so glad, and I have come as your oldest friend, to offer my warm congratulations, and good wishes."

"Thank you, yer ladyship!" said the girl faintly.

"Oh, *you* are the ladyship now, Mary," she rejoined, with an affable smile, "and this is, I presume, Miss Usher?" And as Miss Usher was only a legal woman, she bowed stiffly, and subsided into a chair.

"And now do tell me all about it, my dear? No one can be more interested than I am, who have seen you all your life, and have met your own mother."

"It's just this, yer ladyship—that I am not Mrs. Foley's daughter at all, but a nurse child she kept, and made out was her own—and buried her girlie instead of me; and now it's all come out."

"And are you immensely delighted?"

"No, I am not; I'd sooner stay as I am, except for a few things. I'm not educated, nor fit to be a lady."

"Oh, you will soon learn, Lady Joseline," put in Miss Usher. "It will all come quite easy; it is so much pleasanter to go up, than down."

Mrs. Doran stared at the speaker, and said, "And what are the few things you wish for most?"

"Nice dresses, and books, and pretty things, and not having to wash clothes, and scour."

"Still, you were fond of poultry?"

"No, I never wish to see another hen; but I do love flowers."

"I suppose you have no plans as yet?"

Mary paused and looked interrogatively at Miss Usher. "I believe we are going to England soon."

"Never to return, eh, Mary?" She asked persuasively, with her head on one side.

"I don't know."

"I presume Lord Mulgrave has a London house?"

"That's more than I can tell ye."

"Because if so, my sister, Lady Barre, will call upon you at once. Will you come up to tea to-morrow? I'll send the carriage for you?"

Mary became scarlet. "Thank you ma'am, no."

"No?" she repeated, in a tone of angry incredulity.

"You see," said Miss Usher, coming to the rescue, "Mary is a little strange as yet, and is very shy and awkward."

"I suppose it's only natural"—appeased. "Well, you won't forget your old friends, will you, my dear?"—rising to go.

"No, Mrs. Doran"—and she looked her in the face—"I won't forget my old—friends."

Mrs. Doran returned the gaze with observant scrutiny—she read in Mary's eyes, hostility and dislike. Evidently there was nothing to be made out of her; and presently she went rustling downstairs.

As the carriage rolled off, the girl ran to the window and said: "To think of me! Offered a seat in that! I'd as soon have expected to be asked to take a seat on a throne. Well, there goes the last of Mrs. Doran, please God!"

* * * * *

The "Glenveigh Arms" was an unpretentious hostelry, standing close to the roadside, from which a narrow strip of gravel and a low laurel hedge divided it—a long, plain, whitewashed house, with nothing attractive in its appearance. Strangers little guessed how comfortable it was within, and what a really beautiful old garden lay concealed behind it.

Motors whirled by in a cloud of dust and ignorance, making for a fine new tourist hotel some miles ahead. Mrs. Hogan did not approve of these "mad" cars, that went racking and tearing through the country, killing dogs and poultry and scaring the cattle out of their seven senses! and made no attempt to secure their custom. The word "Garage" was not advertised along with "Mary Hogan, Livery and Bait Stables."

All the same, about a week after Mary's expedition to Lota, a smart bright red Mercédès car, containing four passengers, halted and palpitated outside the hotel.

It contained two men in motoring coats and goggles, the chauffeur in black leather; a valet sat beside him, and there was a certain amount of luggage, indicating that the party was making an extensive tour. The two gentlemen got out and went into the hotel. The tallest of them, when he removed his mask, proved to be a man of about thirty, with a dark, handsome face, a clean-cut profile, and a pair of sleepy eyes. He was Captain Dudley Deverell, Lord Mulgrave's cousin, and heir. His companion, Sir Harry Coxford, was a tubby little round-faced man with a red moustache and many freckles. The two travellers were ceremoniously ushered into the drawing-room.

"No, we don't want rooms, thanks," said Captain Deverell, in a pleasant drawl. "Want to see Lord Mulgrave—heard he was here."

"His lordship left ten days ago," said a trim, black-whiskered waiter, who looked like a Methodist parson in evening dress. "We don't expect his lordship back at present."

"No"—looking round superciliously—"I should think *not.*"

"But a—any message or letter to his lordship, will a—be forwarded to his lordship?"

"Oh, it's of no consequence. We were in this part of the world and happened to hear he'd been here, and we looked in on chance, that's all."

"Can I get you two gentlemen any refreshment?"

"No"—looking round the low sitting-room with narrow windows and old-fashioned furniture.

"Lord, how it smells of musty hay!" exclaimed Sir Harry.

"And flowers," added his friend. "I say, what roses!—yes, and a garden at the back"—walking over. "I wonder what sort of people come here?" and, staring out at the unexpectedly large pleasance, with its wide gravel walks, and old-fashioned benches, "I say," to the waiter, "what sort of people stay here?"

"The *best* sort, sir," replied the waiter, who had been secretly indignant at the bold, cheap air of these motoring gents. "People comes here that like comfort and quiet. No cheap trippers. There's some took in at other hotels as Mrs. Hogan would have the hall washed after, if they had the impudence to put a foot in it! We have our own farm, the finest poultry in the country, fruit and vegetables, good cars and horses on hire, and"—as a grand climax—"a *bath*-room."

"Dear me!" exclaimed Sir Harry, putting up his eyeglass.

"Yes. At present we have his lordship's sister's man of business here. I mean the man of business' sister of his lordship."

"The man of business' sister of his lordship," drawled Captain Deverell. "What the dickens *do* you mean?"

The cool, superior air of the "young high flyer," as he mentally termed him, inflamed the waiter's wrath; his Celtic temper rose fast; he resolved to give this contemptuous inquirer one for his nob.

"Miss Usher, sir, I mean."

"Oh, old Usher's sister," said the captain, turning to his friend. "Then"—to the waiter—"is Mr. Usher staying here too?"

"No, sir; he left with his lordship some time back."

"Leaving Miss Usher alone?"

"Oh, no, sir. It's not giv' out yet exactly on the papers; but she's keeping company with her ladyship, his lordship's daughter."

Captain Deverell stared hard at the waiter, then looked at his friend and laughed. As he resumed his goggles, he exclaimed: "This Ireland is a funny place, isn't it, Coxy? The land of romance, eh?"

"Yes, one must come to the back of the world for news, I see. Well, now we really must get on. It is past four o'clock."

And the pair tramped noisily through the hall; and presently the motor departed with a triumphant "Tuff, tuff, tuff!"

CHAPTER XVIII

On the occasion of this visit Miss Usher happened to be laid up with a severe cold, suspiciously akin to a touch of the "flue," and was nursing herself in her sitting-room. Meanwhile, her young companion had set out for Foley's Corner, in quest of the white cat, who, despite of his buttered paws, daily returned to his late abode with praiseworthy devotion. It was true that the doors and windows were closed, that there was nothing available to eat or to drink, but nevertheless, he was to be found sitting with pathetic patience on Katty's window, or making the air hideous with his melancholy caterwaulings.

Mary thought but little of the mile and a half distance, and directly after tea she and "Rap" had departed to fetch "Whitey." She enjoyed the walk there, when she could be alone, and think, and as Miss Usher was not about, she sallied forth, as in former times, in her "hair"—that is to say, bareheaded, with her hat slung over her arm. She wore a white spotted cotton dress-an old friend, made by an old friend—the weather was much too warm for crêpe and wool; and the same friend, Maggie Kane, met her, and walked part of the way with her, and said good-bye at the cross above the corner. Maggie's manner had been a mixture of constraint and freedom, and Mary had begun to realise the bitter truth of Miss Usher's prophecy. Old comrades and schoolfellows were changed—if she was really her ladyship, she had no call to mix with them as one of themselves; she had a right to go away. They were no longer at ease with Mary, nor she with them. Yes; Miss Usher's plan was working to admiration. Formerly she went in and out among the neighbours, and they were only too glad to welcome Mary Foley; but this grand Lady Joseline was another person. At one time—even three weeks ago—Mary would have felt broken-hearted to leave them all. Now, much as she still liked them, and much as she dreaded her future, she was secretly impatient to depart. Wise old women had given her advice, and Mrs. Hogan, her former patroness, had said to her privately, "See here, Mary, me dear! ye have no part nor lot among us *now*; you're a lady born, and a titled lady; sure, look at your finger-nails yerself!—and ye must just make the best of it. I've no call whatever to be talking so free with ye, and I know it; but I'm fond of ye, lovey, and proud—and so is all the countryside: and we think you should just go quietly to your own, and get the education, and the airs, as is your *due*."

"But I'd ever so much rather stay here!" she protested with tears.

"But you can't, me dear—ye cannot be fish and fowl at the wan time. Sure, ye haven't a soul over here belonging to yer; and it makes people unaisy in themselves, to be sitting talking to ye, cheek by jowl, as Mary Foley, knowing as 'tis standing up and dropping curtseys to her ladyship as they should be half the time. Sometimes I declare when I think of the liberties I've took wid ye as a young girl, I break out into a cold sweat, saving yer presence."

"Then I must go," she cried. "And none of ye want me!" and she burst into sobs. "Oh, I'd never have believed it of ye!"

"If 'twas only Mary ye wor, we all want ye; and the young boys, especially Tom Grady, and poor Dan that's heart-broke, and Patsie Maguire, that's killing himself with bad whisky for your sake."

"Tom! Dan!" repeated the girl; and her face grew scarlet.

"Yes,—see now, the very names brings all the lady's blood in yer body, to yer face! 'Tis her ladyship coming out, and proud and haughty, as is fit for an earl's daughter."

"An earl's daughter!" echoed Mary. "It's all like a dream. I was better as I was before, a thousand times!"

"So we would have ye, my dear; but ye must make up yer mind to the other lot in life. Faix, and it will come aisy. The ould wan above" (she meant Miss Usher) "know's what's what, and will put ye in training. I'd be entirely said and led by her if I was you. You look a lady when ye have the hat on, and ye will *be* a lady yit!"

Mary was thinking over this conversation as she leant against the gate at Foley's Corner with "Rap" and the cat sitting sedately beside her. Miss Usher had talked of leaving as soon as her cold was better, and as it might be that she was now standing at her lifelong post for the last time, she fell into a dreamy meditation. The various faces she remembered seemed to pass the gate in single file. Master Ulick, on his bay hunter; Old Mike Daly; Kathleen Sullivan, her friend, who died of a decline, and the match made up and all; Bridgie Curran, her schoolfellow, whose boy was in America; Timmy Maher, who had asked her to marry him here at this very spot; Johnny Sugrue, who was killed in the war; and scores and scores of others. All that life was behind her, as much as if she were dead. No one would ever come to speak to her again at the gate. No one—*ever*! She had taken leave of the cottage which had been the home of many joys and sorrows—and kissed the little star on the window in token of farewell: for years she had never slept without first pressing her sweet red lips upon the irresponsive glass; but of late she had relinquished the habit. What was Mr. Ulick to her? Or she to Mr. Ulick? The scar was healing—time and silence are great physicians; yet "the tender grace of a day that was dead" occasionally stole into her heart, and it was a fact, that the sudden mention of one name invariably brought the colour to her cheek. Since Ulick Doran went away he had never sent but one sign; and that, thanks to the delinquencies of the local post, was fifteen long months, in reaching its destination.

Judy Flynn was the mistress of a secondary makeshift post office, where the mail car picked up a small bag, en route from village to village; and Mrs. Flynn held a licence to sell stamps, as well as tobacco and tea. Judy was a widow—a character, and a notorious gossip. All the news in the county emanated from "the cross." And if tales were true, no wonder. Judy kept a kettle handy and opened and read every letter that seemed to her to be of general interest! It was she who made known how John MacCarthy was owing for seed-potatoes nigh on three years, and likely to be put in court. How Mary Hannigan's boy had gone back on her! Why the Connors were leaving Moreen, and when old Murphy had married his cook. Her shop was a place of the wildest, maddest confusion; behind the little counter letters, parcels, canisters of tobacco, pipes, old newspapers, herrings, and packets of tea, were inextricably mixed with portions of Mrs. Flynn's wardrobe.

"If ye will only lave me alone, and don't moider me, I can lay me hand on everything," was her invariable boast. Her business methods were at least original. Sometimes she went out, locked the door after her, and left the yawning post-bag hanging on a nail, where the passer-by might post (or extract) letters, precisely as he or she pleased.

But Judy Flynn, stout survival of old times and ways, continued to flourish in spite of numerous complaints from afar. When brought to book, she wept torrents of tears, assuming the attitude of a persecuted, hard-working widow woman. She had strong local interest; her backers were sensible that if Judy was superseded, they would lose much exciting and unexpected information; and as her office was a mere cross-post, serving a small insignificant district, Judy remained.

One beautiful June afternoon Judy beckoned to Mary Foley, who was passing her door.

"See here, acushla," she cried, "there's been a bit of a parcel for ye this whiles back. It come one evening, and I put it up safe, and forgot it, till I found it 'ere last week behind the meal-chest, when I was looking for a spool. Being a parcel, it's no harm; if it was a letter I'd be main sorry; an' here it is"—dusting it as she spoke.

"For me?" said Mary incredulously.

"Yes. Ye don't trouble the post much; all yer boys are within spakin' distance of ye. That thing looks like a book, and is from India."

"India!" repeated the girl confusedly. "Sure I know no one out there!"

"Oh, yes, me darlin', ye know *wan*," replied Mrs. Flynn, with a significant nod. "I can't say if it's in his writing, for the Castle letters does not come this way."

Mary made no reply; she tucked the parcel under her arm, and saying, "Good evening to ye kindly, Mrs. Flynn," stepped forth.

Poor disappointed Mrs. Flynn remained staring after her, till a turn in the road hid her figure from sight. Subsequently she told a neighbour that "Mary Foley was getting a bit crabbed in herself, and looked like a girl that had something on her *mind*."

Mary desired to be alone, and far away from every human eye, when she opened her parcel; she felt instinctively that it came from Mr. Ulick; he and she had often talked of books; he had offered to lend her several; he knew that she was a great reader. Anyhow, this book was a sign that he was thinking of her still. She crossed several fields by a narrow footpath, and at last, at the back of a stile, rarely used, halted and proceeded to investigate her treasure. She studied the writing, the cover, the stamps; finally she cut the string with her excellent white teeth, and a little volume of poetry was disclosed—*Songs of the Glens of Antrim.*

Then she sat down in the long grass, and began to examine it carefully. No name was inscribed within. As she turned over the pages with hasty, tremulous fingers, she came to one, on which was scrawled, in pencil, the word "Mary." Below ran the title: "I mind the day."

"I mind the day. I wish I was a say-gull flying far,
For then I'd fly and find you in the West;
And I wish I was a little rose—as sweet as roses are,
For then you'd maybe wear it on your breast.

I wish I could be living near to love you day and night,
To let no trouble touch you, or annoy,
I wish I could be dyin' here to rise a spirit light,
If them above 'ud let me win you joy.

And now I wish no wishes, nor ever fall a tear;
Nor take a thought beyond the way I'm led:
I mind the day that's overby, and bless the day that's near,

Then be to come—a day, when we'll be dead;

A longer, lighter day, when we'll be dead."

Mary read this quickly, with a catch in her breath; then slowly; finally with eyes so dim, that she could scarcely distinguish the words, and her tears pattered down upon the pages.

This pathetic and touching lament reopened the gates of the poor girl's grief. Misery stalked in, and resumed the seat from which, time, youth, and summer, had almost dislodged her.

Fifteen months previously, a brother officer on the trooper had given the book to Ulick. Ulick, still smarting from his separation, had found that the lines exactly interpreted his own feelings, and in a spasm of imprudent impulse had posted the book to Mary the very day he landed in Bombay.

And now Mary had received it at last. The poem recalled a bygone ecstasy that could never, never return, and in a passion of despair, anguish, and rebellion she cast herself face downwards in the soft June grass. She might have been lifeless, she remained there so long, and lay so still; but the birds in the thorn hedge and the bees among the clover knew better. They heard her low, stifled sobs. It was only a girl who had lost something—or who had been robbed of her all. Well, they had known the experience themselves!

The June evening was five years ago, and Mary, like the birds, had outgrown her heartbreak.

As she stood leaning on the gate for the last time, dreamily reviewing the past years, there was a loud rumbling, whizzing sound, and a red motor shot by, leaving a cloud of dust and a hideous smell of petroleum. This same motor had not travelled half a mile before it broke down. The by-road was covered with sharp, loose stones, and a tyre was punctured.

"It will be nothing much," announced the chauffeur, "but it will take time."

"What do you call time?" inquired Sir Harry Coxford.

"About an hour, sir."

"An hour! How is that hour to be killed?" drawled his companion and host.

"I know"—slapping his leg. "I noticed a pretty girl at a gate about a quarter of a mile back—just below a cottage. Let us go and have a look at her, and a talk."

"Let us go anywhere and stretch our legs, as long as it is not far."

"You lazy beggar! I never met your match. You wouldn't walk half a mile to look at a pretty face, eh?"

"Not five yards to look at the prettiest face in Ireland. Come on. Lead the way to the miraculous beauty at the gate. I bet you a sov. she is ugly, or she has gone."

"Done!" rejoined Sir Harry, and they strolled along down the straight road towards the corner.

"No; there she is!" cried Sir Harry. "I see her dress."

There she was indeed, still leaning on the gate, so absorbed in her own thoughts that the two gentlemen were within a few yards of her, when she realised their presence with a violent start.

"Good evening," said Sir Harry, taking off his cap. He had an affable manner of talking to refreshment-room young ladies. "You seem buried in meditation. I'm afraid we disturbed you."

"Oh, no, not at all," she answered briskly. Here were some people to talk and chaff with—her very last visitors.

"I expect you were thinking of *him*," he suggested, with a significant glance.

She coloured to her hair, and looked haughty.

"Come, come. A pretty girl like you is bound to have a score of lovers."

"That's true!" she assented, with a touch of her old sauciness, suddenly resolved to act the part of Mary once more—"but *she* need never trouble her head to think of them."

"What were you thinking of, then? I say, if you'll tell me the honest truth I'll give you a sovereign, or rather, this other gentleman will, for your thoughts."

"My thoughts are not for sale. They are my own."

"Very sweet and beautiful they must be."

"Sometimes."

"How proud *I* should be if I might have a place in them!"

She smiled derisively. Really, for a country girl she had a wonderfully short upper lip.

"Are you often at this gate?"

"I used to be."

"For any particular reason?"

"Only to see my friends, and pass them the time of day!"

"To see your friends? Yes; but I am sure they found it difficult to *pass*. The road must have been blocked from end to end!"

"Well, there's not many about now, as you may notice."

"Is that thing a cat you have beside you?"

"Yes; it's the newly-invented Chinese breed."

"Where did you rise it?"

"It came to the house as a stray kitten. A stray cat coming in like that brings luck."

"Well, it's more like a dilapidated old weasel."

"Don't abuse it, sir, if you please, for it has something in common with your friend, the other gentleman."

"What do you mean?"

"Why, the poor creature is dumb!"

"Ah, ha! There's a compliment and a challenge for you, Dudley," he exclaimed, with a boisterous laugh. "You must pick up the gauntlet."

"May I ask why you suppose I am dumb?" inquired Captain Deverell, in his slow voice, looking her over with supercilious eyes.

"Sure I had no reason to suppose otherwise till now."

"My friend here invariably talks for both. He enjoys it."

"Yes, and saves your lazy self, a lot of trouble," amended Sir Henry.

"Conversation is a fag. Do you live here?" he added, looking straight at Mary.

"I've spent my whole life in that cottage."

"But it looks as if it were unoccupied."

"It is so."

"Are you, then, a disembodied spirit or a witch? If so, the cat is the wrong colour."

"I am not sure what the word 'disembodied' means, but I understand the word spirit, because I have one."

"I am glad to hear that," broke in Sir Harry. "Tell me where you live; where is your home?"

"My home? Oh, I don't know where it is, so I cannot oblige ye."

"Come, come! think again, and I'll give you a sovereign."

"You are very free with that sovereign, sir."

"Yes. This particular one doesn't happen to be mine. I won it as a bet from the dumb gentleman. He bet you would not be here. I saw you as we passed. And he bet something else, too."

"What else?"

"That you would not be pretty."

"Neither I am—no more nor yourselves. Are you the two frights in goggles that went by on the motor? What has become of it?"

"It's rather delicate just now."

"Well, then, I'm glad, and I hope it may die. I hate motors!"

"Really. And why?"

"Because they go hooting through the world, never caring what they do. One of them killed our neighbour's old dog Joe, too stiff to clear out of the road; and as to the fowls and ducks they run over, and those no use after, there are scores!"

"Would you permit me to take a photograph?" said Sir Harry, suddenly swinging round a small snapshotting camera.

"Certainly, sir. You may take the cat. Here he is," pulling him up, "and proud to sit for you"—and she held him in her arms.

A pretty picture! Snap! It was done—"Beauty and the Beast."

"And now for yourself!"

"What do you want it for, sir?"

"To keep as the portrait of the prettiest Irish girl I've ever seen."

"What would you say, if I told you I was not Irish?"

"Oh, I say! Come"—and he laughed; "you can scarcely expect me to believe *that*! Now, please stay still for one moment. There! I've taken two."

"What's going on here?" said a hoarse voice, and Patsie Maguire came suddenly through a gap in the opposite wall. Patsie, in his dark blue Sunday clothes, looking handsome, ill-tempered, and excited.

"I'm after having my picture took," explained Mary.

"This is a queer sort of business," he growled, stepping over the stile, and standing beside her within the gate.

Patsie had "a drop taken," as the saying is. Raw, bad whisky was working in his veins; his brain was in a state of wild confusion—jealousy and vanity were seething within him, and he had come to the conclusion that he would not let Mary Foley stir a toe out of the place, dead or alive.

"So yer at yer old games," he began, in a blustering voice, addressing himself to Mary, "talking at the corner, talking to any one. Faith!"—to the strangers—"she's the gabbiest little divil in Ireland!"

Mary glanced at him furtively. Patsie Maguire was drunk.

"An' now she's pratin' to gentlemen no less; and for a change—but let me tell ye,"—here he paused and swayed a little—"yer—not—the first gentlemen—that Mary here—has talked to. Aye"—and his wink expressed malicious significance—"Mary knows that I'm telling the holy truth, don't ye, Mary, me darlin'?"

The girl's colour had faded; there was a momentary tightening of the lips, but she merely said—

"Patsie, I'll thank ye to behave yerself! You don't know what yer saying." What was the use, she said to herself, in argufying with a man who was not sober? Patsie, when in such a state, was more or less mad. Had he forgotten, that she was not Mary Foley, now?

They were an uncommonly good-looking couple in Sir Harry's opinion, this Irishman and his sweetheart—the one, so fair, vivacious, and in a way brilliant, with wonderful hair; the other, dark as a Spaniard, with equally wonderful eyes, undeniably well-favoured, and undeniably jealous. So this was the fellow she had been thinking of, and expecting. The gate was their trysting place, and without permission Sir Harry took a joint photograph of the couple.

"Ye'd no call to do that!" cried Pat. "It's a shame to steal a person's face unknownst."

"Do you think so?" rejoined Sir Harry airily. "I've not the slightest objection to any one stealing mine."

"No, for yer quite safe! No one would be at the trouble of taking off your picture; it's ugly enough to break the plate!"

"I say, my good fellow," he cried, colouring up, "don't presume on my good-nature. Don't go too far!"

"Go back to your motor that's lying up the road there on its belly, and take a picture of that!" scoffed the Irishman.

"Yes, I suppose"—ignoring this insult, and turning to his companion—"that we ought to be moving."

Captain Deverell had made himself comfortable on the wall, and was smoking a pipe.

"Before I go, won't you tell me your name?" said Sir Harry, appealing to Mary. "You are better-looking, and better fun, than half the girls in England."

"Thank you kindly, sir, for your good opinion"—and she dropped a curtsey. "My name is—a secret."

"I see"—looking significantly at her; "you are soon going to change it."

"I am—so."

"May I be permitted to kiss your pretty little hand?"

"You may, if you please," and she held it out across the gate.

Sir Harry took it in his, gazed at it in surprise, and pressed his lips on it. Then he turned it about and squeezed the sovereign into its small, rosy palm.

"Throw away his dirty money, Mary!" cried Pat. "Tell him yer able to buy and sell his likes! Throw it in his face, I tell ye!" he shouted passionately, "do ye hear me!"

These men belonged to the very class who would now come between him and Mary; he hated them both furiously.

"I tell you what?" said Sir Harry, who had lost his easily mislaid temper, pushing back the gate as he spoke, "I see that I will have to give you a thrashing; you are spoiling for it, as they say here"—and he seized Pat roughly by the coat.

Pat, nothing loth, tore it out of his hand, flung it on the grass, squared himself, and said: "Come on, me little man! and I'll soon knock the head off ye."

Hearing this challenge, Captain Deverell jumped down with unexpected agility, caught hold of his companion, and dragged him through the gate, struggling violently, saying: "For heaven's sake don't make an ass of yourself! Come along, come along—leave the fellow alone. Why should you interfere with his girl?—how would you like it yourself?"

And the girl called after him, in a clear voice: "Yes; you take your wan off quietly, sir, and I'll see, that Patsie Maguire here, keeps himself in bounds!"

CHAPTER XIX

After the separation of the would-be combatants, and when the dumb man had, with unlooked-for energy, dragged away his furious struggling companion, Mary found herself *tête-à-tête* with Patsie. He had on several occasions waylaid her in the hotel garden; now he had tracked her to "the Corner," and for what good? If Patsie was not pleasing as a lover in the sight of Mary Foley, how could he expect to be acceptable to the same young woman in a much loftier station? What description of a husband would he make for Lord Mulgrave's daughter and heiress? Why, the thing was ridiculous on the face of it! He realised this instinctively, and yet he would not suffer her to depart without some sort of interview, even if the interview led to nothing. Pat was impulsive, sensitive, warm-hearted, and very vain. It would satisfy his heart, and gratify his vanity, to have a real sort of storybook parting with his sweetheart, and all the world—that is to say, his own little world—would know that she had talked to him as equal to equal, and bidden him good-bye.

This, encouraged by bad whisky, was Pat's motive in following Mary. Mary had a patrician horror of scenes. A scene was impending. She read its approach in her suitor's tragic blue eyes; and she was annoyed, not only with him, but herself. She had been led away by some impish spirit to fall into temptation, to play the old part of Mary of the gate to two totally strange gentlemen; and the two strange gentlemen had departed, carrying with them, an entirely wrong impression.

"Well, Pat," she began, on the principle that the first blow is half the battle, "what has brought ye—I mean you"—correcting herself—"up here?"

"To see you, of course. Sure, I never can get a word with you below."

"An' why should you?" she asked, with some asperity. "Ye are very big in yerself!"

"See here now," he began, in a loud, hoarse voice, "which are you at the present moment—Mary, or her ladyship? For I'd like to know where I am."

"I am always Mary here"—and she glanced back at the cottage, which, even in a short time, had assumed a forlorn and deserted appearance. The poor old place! Already the weeds were flourishing in the garden, and the kitchen, when she entered it, smelt of damp, and soot.

"Then it's to Mary I'm talking. Mary, wid all your grandeur and money, you won't buy love, mind you *that*, and you will never find any one, if you were to go over the wide world, that will love you the same as I do."

"Perhaps not, Patsie."

"Ah!"—and his tone was triumphant.

"But what is the use of it, Pat, when I cannot—never could or would or should—love *you*."

"Ye never tried!"

"One does not *try* to love, I believe. I like you, and as a friend I will not forget you or go agen you. You are mixed up with all my life here, and I am friendly with yer mother and Lizzie; but if I'd lived here to the end of my days, I'd never have loved you, Patsie."

"You'll go off and marry some one else—some one of the pattern of the little red-faced blackguard."

"No, I think not; I'm not such a fool!"

"Faix, I don't know about that," he sneered. "A long while back there was Mr. Ulick—ye were near making a fool of yourself with him!"

"I was not!" she retorted with passion. "How dare you bring in his name—how dare you?" she repeated, and her face was white.

"Oh, I dare most things when me blood is up. And now, I'd like ye to promise me one thing."

"What is it?" she asked impatiently.

"That ye will never marry any one at all," he answered, raising his voice, and his eyes blazed into hers, "but be true to Ireland—and to *me*."

"True to you—what balderdash! Sure, don't ye know well I never cared a thraneen about ye?"

She glanced up at him suddenly, and noticed that his dark, expressive face was working with passion. What ailed him? He looked murderous. Was he going to kill her? It was a lonely enough spot. A man had been beaten to death in that very road.

"See now, I'll promise you one thing, Pat," she continued, dissembling her fears, "for old times' sake. If ever you are in any trouble, or want a good friend, I'll help you. And as to marrying me, ye know there's a dozen prettier girls in these parts just *aching* to have you. I can't think why you are so set on *me*. Come, Pat, carry the cat for me, and we will be going home."

Pat turned about; his expression startled her—the hard look in his eyes, the tightness of his lips. Her heart beat convulsively, but she kept a brave front and faced him as she would some dangerous animal, from whom she could not escape, and was therefore bound to overawe. Pat was crazy drunk; the raw whisky had taken effect; there was a mad look in his eyes. Did he mean to murder her? The sudden sound of voices and approaching footsteps filled her with a sense of profound relief. It proved a party of neighbours going towards Glenveigh; and before Pat could interfere, Mary had snatched up Whitey, opened the gate, and darted after them.

And Pat, thus left alone, sat down suddenly on a stone and burst into a passion of maudlin sobs. Why hadn't he killed her, and then himself? A cheap revolver was in his pocket; it was loaded in four chambers. If the Connors had been three minutes later in coming down past Foley's Corner, the chronicle of Mary of the Gate would have concluded here.

*　　*　　*　　*　　*

The cold Miss Usher had contracted "held her," to use an Irish term, for one whole week, and during that time, she had a most tender, thoughtful, and assiduous nurse in her young protegée. Mary was afraid to venture into the garden. Pat might waylay her again; also she experienced a certain shyness with respect to mixing with her old friends, and she spent a good deal of her time in the sick-room, reading aloud to the patient, answering notes—she wrote a fine hand, thanks to the School Board—and concocting drinks, possets, and poultices with much skill. Her attendance was so quiet, her little hands so deft and quick, her soft voice so sympathetic, that the invalid felt herself becoming warmly attached to this treasure-trove; and as she lay in bed, waited on by Mary, she instilled into the girl's mind some practical hints, without seeming to be continuing her much-neglected education.

As Mary read aloud the papers Miss Usher threw in remarks and information. It was socially she was so desperately wanting—yes, in the common A B C of deportment and conduct. Otherwise the good lady was surprised to discover how well the girl was posted up in the most unexpected subjects. She had read widely for one of her station. Tennyson, Sir Walter Scott, Thackeray, the Brontës, some of Victor Hugo's works, Hans Andersen, Macaulay's history and essays, Carlyle's *French Revolution*, with a fair knowledge of history, geography, grammar, and arithmetic; she was not too badly equipped. Questioned, she could tell a good deal about the Crusades, the Wars of the Roses, and was eloquent respecting the battle of Clontarf, which was a new name to Miss Usher; but then, she had never studied Irish history.

At last Miss Usher was sufficiently recovered to start for Dublin, where Lord Mulgrave was to meet his daughter and convey her home. Her chaperon had suggested at least a week in the Irish capital, in order that, before she was actually launched into her new life, Mary, the ignorant child of the pastures, might see things; such, for instance, as a large city with its traffic and shops, a fashionable hotel, a regiment marching, a theatre, a picture-gallery, and a good milliner. Before she crossed the Irish Sea she must be suitably dressed. At present she was merely clothed.

As the day of departure approached, Mary's slender wardrobe was packed; she had been persuaded to leave the cat as a parting legacy to Mrs. Hogan, but the dog, "Rap," must accompany her wherever she went. On this subject Lady Joseline showed an amount of decision that had never been evinced by Mary Foley—indeed, she was, as her friends knew, just wrapped up in the creature. No doubt he was a fine, handsome terrier, who had belonged to poor Katty; but Mrs. Hogan's memory was long; she recalled a time when "Rap" had been the property of a young gentleman. Was Mary still faithful to that first fancy? Now came the final good-byes. Her numerous friends flocked to the hotel to say God-speed to Mary. These included Father Daly, Mr. and Mrs. West, Mary's schoolfellows, neighbours, and lovers. When it came to the last words and handshakes, Mary broke down and wept unrestrainedly. She wept all the five miles to the station—such a capacity for grief was beyond the bounds of Miss Usher's experience—indeed, the girl's condition remained very tearful and subdued throughout the entire journey. Mary had been twice to Cork on a three-shilling cheap excursion, crammed with many others into a third-class little better than a cattle-truck; this was a new conveyance, a carriage with beautiful cushions and "Reserved" printed on the window. Once in Dublin, they drove to the "Shelbourne," the grandeur of which struck the poor creature dumb; the lift proved a paralysing novelty, also the smart and superior chambermaid who addressed her as "your ladyship." However, she was completely worn out with her journey, her emotion, and the novelty of everything, and, refusing dinner, retired at once to bed, and in sleep, forgot all her joys, sorrows, and fears.

The next morning the new arrival felt fresh as a lark, and ready to witness any amount of novelty. Concealed in a hired brougham, Miss Usher carried her charge to a well-known establishment, and there spent the flying hours in fitting her out in a manner becoming, not only to her, but to her new position. She was fortunately easily suited, being of a "stock size," and with slight alterations she became possessed of a smart tailor-made, a black evening gown, a French model, crêpe-de-chine, a travelling cloak, tea-gown, luggage, hats, gloves, shoes, and furbelows. It was almost like buying a small trousseau; but Miss Usher had "carte blanche" from his lordship, he was coming in three days to claim his child, and she was resolved that she should do him credit!

After this morning's hard work and lunch, the two ladies drove together out to the park, and Mary saw a number of wonderful things; she was strangely quiet, and talked hardly at all, but her glances were in every direction, observant, critical, and amazed.

When they returned, they discovered that some of the purchases had already arrived; in fact, the young lady's room was half full of cardboard boxes.

"You will have to put on the black gown," announced Miss Usher. "I'll dress you myself, and we will dine at the table d'hôte."

"Oh, no, no," protested the other, in an agonised voice, "I dare not."

"Oh, but yes; you must begin some time, and the sooner the better, and learn how girls of your own rank look and behave themselves. Don't you wish your father to be pleased when he returns? Don't you wish him to be proud of you?"

"Is it proud of *me*! You're making fun," she scoffed.

"Not at all. I want you to do me credit. And you will follow me into the room, and copy what I do as regards knife and fork and wine-glasses."

"I expect I'll do something awfully bad—upset the things, I'll be so nervous, and have all the servants laughing at me."

"Well-trained servants never laugh; and please remember that you are no longer, as you seem to think, on equal terms with them. They don't understand familiarity; they have their own dignity. There is a story of a gentleman who had socialistic ideas—all men on an equality sort of thing; he insisted on shaking hands with his butler. The butler did not like it; he gave warning."

"Ah! I suppose that was why the tall chambermaid stared at me, when I said how nicely her fringe was done!"

"Of course; she must have been horrified! Now go and do your hair, and when you are ready I'll come and help you into your new gown."

"The girl has a taste for dress," reflected Miss Usher, as she arranged her own thick grey locks. "I suppose it comes from her French relations. It was really marvellous, the eye she had for a suitable purchase, considering that everything is as new to her as if she came from another planet. She is wonderful, poor child!"

Before Miss Usher had completed her toilette there was a timid knock at the door, and she gave a faint scream, as her charge trailed into the room. What a transformation! The well-cut bodice set off a willowy and graceful figure; the sweeping skirt lent dignity; the black gown was entrancingly becoming to the soft white skin and ruddy hair of Lady Joseline. Yes, she was Lady Joseline, indeed—an aristocrat every inch, from her neat black velvet shoe, to the crown of her thick hair. Mary Foley, in a clumsy serge, had quitted the apartment half an hour ago for ever, and this graceful young personage, had taken her place!

"Will I do?" she eagerly inquired, in her soft southern brogue.

Yes; outwardly she would do extremely well. She seemed to possess the natural art—a valuable one—the art of knowing how to put on her clothes.

"Yes"—turning round and then standing up—"nothing could be better, Lady Joseline."

"Oh, for goodness sake——"

Miss Usher made a gesture of interruption, and continued.

"For the future you must remember that such is your *real* name. You have now taken upon you your new character. May you adorn it, be happy, and make others happy, my dear!"

And as she spoke, she went over to the girl, and kissed her on both cheeks, French fashion.

"You are half French, you know," she explained; "your grandfather was the Duc de Hernoncourt, a French nobleman."

"My grandfather! Sure I always think of old Joe Foley as that!"

"Yes. You will soon get accustomed to your relations. Mary Foley is gone; we will never see her again; we will forget her, and give her dress and boots and hat and clothes to some poor woman. And now we will go downstairs together, and eat our dinner."

"Oh, dear me, I'm so frightened, I'm all of a tremble; the legs is giving under me."

"Your ladyship should say trembling—not all of a tremble; and you need not mention your legs. Come, there's nothing to be afraid of."

"That's what Mrs. Hogan said; her last words were to hold up my head, and not be afraid of anybody—but sure, talking is easy!"

"You are not afraid of the lift now, are you?"

"No, I like it finely. I love going up and down in it."

"Everything will be the same in time, my dear girl. Just keep a cool head, and wait."

"Oh, I declare I feel all goose-flesh!" whispered her charge.

"Never mind; follow me closely. This way. Our table is in a corner"—and as she spoke the chaperon entered the brilliantly lit dining-room—already crowded—and proceeded to steer Lady Joseline into society for the first time.

CHAPTER XX

"I don't rightly know whether I am on me head or my heels!" declared her ladyship, when she had taken a seat in the corner, with her back against the wall, and proceeded to gaze about her. "What a power of people! I suppose this is a glimpse of what Father Daly calls 'the world.' No," to the ready waiter, "no broth!"

The man, with blank, impassive face, bowed, and offered soup to Miss Usher.

"Dear child," she murmured, when he had departed, "this is *soup*; we don't call it broth."

"Very well then, I won't"—taking up the ménu, and looking over it. "I declare to goodness if it isn't in a foreign language! Will ye tell me, what's the use of that?"

"I'm sure I cannot give you any reason, but it's the fashion. You will find it everywhere."

"And such a lot of things. I can guess at some names: 'enter' and 'relieve'—hunger, I suppose."

Here Miss Usher leant across and carefully explained the meaning of 'entrée' and 'relève'—the names of the courses; whilst the girl listened, with both elbows firmly planted on the table.

"You should not sit like that, my child," suggested the teacher of manners.

"No? But there's a girl doing it over there," argued the pupil; and, pointing with a taper finger, she indicated a young woman in a loud tea-gown with a towzled head and arms bare to the shoulder, who was holding forth to a shiny-faced, dissipated-looking man.

"Never mind, my dear, you need not take her for a model. Look at those two nice girls in white. Now have some fish?"

"Claret or Chablis, my lady?"

"No, thank ye," she responded, "I never drink wine at all; but I'd be glad of a glass of spring water, or"—as an afterthought—"if ye have such a thing as a sup of fresh buttermilk?"

Without relaxing a muscle, the waiter replied: "We don't supply buttermilk, my lady, but the water is the best."

Lady Joseline ate little dinner, but devoured the company with a pair of eager, childish eyes. One lady she stigmatised as "a play actress," another as "an old show, with feathers in her hair and scarcely a tack to her back." Most of the men were "as like the waiters as two peas." Then, to their special attendant—

"No meat whatever. Sure, man alive, 'tis a fast day!"

"My dear, there is no occasion for an explanation," remonstrated her *vis-à-vis*, when the waiter had retired.

"Sure, won't he think it uncivil, just to say no or yes?"

"Not if you add 'please.' The salad is nice and fresh, but you should not eat it with your fingers."

"It tastes more natural like!"

"Possibly; but you don't wish to be remarkable, do you?"

"No, indeed. Am I? Tell me, please, is there anything *on* me? or queer about me? Is anything sticking in me hair?"

"Why, certainly not. Why do you ask?"

"I've noticed quite a lot of people staring over at me, as if they knew I was no great shakes, and had no call to be here; and there's a man near the pillar that has a pair of eyes like two big black slugs. I declare they make me curl all over!"

Miss Usher was agreeably conscious of the fact that her charge had made considerable sensation in their neighbourhood. No one could look more elegant and distinguished, than the pretty girl in the corner. There had been whispers, glances, and a turning of heads. These admirers had not heard the beauty's soft common brogue, nor witnessed her difficulties with forks and wine-glasses. "But, considering all things, she was wonderful," said the chaperon to herself, as she rose from the table, and ordered coffee in the hall. The more her ladyship rubbed off the raw edge of ignorance, and the sooner she encountered and vanquished startling first impressions, the better for her, and her kinsfolk.

As they sat down at a little table, and the coffee made its appearance, the girl said in a loud voice—

"I'm not partial to coffee. I'd sooner have a cup of tay!"

"But coffee is better at this hour. No one drinks tea immediately after dinner; and, my dear, you really must begin to drop such words as 'tay.' Now sit here quietly, and listen to the way other girls speak."

"And take a lesson for nothing?"

"Yes, and profit by it. Remember that your father arrives to-morrow."

"Oh, Miss Usher dear, I'm terribly scared of him!"

"You must put that feeling out of your mind, and you will soon learn to love him; he loves you already."

"What? Oh, balderdash! Now, how could he love one that he's only set eyes on a few times."

"Quite naturally, as a matter of course, for your mother's sake."

"You mane, because"—lowering her voice—"I'm so like her?"

"Yes, in appearance; and you must strive hard to resemble her in other ways."

"I will so if I can. But what ways?"

"She was most unselfish and thoughtful, good to the poor and the aged, kind to animals, very gay and gracious in her manners, sweet-tempered, clever, and fascinating."

"Oh, but fancy the likes of me being clever, and fascinating!"

"Why not? But you will soon begin to learn to speak like other people. To-morrow I shall write down a list of expressions you are not to use. You are not to say 'ould' for old, 'ye' for you, 'the likes of,' 'sure now,' and 'by your leave.' Talk but little, listen, and read a great deal."

"I see what you mean; I'm to keep my ears cocked. I'm not too bad to look at, but when I open my lips I am like the girl in the fairy tale, and my mouth drops toads and serpents."

"There are no toads or serpents in Ireland you know. Still, just at present, until you see and hear a little more, I think you will find that, except between you and me, silence is golden."

After a considerably long silence, during which Miss Usher knitted steadily and her charge stared about her, the latter said—

"Well, I've been listening to those two girls in blue carrying on with the nosey young man; and the little one told him he was 'a rotter' and the other said he was 'pulling her leg.' What sort of chat, do ye call that?"

"Oh, they are not ladies," explained Miss Usher, who was distinctly disconcerted.

"Yes; but how am I to know the differ between the talk of ladies and the talk of them as is not?—not being a lady meself."

"Oh, you will soon understand."

"But those two are dressed as well as I am, and better," protested the girl, "and how——"

"Dress reminds me," interrupted Miss Usher, "that you have several fittings to-morrow, and a busy day"; and, suddenly rising to her feet, she added, "It is getting on for ten o'clock. Shall we retire?"

On the way to their rooms, the two paused on a landing before a great mirror; they halted involuntarily, and gazed at themselves as they stood side by side; or rather, they both gazed at the reflection of Lady Joseline Dene.

"I'm just a daw in peacock's feathers!" she exclaimed at last. "It's all mighty fine, my beautiful dress, and my hair done up in the fashion. Oh, dear me! I'm a regular take-in. I shall never be as nice as I look."

"Yes, you will," said her companion, leading her into her room; "and remember, dear child, that you are nice to your father when he comes to-morrow."

"I'm all in a tremble, when I think of it. How can I be nice?"

"By not being shy and shrinking and plainly afraid of him. He is a shy man himself—people call it reserve. For years he has shut up his real self, and no one has seen it. I believe that you hold the key."

"But I shall never dare to turn it in the lock."

"Why not? You are his daughter, a gift given back to him to cheer and brighten the end of his life. Mind that you do it."

"I'll try. Anyway, I'll put it in my prayers."

"Do," replied Miss Usher, as she closed the door.

CHAPTER XXI

It was with a feeling of repressed excitement and unusual trepidation, that Lord Mulgrave, who had come over by the evening boat, walked into the hotel and inquired for Miss Usher.

"Miss Usher and her ladyship were in," said the porter; "in fact, they were in the hall." Yes, he recognised Miss Usher's black-and-white check gown, and her broad back; the girl with her—could it be Joseline? What a transformation! Undoubtedly clothes had done wonders; but her manners were as pitiably timid and uncouth as ever—she was actually shaking with nervousness. By Lord Mulgrave's desire the little party dined in a private room, where he and Miss Usher talked, and did their utmost to promote the ease of their companion, who, in spite of her smart white gown and fashionable coiffure, was still the peasant in her heart. She ate but little, and scarcely opened her lips, fearing to be guilty of some awful blunder, and shock this handsome grey-haired gentleman!

After the meal was over Miss Usher effaced herself with a murmured excuse about letters, and left the father and daughter to talk to one another alone.

"Come here, my dear," he said, drawing up a chair, "and let us endeavour to know one another. Talk to me, won't you."

Joseline accepted the seat in trembling silence. What could she talk to him about? The price of calves, the Hennesseys' wedding, the mission at Glenveigh, her new clothes? Cleverly, and by degrees, her father drew her out, and prevailed on her to thaw—to speak of herself and her upbringing; and as she became more familiar with his presence and the sound of her own voice, she talked a great deal, and unwittingly displayed her simple mind, and simple heart. She was a dear, sweet, good girl—the image of her dead mother; but twenty-one years yawned between him and her, and as he listened to her artless conversation, he felt overcome by the appalling state of her ignorance of what may be called, "life above stairs."

"Yes, I've had good schoolin'," she was saying. "I can cast up figures, and knit, and mend lace; the nuns taught me."

"Yes; and anything else?"

"I can sing—I was among the altos, and once I sang at a concert, and many a time at a dance."

"I'm glad you can sing. Will you sing to me now, my dear?"

"Is it here?" she faltered. "Sure, I've no concertina."

"That is no matter."

"Oh, I'd be afraid, so I would. Oh"—twisting her hands—"I dare not."

"Now listen to me, Joseline" (how many years since he had uttered the name!). "If you are going to be afraid of *me*, I shall be afraid of *you*, and that will be a terrible misfortune. You have your mother's face; if you have her nature, I don't care one straw for accomplishments. I think you may have her voice. Will you not sing to me, my dear, and give me pleasure?"

He pressed her little hand tightly; he felt her trembling; and then, all at once, in the dusky room, the sweet, low, quivering notes began, at first faint and husky, but gaining strength and volume as they went on. Oh, such a heart-piercing, exquisite air! The words were unintelligible, for she was singing a well-known Irish lament, which, rendered into English, was something like:—

Wail, wail, ye, for the mighty one!

Wail, wail, ye, for the dead!

Quench the hearth and hold the breath, with ashes strew the head!

How tenderly we loved him! how deeply we deplore!

Holy Saviour, but to think, we shall never see him more!

Wail, wail him through the island! Weep, weep for our pride!

Ye know that on the battle-field our gallant chief has died.

Weep the Victor of Benn Burb! Weep him, young men and old!

Weep for him, ye women! your beautiful lies cold.

Soft as a woman's was your voice, O'Neil; bright was your eye.

Oh, why did ye leave us, Owen? Why did you die?

Your troubles are over; you're at rest with God on high.

But we're forlorn and sad, Owen. Why did you die?

As she concluded with a low sob of supreme dramatic effect, Lord Mulgrave drew a deep breath, and, carrying the little cold hand to his lips, said, "My dear child, do you know that *my* name is Owen? Your singing is no mere accomplishment; it is a great gift."

"Did she sing?" she asked faintly.

"Yes. It was the same voice"; and he sighed as he released her fingers.

"Does Lady Mulgrave sing?" she continued, in a bolder key.

"No"—and he gave a slight start—"but, Tito, her daughter, is fond of music; she is nearly your age, or a little older. You will be, I hope, capital companions for one another; she's a bit of a rattle, but a good-hearted girl."

"Is she pretty?" she asked.

"Not exactly; but rather attractive and piquante."

"I never heard that word before; I suppose it means something nice?"

"Yes. You will see for yourself. She and Dudley are great friends; he is my heir, you know, and your cousin; we see a good deal of him."

"And what is he like?"

"Oh, fairly good-looking, but a lazy beggar. He did well in South Africa, but got enteric, and was laid on his back for so long I believe he fancies he is still there. You have put his nose a bit out of joint, for some of the estates will now go to you."

"Is it to me? Sure I'm not fit to own land. Once they wanted to make up a match for me with a strong farmer; his people were eager for it, on account of the fifty pounds."

"But you said no?"

"Bedad, I did—a great fat man, with a bald face, and a pearl on one of his eyes." She meant cataract.

Lord Mulgrave gave a short laugh; then he said, "So, Joseline, you've never had a lover?"

"Is it me? Why I had a couple of dozen or more making shapes at me!"

Her father sat up stiffly in his chair, apprehension in his attitude; the expression of his face was disturbed.

"But sure, I didn't care a hair for one of them," she added reassuringly. "I only liked them just for joking and dancing—nothing more, I give ye me word. But I'd fine work keeping them off; they mostly wanted to marry me!"

"You say you had many admirers, my dear. Did you not care for one of them? Come, now, do not be afraid to speak."

"No. Sorra one of them!"

"And yet you are past one-and-twenty! It is strange that my little girl's heart has never been touched," continued Lord Mulgrave, in a meditative tone; "but I think I can explain it. I believe it was a case of like to like, and you instinctively shrank from the claims of a race to which you did not really belong."

"I expect there was something in that," assented Joseline. "They said I was too particular, and all for picking and choosing."

"Now, supposing you had come across a gentleman wooer?"—and Lord Mulgrave paused interrogatively. (Did he notice that Joseline was very pale?) "I wonder how it would have been? Perhaps you and I would not be sitting here to-day, Joseline. I am thankful that you belong only to me!"

A long pause ensued.

Joseline was conscious that her mind was in a tempestuous state of indecision. Should she speak? Should she disinter and lay before her father, the poor little skeleton of her own romance? Should she or not? After all, there is something that belongs to ourselves. And yet—and yet—— Her large eyes gazed into vacancy.

At last she faltered, in a low and shaken voice, "Well, father, there *was* some one once. You are right. A gentleman—and—he was—a real gentleman. He went away six years ago, when I was but a young slip of a thing, and it nearly broke my heart. And that's all."

"What was his name? Who was he?" he asked under his breath.

"Sure there's no need to tell ye that, for"—and her face quivered—"I'll never come across him again."

"Irish, of course?"

She nodded. "There now, I've told ye, and ye know all there is to know about me. Promise me ye will never let on."

"I promise faithfully. Did he give you the red dog?"

"No, he gave him to Mrs. Foley. And now we will never spake of him again." Here two tears, which had been gathering, fell. "You have me only secret."

As a servant entered with a telegram and turned up the electric light, her father looked searchingly at Joseline. Her face was white and haggard. "My little girl is tired?" he exclaimed.

"Yes; I feel as if the feet were falling off me. I was standing so long to-day being tried on."

"Then you must go to bed at once. To-morrow we will do a drive and the theatre. Next day we go home. You are no longer afraid of me, are you, dear?"—and he bent down and kissed the hair over her brow. "You must not. You are my only child; all I have, remember."

"I will remember, and you will remember"; and she looked up at him with an expression more eloquent than speech. An undivided and implicit trust, spoke in her beautiful eyes.

END OF PART II

PART III
CHAPTER XXII

Although Lord Mulgrave had given Miss Usher a cordial invitation to accompany his daughter to London, that prudent lady excused herself with the plea of one or two engagements in Dublin. She wished to give the father and daughter an opportunity of becoming better acquainted before they joined the family circle. What could be a better occasion than a sea voyage and a railway journey?

"I shall miss you awfully," sobbed her companion of the last six weeks. "I don't know what in the living earth I'll do, all alone. Of course, I have his—his lordship—father; but I mean among the women. And I've a notion they are all going to hate me, so they will."

"That is a foolish idea to start with, my dear. You will find that if you like people, people will like you. Do not be afraid of your relations. Be good—tempered and pleasant, and just yourself."

"Faix, it's easy talking, Miss Usher dear. But which self? I've two, you see. The one that comes natural—the common country girl, reared, as ye may say, on the side of the road, and the new self, that's a grand lady, and must mind her manners and her talk, and hold up her nose as if there was a smell under it!"

"Not at all," protested her counsellor. "I hope you will be gracious and polite to every one; it is only nobodies who give themselves airs. Your father has invited me to pay you a visit later, and I shall look for wonderful improvements and bring you a little prize. You are improved as it is; you have learnt a great deal."

"It will all run out of my head the moment I get among strangers," declared her pupil, in a tone of deep dejection.

"At any rate they will make allowances."

"More likely they'll make fun of me!"

"Nonsense! Now, you must try and remember some of the things you have learnt. Promise me you will not say 'Faix,' 'Musha,' and 'Begorra'; in fact, my dear child, you should endeavour to cultivate silence."

"Sure, don't I know that well! and yet for the life of me I can't hold me tongue. I can't stop myself. I've been so encouraged to talk as much as ever I liked since I could talk at all, the words just slip out of me mouth before I know they are gone—and often words I never meant to say at all. I tell the black truth, and let them take it or leave it—man, woman, or child."

"You must make up your mind to listen and learn," said Miss Usher, soothingly. "You learn quickly. Now, I've a little book for you here." It was a neat edition of *The Manners of Good Society*. "Read this over; it won't tell you everything, but you will find it a help."

Lord Mulgrave, for his part, had a gift for Miss Usher, and the evening before he took leave of her he offered her his heartfelt thanks for her care of his daughter. "I am aware that nothing I could give you, would be an adequate return," he said, "but I want you to accept this as a memento of *Mary Foley*"; and he placed in her hand a blue velvet case—a case containing a string of pearls, which, as a lady friend subsequently remarked with bated breath, "must have cost hundreds and hundreds of pounds."

The travellers left for Holyhead by the early boat; and as Joseline, in the dull grey cold morning, took leave of her friend—her very last tie—she broke down and wept bitterly, and, with her arms tightly clasped round Miss Usher's neck, fell into a sudden breathless sobbing.

"May Heaven forgive me, but I *hate* going, so I do," she gasped. "Oh, Miss Usher dear, I wish to God I was on my way back to Glenveigh!"

* * * * *

At Kingstown the waves were tumbling over the west pier; the water in the harbour was lively. They were likely to experience a bad crossing—a bit of an October gale.

At first Joseline enjoyed her novel experience of the sea, the stinging salt air, the unfamiliar up-and-down motion; but once past the "Kish," when they caught the full force of the wind, she was compelled to seek refuge in the ladies' cabin, where she fell an immediate prey to *mal de mer* and terror. Over and over she believed that each lurch was the end! However, at last Holyhead stack was safely sighted, and a miserable, white-faced girl was claimed from the stewardess by the Earl of Mulgrave. Her head was swimming and aching as she crawled up the gangway, leaving *The Manners and Customs of Good Society* behind her on board the *Ireland*.

During the long day's journey to London Joseline recovered but little, in spite of her companion's most anxious solicitude; her interest in the flying landscape proved feeble, she felt so sick, and so utterly shattered and desolate.

"Would you prefer to stop in London for the night, and go on to-morrow?" suggested Lord Mulgrave.

"Oh, no, no! let us do it all at wance."

"And get it over," he added, with a faint smile. "You need not be nervous, Joseline; every one is prepared to give you a warm welcome."

"But I feel so strange. I know I'll be like a sort of wild plant that is pulled up by the roots, and stuck in a greenhouse, and every bit as much out of place."

"No, for you belong to the greenhouse," he answered, "and by-and-by you will find that you are in your natural atmosphere."

"God send it!" she murmured, as with a gesture of weariness she closed her eyes, and presently fell into a comfortable little sleep.

Her father, who sat opposite, studied the pale face anxiously. Here was the image of his dead wife: her outward form, with the mind, manners, and habits of an Irish peasant. What an unparalleled situation!

The poor, tired child had some formidable obstacles in her future path. Lotty and she would have nothing in common—Lotty, with her bridge and her cigarettes, her society jargon, her *set*, would be terribly embarrassed by this simple, innocent creature. His wife's opinions were decided, her tongue was persuasive, her will inflexible. He had drifted into allowing her to gently lead, to manage, and to set him a little on one side, because he had not cared. Now he had something to care for and protect. He must stand between Lottie, and a girl who embodied many of Lottie's especial aversions—a girl who was a mere child of nature, outspoken, impulsive, uncouth.

Joseline and her father, having dined at the Euston Hotel, made their way down to Ashstead. It was past nine o'clock, a dark, windy night, when they arrived outside the gusty station, where a fine equipage, with two moon-like lamps, awaited them. As she was conducted to her carriage, the girl felt as if she were a second Cinderella going to the ball. They drove away rapidly, Joseline sitting erect, her heart beating with nervousness; her father took her little cold hand, and held it in silence. When they stopped at a pair of great gates, which opened noiselessly and swung back of their own accord as the carriage dashed through, he said—

"This is Ashstead—my dear—your home."

"Father," she gasped, "I am mortally in dread. I feel as if I was going to be killed, or married, when I think of meeting all these grand strangers. I declare I'd like to get out of the carriage, and run in and hide under the hedge."

"My dear, I assure you there is nothing to alarm you."

"It's her ladyship and the young lady that terrifies me, when I think of them."

"Her ladyship is prepared to welcome you warmly. She is——" (What could he say to encourage this trembling creature?) "She is—most sweet-tempered, and full of tact."

"Tact! What is tact?"

"A—the knack of saying the right thing, and keeping quiet at the right time."

"Oh, laws! then she is just the black opposite to me! And the young one?"

"I feel sure you and Tito will be as sisters; she has often wished for a companion. She will show you all sorts of things, and tell you what to do."

"I suppose she has had a grand education?"

"Yes, chiefly abroad. I am afraid she did not make the most of her advantages; her spelling is shocking."

"Oh! Well, anyhow, I can spell," declared Joseline, with a gulp. "It is the other things—the tip-top talking, and the sailing about a room, and the hand-shaking, and looking people over from their shoes up. I watched the ladies in the hotel. You see, I just clump about, and hitch myself on to anything, and say, 'What way are ye the day?'"

"Well, here we are," he interrupted, as the horses came to a standstill under a pillared portico. The door was then thrown open, and the light from a large domed entrance streamed out into the night. Silhouetted against the yellow glare were three tall men-servants. In a sort of daze Joseline stumbled out of the brougham and followed Lord Mulgrave into what seemed to be a royal palace. She paused for a moment, whilst a footman relieved her of her umbrella and handbag, and, turning to her father with piteous eyes, exclaimed, in a voice which the great dome re-echoed—

"I declare to goodness I'm all of a swither!"

To this announcement her parent made no reply, but hastily preceded her across the hall along a wide red-carpeted corridor, lined with paintings and cabinets, to where a murmur of voices came through a half-open door.

Lord Mulgrave had particularly desired an informal reception for his daughter, so romantically restored. Of course, he was aware that the entire neighbourhood were on the *qui vive* to see her; their curiosity must wait. He expected to find merely his wife and Tito. But Lady Mulgrave had arranged otherwise; she had invited Lady Maxwelton and her girls to come and behold the new niece and cousin, and being in London, they had responded with alacrity. Several smart neighbours were added to her dinner-party; but for these the inducement offered was bridge.

Lady Mulgrave was secretly displeased that her husband was bringing "the hog-trotter" girl home—actually straight to Ashstead. She ought, as a preliminary, to have first been sent to some school or foreign convent. It was most irritating to have her dragged into the family; the whole thing was so melodramatic—a sort of penny novelette story; it had got into all the papers, too. The proper thing to do would have been to send the girl abroad, and permit the episode to evaporate. An uncouth peasant-girl was bound to cut a most ridiculous figure; but since she was really coming, her ladyship had invited a surprise party, as a little punishment for his lordship. The presence of so many critical eyes would intensify his discomfort: in addition to the kind and charitable intention of making him ashamed of his daughter, it was also arranged as an ordeal for the girl herself.

Ten o'clock had struck. The small blue drawing-room was set out with three bridge-tables, at which sat twelve deeply engrossed players. Lady Maxwelton occupied a sofa with another lady; they were discussing missions.

"Mother," said Tito, suddenly throwing down her hand, "I'm sure I hear the carriage! Yes; they have come at last!"

"Nonsense! It is the wind. They won't arrive to-night," replied Lady Mulgrave, from another table. "Of course they will stop in London." As she spoke, she ceased to sort her cards, and announced, "I make no trumps."

"It *is* them," persisted Tito, rising. "Mother, aren't you going out?"

But her mother merely took up her cigarette and blew a cloud of smoke. As she did so the door of the drawing-room was pushed open by some one, and a graceful girl in a long sable-trimmed cloak and a French toque came slowly into the room, ghastly pale, and yet so pretty! She looked distinctly dazed—no wonder, poor alien!—as she contemplated this brilliantly lighted room, the crowd of gaily dressed people all playing cards and smoking cigarettes. Even Joseline was sharply sensible of the strangeness of this new life—so near, yet so unknown. Directly facing her, a yellow-haired woman—her beautiful bare shoulders emerging from a hazardously low yellow gown—with a cigarette half-way to her mouth, stared at the new-comer with eyes of stony incredulity.

For about the space of ten seconds a deadly stillness reigned. The arrival paused, and in that time Lady Mulgrave saw and realised, the amazing likeness to a certain picture in the red saloon; also that this graceful, well-dressed personage was the bog-trotter girl, as she mentally called her. Her husband, who was now in the room, said—

"Lottie, here is——"

"Oh ... I know.... I see," she answered quickly, and, putting down her cigarette, she rustled forward, took her stepdaughter's hand in hers, and administered an elaborate embrace. "Dearest, you are welcome—so welcome. And here is my girl Tito," she added, in her sweet voice, waving forward a petite figure in a bright red gown, with bright, dark eyes.

For a moment Joseline hesitated, and then she stooped and kissed Tito, murmuring in a soft, broken whisper, "I do hope you will like me, me dear! and we will be friends."

Tito was taken completely aback, but from that moment her heart was enlisted by this sweetly pretty creature, with the lofty air and ridiculous brogue.

"Elgitha," said his lordship, "let me present your niece to you," and he led her formally to a sofa, on which was seated the stately dowager in velvet, with her beautiful white hair turned off her face over a cushion.

The marchioness rose and warmly embraced the girl, and added, in a subdued aside, "What a *likeness*!"

There were more introductions, a little talk, chiefly carried on by his lordship, and then he said—

"Tito, will you take your sister away to her room and look after her? We had a hideous crossing."

"I'm sure you must be dead," said Tito, leading the way, "and glad of a rest and supper. I'll introduce you to your room and your maid."

"Maid? Oh, no. For goodness sake——"

"Why, of course a maid! Mother has two—one for her clothes, and one for her hair! Here we are"—and she ushered Joseline into a lofty bedroom on the first floor. "Is it not nice?"

"'Tis elegant! 'tis grand"—gazing about at the silk hangings, silver looking-glass, and French furniture. "Just beautiful."

"Do let me help you off with your wraps! Dear me! how different you are to what we expected!"

"Yes?"—sitting down wearily. "What *did* you expect?"

"Oh, a sort of bare-legged girl, with a turf creel on her back."

The new-comer laughed hysterically as she removed her hat-pins. "Oh, well, I never was just as bad as that!"

"I think you have made a most successful first appearance. You carried the house by storm, and, figuratively speaking, will have splendid notices in all the morning papers. You don't understand my jargon? And you are worn out. Ah! here comes your maid. Justine, this is her ladyship. I see you have brought up some soup. You will look after her? She is frightfully tired. What time do you get up in the morning?"—turning to Joseline.

"Half-past six!" was the prompt reply.

"Half-past—horror! I generally emerge about eleven. To-morrow, I'll come and look you up early, and we will go round the grounds together whilst Justine unpacks. Of course you breakfast in bed!"

"Is it me? Never in my life!"

"Well, I'm really going now. Good night." Kissing her, she whispered, "sleep well, and dream happy dreams. I expect they will all come true!"

CHAPTER XXIII

Joseline, who was worn out, both bodily and mentally, slept a sound and dreamless sleep, from which she was aroused by the sound of careful footsteps, a rustling of starched petticoats, and a gentle opening of heavy shutters. She stared about the unfamiliar, lofty room. Where was she? As her gaze fell on the pale satin counterpane, the dignified dressing-table, beyond it a tall housemaid in a stiff print gown, cautiously raising the window-blinds, she closed her eyes. Would she open them on her own little quarters in the cottage loft?—a room with a wooden bed and patchwork quilt, a rickety washstand, and one chair? No, no—and she sat erect among her pillows—it was not a dream; she was at home—her real home. Sleepily she watched the clever housemaid arrange her bath, and carry in her tea in a dainty canary-coloured service.

"At what time will you have your breakfast, my lady? Her ladyship said you would have it in your room."

"At nine o'clock. Just a bit of anything that's going—I'm partial to stirabout."

"Very well, my lady."

Enter Justine the maid, with her smart lace-trimmed apron and air of critical inquiry, who began to arrange and put away and take out things in a sort of stealthy silence. Presently she came forward and asked—

"When will your ladyship get up?"

"Oh, now," she answered, "it's all hours."

"When shall I come back?"

"I can dress myself, thank ye."

"But your hair, my lady?"

"Yes, I always do it meeself."

"Then you will ring if you want me. I've left out your blue cloth; it"—pause—"fastens up the back."

As Justine closed the door, her ladyship slid out of bed and ran, barefooted, to the window. Before her eyes lay a heavily timbered park, so large, that it gave her the impression of being boundless. A silvery frost sparkled on the grass. Beneath the window was a pleasure-garden with gravel walks and marble steps and statues, where three men with brooms and a barrow were languidly sweeping up the dead leaves. Somehow the stately spacious outlook, impressed Joseline, even more than the interior of the house.

When breakfast arrived, she was already dressed, all but the fastening of her gown, and, unaware of the enormity, she requested the housemaid "to give her a hook up." Of course it was not Marston's business, and she might get into trouble with Ma'mselle; but the new-comer had no idea of the hard and fast lines of domestic service—or indeed that there were any lines at all. After a hearty meal, Joseline ventured forth into the wide corridors, down a grand staircase, and was presently lost among the intricacies of an immense, rambling mansion. There were long passages, lined with sporting pictures, and covered with thick red carpets, where she encountered soft-footed men-servants, who stared and stood aside. She discovered a billiard-room, then, opening a swing door, a cloak-room, and suddenly found herself in what appeared to be the butler's pantry, where two youths in shirt-sleeves seemed not a little startled by her visit. She had opened the wrong swing door, and, in beating a nervous retreat, came face to face with her father in shooting kit. He seemed surprised and pleased, as he exclaimed—

"Hullo! you early bird, what are you doing in this part of the house?"

"Faix, I believe I've lost me way. I wanted to find you, and—all the other people."

"At any rate you've found *me*. I hope you are rested?"

"Yes, thank you. And where are the rest of them?"

"Scattered about. Some are playing golf, some are in bed. I've been interviewing the steward." Then, as he ushered her through a doorway, "Would you like me to show you the house?"

"Yes, indeed; I would love it."

To introduce Joseline to the home of her forefathers was a task after Lord Mulgrave's own heart; he was a man of cultured tastes and a well-known collector. He had a fine show of old arms, old ivories, old cloisonné, some exquisite French cabinets, and the finest snuff-boxes in England. By degrees he piloted Joseline through a suite of reception-rooms, and showed her many rare and costly objects among his heirlooms and his treasures; he was eloquent over his relics of the Armada, his Sèvres cups, "Mary and William" tankards, and was conscious of a sharp spasm of disappointment, when he found that the object that claimed his companion's admiration and awe was the stuffed brown bear, which held a cigar-tray in the billiard-room! In short, as far as knowledge and appreciation of art went, Joseline might be a child of six. In the red saloon, a room panelled with damask and pictures, she came to a halt before a fine painting of the Madonna and Child, which Lord Mulgrave had picked up at a curiosity-shop in Pisa; it was said to be a Raphael—at any rate, it was of his school.

Joseline gazed for some time, and then crossed herself devoutly.

"Oh, it is real beautiful," she remarked at last—"a deal better than the one in Glenveigh Chapel. I wish they had the likes of it. An' wouldn't Father Daly be the proud man!" She paused, coloured, and exclaimed, "Oh, I was forgettin'."

"Forgetting what?" inquired her father.

"I'm afraid my being a Catholic is a shockin' upset; but I tell ye, for ye bid to know"—and she surveyed him with solemn eyes—"I'll never change my religion."

"No, of course not, my dear. It is true that our family have always been Church of England; but I am thankful that you have a religion; it is an uncommon possession in these days."

Was he thinking of his wife, with her Sunday card-parties?

As they talked on many subjects, they were moving slowly down the saloon, and at the end, he came to a standstill. Lord Mulgrave had instinctively felt that there was no use in exhibiting the priceless Vandycks, Romneys, and Hoppners, to this uneducated child as yet; but here was a modern picture, bound to enchain her. Joseline looked up at a full-length painting of a lovely girl, robed in a filmy white gown, with delicate touches of blue. The portrait had been taken at a happy moment, and seemed to exhale the very breath of life and youth. No need to explain. Instinctively she was aware that she was face to face with her mother. The picture was a gem, the "chef d'œuvre" of a French artist who, like his model, had died young. The face was so vivid, so full of animation, it seemed to stand out from the canvas, as if alive. A truly speaking likeness! Joseline recognised her own shade of hair, the colour of her eyes, and brows—her very mouth—she was looking at herself as in a mirror.

"You are like her," said Lord Mulgrave, in a low voice. "You can see it?"

"I am, in face," she answered, with an effort. "But in mind and ways I'm just an awkward, common flahoola of a country girl!"

She had spoken the truth; her father could not contradict her. Again he was penetrated with the conviction that, with the refined face and figure of his beloved Joseline, the charming daughter beside him, had the manners and vocabulary of the Irish peasantry. (Unfortunately for Lord Mulgrave, his nature was dominated by the critical faculty.) Would she ever outgrow or live down her plebeian youth, and those twenty-one years of poverty and hardship, which yawned between her and him?

"Oh! you will improve," he said, with a stifled sigh.

"I'm afraid I'm too old. However, I'll try."

"And here," continued Lord Mulgrave, indicating a patrician individual in splendid uniform, "is your grandfather, the Duc de Hernoncourt."

"Holy Moses! Fancy that my grandfather!" she murmured, staring into the face, "and him a duke, no less!"

"Yes; he had the royal blood of France in his veins. So"—looking at her steadily—"have you."

"Is it me?" she repeated, opening her eyes. Then she burst out laughing. "Well, to think of that now! He looks terribly stiff and stand-off, does my grandfather, and as if he did not want to know the likes of me."

"This is the little boudoir," announced Lord Mulgrave, suddenly opening a door into a small, bright room, where a great wood fire blazed up the chimney. Before it was drawn a sofa, on which a recumbent figure lay extended at full length, displaying a generous view of red silk stockings and buckled shoes, the head buried among soft silk cushions; and when the head turned, it displayed the face of Tito—Tito with a cigarette between her lips, and a yellow paper-bound book in her hand.

"Hallo!"—suddenly sitting up. "Good morning, pater." To Joseline: "So you are down?"

"Yes, long ago," she replied. "I'm sorry you are sick. What ails you?"

"I sick? Certainly not! Pray why on earth should you think so?"

"Because you are lying stretched."

"Oh, that's nothing. I'm taking it easy. The Max girls and the men are playing a foursome, and I'm off duty"; and she snuggled down again, and replaced her cigarette.

"Duty reminds me that I'm to meet Ross, the head keeper, at eleven-thirty," said Lord Mulgrave, "so I must be off; and I leave you two girls together. Tito will take you in hand, Joseline, and coach you a bit. I'll see you at lunch." And he went out.

"Sit down in that comfy chair," said Tito, extending an authoritative cigarette, "and let us have a talk. I suppose the earl has been doing the grand tour. Tell me what do you think of the pictures? Aren't they splendid?"

"Oh, yes," she assented, without enthusiasm, "grand."

"The Cavalier on the black horse is worth ten thousand pounds."

"Holy saints! Did father pay all that money?"

"No, goosey. The Cavalier is an ancestor—a most valuable one, too. If he were mine, I'd sell him like a shot. They are all your ancestors."

"How strange! I never heard the word itself spoken till last week. Where are the other people?"

"Mother is in bed; she never shows till lunch; she has her toilette, and her little dog, and her letters. Lady Max is an early bird, but she breakfasts in her boudoir; she has a mighty correspondence—political and philanthropic. The girls are out—both golf mad. Griselda is a champion; the rest of the crowd were only neighbours. There is another big spread to-night, and a shoot to-morrow."

"Oh!"—and Joseline relapsed into silence, and sat staring at the fire.

"Now, come, let's talk, and get to know one another," said Tito briskly. "You begin."

"Faix, it takes a long while to know people," rejoined the other, in her soft, musical drawl.

"But in my case I become an intimate, or an enemy, within the first half-hour."

"Faix, then, I hope you won't become my enemy."

"No—though of course I ought to, after your turning up, and giving me the back seat!"

Joseline became crimson, and looked uncomfortable and distressed.

"Bar jokes! I mean to do you a good turn, and tell you things."

"I'll be thankful to you, for I'm as ignorant as a young crow. What sort of things?"

"Family news, family politics, family secrets that you would take ages to discover. Also I'll be your child's guide and adviser—for though I expect you are only a couple of years younger than I am, I am old enough in worldly ways to be your grandmother. You call me Tito, of course."

"Yes, of course. And your mother; what am I to call her?"

"Um," muttered Tito into the stump of her cigarette.

"Um?" repeated her pupil. "Do you mean *Mum*?"

"No. I'm considering," she answered, with half-shut eyes. "I'll let you know later. Did you do your hair yourself?"

"Yes; av course I did. Why? Is it a holy show?"

"No; ripping! Tell me, has the earl said anything to you about money, or an allowance?"

"Yes. He said four hundred a year. It's far too much."

"Too much!" suddenly sitting erect. "Not half enough. You could never do with it—that is, if you are to be dressed. Why, look at me!"—gesticulating. "Do you see this serge gown I've on? It cost twenty guineas—not paid for yet. My shoes"—she flourished her pretty feet—"three guineas. As to my evening gowns, that wretch 'Du Du' won't let me have anything under thirty-five pounds, and then it's sham lace, and looks like a rag in a week! Do you know that my winter coat cost one hundred and twenty pounds? That makes a big hole in four hundred pounds. I've the same allowance too, and I'm drowned in debt."

"*You* in debt? Why I thought it was only poor people that owed!"

"Well, I'm poor. I've nothing of my own but a hundred a year. Oh, I owe bills I simply dare not think of. Such piles—especially in Paris. Mother is even worse; she owes thousands! Of course, then there's her bridge losings, and her new motor, and Monte Carlo and all that. When she married his lordship she had a thousand a year, and a little girl. She has the little girl still—but the thousand a year has departed."

"But is not father rich?"

"Yes. Nothing much for all he has to keep up. He says he is a poor rich man. Lots of the farms are on his hands. There is the big London house, the villa at Cannes, this place, with fifty servants. And mother is a bad manager, and frightfully extravagant."

"Well, av course I've always been poor, and twenty pounds seems a fortune. Tell me, Tito, why do ye spend so much on yer back?"

"Because I must be in the swim. One cannot be seen over and over in the same gown. When I go on a three days' visit, I take at least a dozen frocks. Then, I'm plain—I require dressing. Now *you* could wear anything."

"Is that so? or are ye joking?"

"Why, you know you are most awfully pretty! I say"—and she pulled up a cushion with a tug and selected a fresh cigarette—"don't you feel a bit funny? Outside you look all right"—she paused and surveyed her companion critically, then resumed, "but how is your mind? How are you *inside*?"

"Faix, then I'll tell you! I feel just as you would if, after being reared in grandeur all your life, you were suddenly struck down below stairs, among a pack of strangers, and told to scour the pots, and wash up dishes."

"I'd be bound to smash everything before me."

"That's just how I feel," said Joseline with fervour. "I'm sure to break lots of things."

"You mean the laws of good manners. Well, you will soon learn; you see, you are a lady born."

"But I've lived all my life as a working girl"—and she held out her hands. "I may be Lady Joseline to look at, but I'm just Mary Foley dressed up."

"There is one thing you'll break, my dear, and that is hearts."

"Arrah, go on with you, and your blarney!"

"Go where?"—laughing. "I really wonder you were not married long ago."

"Faix, there is more nor you wonders at that," she answered sedately.

"Who pray?"

"Why, the boys I would not take!"

"Do tell me about them?"

"Augh, sure, they were only just common chaps."

"What a providential mercy you did not *take* one of them! That would have been a fine complication!"

"Have you any chap, Tito?"

"Oh, heaps of a sort. Of course, I've played about."

"What's that?"

"Sitting in corners and writing little notes and having jokes, but nothing serious. Mother thinks it is time there *was* something serious; you see, I'm twenty-three"—and she blew a cloud. "And I've no looks or money; I'm only smart and bright and well turned out, and an A1 dancer and bridger."

"What's a bridger?"

"Oh, you poor dear innocent, you'll soon know! Well, as I was saying, I'm not a very marketable article, and here you come and take all the wind out of my little sails."

"There's no fear of that! You can't understand the dread I'm in of all the strange grand folk. When I think of things I'm scared; and as to the servants, I declare they just paralyse me!"

"How ridiculous! You must really learn to hold up your head and be self-confident."

"I never could. Now, there's your mother; she's a real lady; any one can see that with half an eye."

"Of course, mother comes of a good old family, and is proud; but she was only a parson's daughter—second son—family living, you know?"

"No, I know nothing. I've heard of a living family, never of a family living. I'm afraid her ladyship will mislike me."

"Oh no, she never mislikes any one; and don't call her her ladyship, for mercy's sake!"

"No; and I'll be very thankful to you if you'll correct me when I'm wrong. Now, tell me, what my father likes?"

"Peace, with a big P, and sport and books and pictures and curios. I am happy to add, he likes *me*."

"And your mother?"

"Society, society, and again society—lots of nice boys, and smart married women without their husbands, married men without their wives. She adores bridge and cigarettes, motoring, and pretty clothes; she likes to give the best house-parties, and to feel that she is very popular. By-the-by, I wonder what Dudley will say to *you*?"

"Dudley? Oh, yes, I remember—father's cousin. Do you like him?"

"Pretty well: he is decent enough. Mother adores him."

"Why? Sure she is no relation!"

"No, if he were she might loathe him. She likes him because he is rich, and run after, and good-looking, and the next heir—and so deliciously casual and cool; and because"—here she took the pillow from beneath her head and thumped it vigorously—"she wishes him to marry"—a violent thump—"*me*!"

"Well, and why not?" inquired Joseline, in her tranquil voice. "I see they do draw down matches over here, with all their laughing at us in Ireland."

"*Us*, in Ireland!"—throwing herself back. "You have no more to say to Ireland than the parrot or your terrier. By the way, why did you import him?"

"I was lonesome like."

"I believe he has chased the housekeeper's best cat; and that cat is a personage, I can assure you."

"I'm sorry; but he was always a terror for cats."

"What a funny expression!"

"Well, when I'm too funny entirely, will you, for the love of goodness, give me a wink or a pinch. I know I just talk like the purest commonality—I'm not fit to be a lady."

"You can't help yourself; you *are* a lady."

"I'm better than I was, thanks be to Miss Usher; she made me read aloud to her every day. Now, do tell me, when are you going to be married to my cousin?"

"Most probably never—though it would be a splendid match for me."

"Then why not give in to it?"

"I expect there would be two words to the bargain. Dudley is in no hurry; he knows his value, and that he could marry almost any girl in England. Perhaps he may take it into his head to marry you! I'm sure your father would fall in with that arrangement."

"And what about *me*?"

"Oh, you! It would be like a political marriage; you'd have to consider yourself highly honoured. He is the most fastidious creature I've ever seen."

"Tell me some more about him," urged Joseline, suddenly sinking on to the big white rug, and clasping her arms around her knees.

"Yes, with pleasure, if you will wait till I light a fresh cigarette."

"But you have smoked two already," remonstrated her companion.

"Oh, that's nothing"—carelessly striking a match. "Why, mother smokes dozens a day, although the doctors have forbidden her to smoke at *all*, she has such a weak heart; and they declare she will kill herself, but she does not believe them. As for Dudley, he has been in the army—the Duke's Lancers; he was out in South Africa, and got enteric, and nearly died; he is awfully faddy about his health, and takes a real interest in his tongue and his temperature; then, he is shockingly flattered and run after, for, besides being heir to the pater, he has a big property in mines, which, needless to say, he never goes near; he is supposed to have tremendous taste in some ways, and sets fashions—he was the first man to wear a silk muffler with the point outside, and to lunch at his club on bread and milk. Now I hear that bread and milk is the rage!"

"And what else does he do besides eating slops?"

"Oh, he travels, and motors, and shoots, and sleeps, and nurses himself, and says nasty, cynical things—and sometimes does kind ones. He is rather decent—the earl likes him; by all the laws of propriety he ought to hate his heir, but they get on capitally; they neither of them talk much; they just sit and smoke, or walk and smoke. Dudley is accustomed to be talked to and amused; you see, he is a great catch."

"Does he flirt, or play, as you call it?"

"Yes; but only with married women."

Joseline stared; her face expressed shame and disapproval.

"Oh, my dear little lambkin, it's all right. No scandal! Just a few dresses, and a kiss or two."

"I don't understand."

"No, but you will, darling. Now tell me, between ourselves, have you ever had a real lover?"

No answer. Joseline's eyes fell, and her colour rose.

"Look here, we will exchange experiences. I will tell you my secrets; you shall reveal yours. Come now; has a man ever kissed you?"

Joseline's colour increased, and crept up to her temples.

"Ah, ha! I see! Oh, your face is a shocking telltale!"

"Then it's telling a big lie!" she protested with energy.

"It looks to me like the truth. *Some one* has kissed you. Come now, own up!"

"If I do, you will swear"—and she rose to her knees, and leant against the sofa—"to keep my secret?"

"Yes, I swear—a million times over!"

"Well—I've no call to be ashamed; it was six years ago, and I was only a slip of a thing; but a man did kiss me, and I kissed him"—a pause—"through a pane of glass!"

Tito sat erect, stared incredulously, and burst into a scream of laughter; it rang through the room, peal after peal. At that moment Lady Grizel appeared in the doorway, where she stood for a moment in startled silence.

"Why, Tito, you have nearly drowned the luncheon gong!" she said. "What *is* the joke?"

Tito, still gasping for breath, scrambled off the sofa and replied: "The best joke I've heard for years!" and drying her eyes, she repeated, "The best I've heard for years! I must refer you to Joseline!"

But Joseline had already sprung to her feet, and fled.

CHAPTER XXIV

Lady Mulgrave and her guests were already seated, when two late arrivals joined them with hurried apologies.

"Good morning," she said, tendering a dainty hand to Joseline, and offering her ear to be kissed.

But this ignorant Irish peasant failed to accept the hint, having no conception that she was being honoured with permission to salute her stepmother's delicately powdered skin; and she stood for a moment, undecided and embarrassed.

"Well, there, my dear, go and sit down," said her ladyship, indicating a place next to herself. "I hope you are rested?"

"Thank you, I'm finely to-day."

"I suppose you have been round the house?"

"Yes. It's wonderful; it's grand. I never saw the likes of it."

Lady Mulgrave smiled faintly, and said, with half malicious emphasis, "No, dear, I should imagine *not*!"

Her look was significant, though her smile was enchanting. Joseline instantly withdrew into herself and proceeded to eat her lunch in nervous silence. Whatever she said or did was bound to be wrong. She read—she was quick in such matters—criticism and ridicule in the other woman's eyes.

Those same eyes watched her from time to time with a curious, scrutinising gaze. Seen in the broad light of day, the girl's extraordinary resemblance to her mother came home to Lady Mulgrave like a shock. She had never ceased to be jealous of that exquisite portrait! And here was the picture alive, a brilliant and emphatic reality, seated beside her at table, and, oh! small sweet consolation! eating French beans with a knife!

Although Mrs. Dawson had secured a splendid position for herself and daughter, her affection for Lord Mulgrave was lukewarm; she had, however, acted her part to perfection. By-and-by it had dawned on her husband that there was no sincerity behind all those honey-sweet words. Gradually he had withdrawn into himself, and they had drifted apart, having nothing whatever in common.

Then there had been disagreements respecting expenditure, arrangements, guests of which he disapproved; but in these little encounters, the lady had invariably the best of it; she never lost her self-command, or her temper; but she wept in a subdued and becoming fashion, and Lord Mulgrave was a coward in the presence of a woman in tears, therefore he relinquished his sceptre for the sake of peace. And yet, though he was indifferent to her, she was jealous—jealous of the beautiful French wife, whose memory he had enshrined, jealous of the poor little treasures which he hoarded, of the miniature that he carried with him whenever he left home, were it but for a day!

Now, like a thunderbolt from the skies, this Frenchwoman's daughter—her living, breathing image—had crossed the threshold of her life. Already she was sensible of a hot dislike of the girl (though, of course, no one should ever suspect it). She would play her cards cautiously, pose as the sweetest of stepmothers, and, as soon as possible, marry her off. With that face and figure there would be little difficulty, unless the creature was an absolute idiot!

She could see that Joseline was pitiably nervous, and no doubt would have been a thousand times happier in the servants' hall. It was true she ate but little; and by degrees ventured to look about her. The presence of her father at the foot of the table—of Tito, chattering directly opposite—emboldened her, and she glanced at the company one by one. There was her aunt, handsome, gracious, and stately, with her white hair beautifully waved, her plump hands sparkling with rings; she looked kind. There were her cousins—fresh Scotch girls—wearing tam-o'-shanters and tweeds; three clean-shaven young men, rather like a set; and a pretty dark girl from the Rectory. They were all eagerly talking golf—discussing putting, ties, bunkers. To Joseline it was the purest gibberish, but to the company it seemed a topic of the most vital interest. Even Lady Maxwelton was eloquent, and bragged of "our greens."

Her immediate neighbours had only addressed one or two remarks to the new importation. They were charitable, Christian people, and realised that it was kinder to leave her unnoticed—and to permit the poor girl "to find herself."

After lunch, the six ladies adjourned to coffee in the little drawing-room, and here the marchioness and her daughters gathered round and made friends with their new cousin.

Such a pretty, blushing, timid creature, with her soft southern brogue! And what a likeness to her mother!

By-and-by Joseline rose, in hopes of making her escape; but Lady Mulgrave, with an imperative gesture, motioned her to her side, and, looking up with half-closed eyes, exclaimed, "Now you must talk to *me* a little, dear girl."

Joseline sat down in embarrassed silence.

"Dearest child, I really do think you so wonderful." A pause, and she blew a cloud. "Six weeks ago you were in a cabin. It is extraordinary, is it not?"

"It is," was the humble admission; "but it was not altogether what you might call a cabin."

"No? And what, then—a hut?"

"Just a decent slated house with two good bedrooms, forby, a loft, and a fine kitchen and scullery."

"Where did *you* sleep?"

"In the loft."

"But, dearest, you said there were two bedrooms."

"Yes, but we kept potatoes in one, and I liked being up high. And now, with your leave, I'd like to go away and write a few letters."

"So then"—with a playful air—"you can write?"

"Oh yes, and read, and cipher. I had good schooling."

"And what are your accomplishments, Joseline?"

"Not much to brag about."

"Still, I'm confident you are clever at some things."

"I can sing, and play the concertina."

"Oh, the concertina!" repeated Lady Mulgrave, with a faint shudder.

"And I can knit and dance; and I'm a good milker—if that counts."

"So, then, you had a cow? Any pigs?"

"No. We had three, and sometimes four, cows. We kept the Rectory in milk, and the police barracks as well."

"Did you do all this yourself—no assistants?"

"Me mother—that's"—becoming scarlet—"Mrs. Foley,—wasn't up to much, and I used to have a girl in on weekdays to lend a hand, and a boy of a Sunday—but I got shut of him."

"And where did you shut him? And why?"

"Oh, because he was always in a hurry to be off, tearing at the cows at two o'clock, instead of six, because, being Sunday, he wanted to do the bona fide on his bicycle."

"Dearest, what *do* you mean?"

"The bona fide traveller, you know, is allowed refreshments. He would take a spin of six or seven miles—get a drink at a public-house. May I go now, please?"

"Yes, of course, dear." And as the girl crossed the room and disappeared, Lady Mulgrave turned to the marchioness and said, with a shrug, "Is she not *too* quaint for words! playing the concertina, and the boy doing—what was it?—the bona fide on a bicycle!"

"I think she is a sweet, simple, good girl," declared her aunt—"just one of nature's ladies."

"Oh, she is simple enough," acquiesced the other; but in her voice there was a belittling and malicious note.

Joseline spent an hour in writing letters to Miss Usher, Peggy Carroll, and Mrs. Hogan—letters written on beautiful thick paper, and ornamented with a neat gold crown. After these had been despatched, she accompanied her father on a tour of inspection round the grounds, the gardens, and the stable-yard. It was a bright, frosty afternoon, and she felt invigorated and even gay. The two made steady progress in intimacy; her awe of him had entirely abated, and she talked freely, expressing her delight in the greenhouses and horses and dogs with truly Irish enthusiasm. As they walked away from the golf links he said, "You must learn to play golf and billiards. I will teach you—yes, and to ride too."

"I've everything to learn—and that's the truth."

"I am glad you and Tito seem to hit it off."

"Yes, indeed; she's queer notions, but she is real kind-hearted. I've asked her to correct me when I'm doing the wrong thing."

"She's so feather-headed, you must not rely on her; better come to *me*."

"So I will, with a heart and a half."

"You will soon become accustomed to us and our ways. Be yourself—be gay, my dear; another young voice in the house is a great pleasure to me."

"But not a South Cork brogue! Ye can't call *that* nice?"

"Yes, I can; it reminds me of old days. Your mother had most wonderful spirits; she was the happiest——" he stopped. "Well, here I see her ladyship coming in her motor; you had better go and get ready for tea; she likes young people to be punctual—remember that, dear."

"Yes; and we were so late for lunch! But I had to tidy my hair; it was like a furze bush. I won't have any tea. I must unpack, and tidy up my things; but I'll come down early."

"If you do, then we can have a talk. Dinner is at eight. I believe Dudley is expected."

Joseline, having arranged her belongings in her own way, dressed early, and descended to the yellow drawing-room, in order to have a good half-hour with the magazines, and the promised talk with her father, before the crowd came.

Absorbed in a story, she did not hear the door open.

Captain Deverell entered; he had just arrived by train. At first he supposed the room was empty, but, seeing a white skirt billowing round the sides of an arm-chair near the fire, he called out, "Hullo, Tito! Is that you? Has the wild Irish girl arrived?"

The figure sat up, rose slowly to her feet, and confronted him. No, it was not Tito, but a far better-looking young lady, wearing a white gown and a turquoise necklace, who replied, "Yes, she has come—in fact, here she is!" dropping a curtsey. "But she's not very, very wild at present."

He surveyed her gravely. "I beg your pardon. So you must be Lady Joseline?"

She nodded.

"And I have the honour to present your cousin, once removed, Dudley Deverell"; and he made a profound, half-ironical inclination.

"Oh, yes, I've heard all about you from Tito"; and she sat down and took up her book with an air of calm detachment.

"I've seen you before somewhere, I think," he announced, after a puzzled silence.

"Have you really?" And again her eyes wandered to the page.

"It is not considered polite to read—er—when you have some one to talk to."

She closed her book, and said, "Excuse me, please, I have not learnt manners yet. I will not read, but I am awfully interested in the story."

"And not in the least in *me*, eh? How crushing!"

She coloured up to her hair.

"I have it!" he shouted triumphantly.

"What have you caught?" she demanded, with brisk curiosity.

"You, bless my soul!" Here he sat down. "Why, you are the girl at the gate. Yes, I recognise your eyes, though you are dressed up. You cannot have forgotten us—the motor people! And my friend Harry Coxford had a row with your young man. Don't you remember?"

"Oh, indeed, I remember it well enough! And you were the dummy! Patsie had drink taken, and I got a queer fright, I declare, when the two were in handy grips."

"What were you doing there, that day?"

"I went up just to fetch back the cat, and to say good-bye to the old place. 'Twas there I was reared."

"Were you? Well, I must say you do it credit. So that was your home, until old Usher ferreted you out?"

She nodded.

"And how do you like your new quarters?"

"Well enough so far, thank you."

"By Jove!"—looking her over—"she is a cool card—might have been here for years"; and he took in the well-cut gown, the dainty little shoe, the turquoise necklace, which so well became her dazzling white throat. Yes, the girl had evidently begun well, and made what is known on the turf, as a "flying start."

It was a singular circumstance that whereas her tone and speech were distinctly common, she had nevertheless an indescribable air of good breeding—the strange, inimitable stamp of social superiority that cannot be acquired by any known process of education.

"And what became of the uproarious young man?" he inquired.

"Oh, he's all right, for all I know," she answered, with supreme indifference.

"Or care," drawled Captain Deverell.

"Yes," she answered coldly, "or care."

"There's a pretty confession."

"Sure! the likes of him was nothing whatever to me," she announced, with an air of serene repudiation.

"No, but you seemed to be a good deal whatever, to him."

"How could I help that? Aren't they all the same?"

"Oh, are they? Does your father know of this Pat, or Mike?"

"No; why should he be bothered with the likes of such nonsense?"

"Nonsense! Well, you are amazing. The man was madly in love with you, and you call it 'nonsense'!"

"People in love are mostly foolish."

"How do you know?"

"Why, from seeing plenty of them," was the unabashed reply.

"In your own case?"

"Yes, they tormented the life out of me, and I was tired of insulting them. But I'll tell you one thing—Patsie only fancied he liked me; it was just because I was going off, and his contrariness. If I'd been stopping on, I don't believe he'd have bothered me, for he is looking for a fortune."

"Yes"—drawing his chair a little closer. "This is most interesting. Please go on."

But Joseline was gazing at the door, which opened cautiously, and admitted Lady Mulgrave in an evening toilette of sea green and diamonds. She rustled forward with empressement.

"There now, and I'll tell ye the rest when we are by ourselves."

Her ladyship distinctly overheard this promise. What a bold creature!—a girl who had met Dudley for the first time. So this was her simple, innocent little Irish peasant! Already spreading her nets for her father's heir. How truly abominable!

"My dear boy, I'd no idea you had arrived," she said, coming over with extended hands. "I see that I needn't introduce you to Joseline"—and she looked contemptuously amused. "Have you been here long?"

"Only about five minutes."

She glanced interrogatively at the girl, who turned towards the mantelpiece, and said, "Fifteen, by the clock."

"Well, it seemed like five," he said; "my new cousin had so many curious things to tell me. Now I must be off and dress"; and he departed, leaving Joseline and her stepmother *tête-à-tête.*

"But, dearest child, I was given to understand that you were painfully *shy,*" she was beginning, when, to the girl's immense relief, the door opened again, and several of the guests came into the room, followed by her father.

"And how has my little girl been getting on?" he asked, as he joined her.

"Oh, very well so far, and I've just made acquaintance with Dudley Deverell."

"And what do you think of him?"

"I cannot answer that just yet; but I can tell you what he thinks—of me."

"Really!"

"That I am a new sort of foreign curiosity. I may be gold, or I may be *brass*! I'm sure he suspects there's a bit of brass about me!"

CHAPTER XXV

Tito's sketch of Dudley Deverell was not altogether a caricature; he was good-looking, selfish, and popular. Social success and an atmosphere of flattery, stimulated his weaknesses, and encouraged him to display the least attractive side of his nature—a cynical air, an amazing indolence, and a cool indifference to the opinions of other people. Life had been made pleasant for him, and he valued it accordingly. As a guest and attraction he was faithless, and had thrown more than one important hostess into a tempest of indignation, by sending at the eleventh hour a lying wire. He travelled, he shot and fished when his health permitted, and was just as bored as other young men, with no occupation, and great prospects.

Some day he was bound to marry, and possibly Tito would do as well as any one! She knew the place, and it would please her people. Tito was good company, and a ripping dancer, but inclined to be rowdy, and confoundedly plain. If he could not remedy one defect—he would the other.

And now there was another girl in the family—he had bestirred himself so far as to journey to Ashstead, to see what she was like? It was an amazing tale. An introduction to this peasant would afford him a novel sensation. New sensations were rare and precious, and he had run down just for one night, in order to interview the stranger; and behold! she was no stranger, but the pretty, cheeky girl who had chaffed him by the roadside in Ireland. The new cousin was uncommon; she was amazing; her manners and accent were abominable. However, she had lovely eyes and a saucy tongue, and he foresaw a considerable amount of entertainment.

These were some of Captain Deverell's reflections as he gazed into his own face and executed a most finished white tie (he had been an Eton boy). Lady Mulgrave, too, had certain thoughts respecting Joseline. She had never seen Dudley so animated and interested, as on this occasion in the drawing-room.

Oh, that would never do! She would nip the intimacy in the bud at once. Dudley rarely remained longer than twenty-four hours, and she would see that he and the girl were kept apart. Captain Deverell slipped into the drawing-room just as dinner was announced, looking the ne plus ultra of the smooth-faced, smooth-headed young men of the period, and was just in time to lead Lady Grizel into the dining-room.

As Lord Mulgrave glanced round the beautifully decorated, well-lined table, he felt secretly vexed that Joseline, who had yet to distinguish between a dinner-knife and a dessert-knife, and to whom a finger-glass was a puzzle, should not have been allowed a little breathing space before being placed on exhibition.

Certainly she looked surprisingly like the rest of the company, save that she was much more attractive. With her wonderful skin, her burnished hair, her fine features, and exquisitely turned throat, it might be her mother come to life. And she was suitably dressed! Miss Usher had proved, indeed, a treasure. Then he considered his wife at the head of the table, a fashionable figure, with wonderful hair and complexion, a generous display of her splendid neck and shoulders, a French gown, the family diamonds, and her best society smile.

Lady Mulgrave glanced frequently at Joseline; she was a remarkable object, and Captain Deverell's eyes strayed to her too. The girl seemed to be both beautiful and discreet. She scarcely spoke, she scarcely ate, but crumbled bread and uttered monosyllables. Once she assured a man-servant that "she wanted no more sauce—she had lashings!" What were lashings? "Oh, if she would only talk!" said Lady Mulgrave to herself. Some one had been advising her to hold her tongue. However, her hands were red; she had upset her neighbour's champagne, eaten her neighbour's bread, and dropped her spoon. Yet, when all was said, the peasant girl had undergone the ordeal of her first dinner-party, with respectable self-possession.

After dinner, Joseline was formally presented to various important dowagers in the drawing-room, who found the girl pretty, well turned out, but oh! so stupid! She scarcely opened her lips.

Then the men came crowding in, conversation became general, bridge-tables were set out, and Joseline found her tongue.

"Do you play bridge?" inquired Captain Deverell, sinking into a seat beside Joseline, whilst another man hovered near.

"No, I never heard tell of it till to-day," she answered; "and is it with a ball, or what?"

"No; with cards." Then, speaking as to a child, "You know cards—playing cards?"

"Yes, and like them finely too. I've never heard of the game you mean, but I know 'spoil fire' and 'beating Jack out of town.'"

"That must be a most exciting game," drawled her cousin. "How many beat him? Not more than one at a time, I hope?"

"As many as likes; it makes no odds."

"Are you fond of motoring?" inquired a man who did not see why Deverell should engross the beauty.

"Well, I'll tell ye after I've been on one. I once got a lift on a traction-engine—me and a girl—I mean, a girl and myself—and I suppose it's the same sort of thing?"

"Only the pace is slightly different."

"Yes; but the noise, and the joggling, and the frightening of horses and cattle, is all one."

"I daresay you are right there," he assented.

"What part of Ireland have you lived in?" inquired a smartly dressed lady, who was seated near Joseline.

"The south, near Glenveigh."

"Oh, yes; a great place for fishing, is it not?"

"I would not say that; but it's where people come *looking* for fishing."

"And don't get it. I see! By the way, does not Mrs. Borrodaile live in that part of the world?"

"She does so, at the Court."

"I suppose you know her—er—by sight?"

Joseline nodded. "I seen her in the chapel."

"Do tell me what she is like?"

"Well, some makes out she is handsome; but I'd call her a very streelish lady."

"Streelish!" she repeated. "You mean stylish?"

"No, no, I do not. She has a great streel on her—long, sweeping things—and looks as if she was falling out of her clothes."

"Really?" she laughed. "I must inquire into this. I've not seen her for ages; she is my cousin."

"Is she so?" rejoined Joseline imperturbably. "I believe she is very good to the poor. Her kitchen-maid was a friend of mine and thought a power of her. Still and all, she *has* a rakish look!"

This newly discovered heiress was a unique creature, with her distinguished face and her extraordinary talk. She was splendid fun; people began to hover near her. Her father watched her with nervous apprehensions. It was too bad of her ladyship to bring the child forward before she had a little experience of society! But her ladyship had her own views; she wished to make her husband uncomfortable and ashamed of his low-bred daughter. He now joined the circle, and with unexpected animation, urged people to seat themselves at bridge.

Bridge, the all-fascinating, soon scattered Joseline's little court; and presently she and her father stole away together to have a talk in the library. They were not missed.

When Joseline had retired, Lord Mulgrave, as he smoked alone, began to ask himself if he would not have been wise to have accepted Lottie's broad hint, and sent the child to a school for a few months, just to rub off the rough edges of her vocabulary?

The shooting party were to have a grand battue the following morning. All the ladies who were not sportswomen were to meet the guns at a keeper's cottage, and there share their luncheon. But some of the women preferred to walk with the guns. These included Tito, who begged Joseline to accompany her to the neighbourhood of a celebrated warm corner, where they took their stand; but after a very short time Joseline and her dog made their way elsewhere. She had no taste for the spectacle. As she struggled through the undergrowth, she suddenly came upon Dudley Deverell, gun in hand, his loader beside him, awaiting the magic words "Mark over!"

"I say, what in the world are you doing here? and with a dog too! If the governor sees it he will be furious," he drawled. "If you don't mind you'll get shot."

"The dog will stick to me, and I'm striving to get out of the wood and doing my big best; but wherever I go there are guns and slaughter. Pah!" she exclaimed, "grown-up men shooting tame pheasants! Why don't you wring their necks, and have done with it!"

Dudley Deverell, who prided himself on being a dead shot and a keen sportsman (when his health permitted), stiffened and coloured with annoyance. What did this girl know of shooting or sport? She really *was* a young savage! "I see you don't approve of us, which is deplorable; for you will have to remain here till the end of the beat."

"Who says so?" she demanded.

"I do. You may get shot. Mark over!" He raised his gun. Bang! bang! went two barrels, and a couple of rocketters came crashing heavily down. One of them fluttered about till it was put an end to. "What do you think of that?" he inquired.

"I call it a horrid sight!" was the unexpected reply. "There is no chance or fair play in it. But I suppose the poulterers have to be supplied!"

"Pray what do you know about poulterers?"

"A sight more than I want to! Haven't I spent all my life, till the last two months, rearing chickens, and selling eggs?"

"Oh! Really! And how did you dispose of them?"

"To the gentry."

"You did not *kill* them I presume?"

"No. I never had the nerve; but I plucked some of them with me own two hands."

"Still, I suppose you made a good thing of it?"

"No then, I didn't; though I had one lady, a big customer—till we fell out."

"About eggs? A bad egg, eh?"

"No. There *you* are out. My eggs were the best. It was over a gold locket and chain."

"How was that?"

"She made out as her son had given it to me."

"And she was wrong?"—smiling. "It was the other fellow?"

"Well, yes, if I'm a fellow, for I gave it to myself."

"And the lady's son—was *he* one of the crowd you——?"

"What does my father do with all the game?" she interrupted brusquely.

"I'm sure I've no idea. He has the best coverts in the county, and that's enough for me. What an odd girl you are!" he said suddenly. "Don't you feel it yourself?"

"I feel I am the odd one out at present. And you are a queer sort of man."

"I—queer? In what way?" he asked, with a touch of hauteur in his tone.

"Oh, rambling about the world, looking for something to kill, same as a boy birds-nesting, and not doing a hand's turn, good or bad."

"Ah, I declare you are a young reformer"—colouring angrily. "And *you* must know such a jolly lot about the world, and men of the world—don't you?" he added ironically.

"There, now you are laughing at me. I'm no reformer. God knows there's plenty of faults in me, and I've no call to be picking holes in you, or the likes of you; but I can't keep me tongue quiet."

"You can keep it very quiet sometimes—for instance, last night at dinner."

"And hard set to do it. I've always been a terrible talker. Tell me, is it true, that, with all the foreign countries you have seen, and the strange places you have pried into, you have never in your mortal life been down one of your own mines, nor seen how things is going with men and beasts that make your money? There! now I see you're real mad. I didn't mean to torment ye!"

Before Dudley could make a fitting and crushing reply, steps approached from behind them, and a man called out, "Hullo, Deverell, what luck? You had a hot corner!" But all that Deverell displayed was four brace. "Ah, you've had a young lady with you I see." As the girl pushed through the laurels, and fought her way on to a path, she heard the voice declare, "They are the very deuce out shooting."

"Yes," acquiesced her cousin, with unflattering emphasis, "an infernal nuisance."

So that was Dudley's verdict. She was an infernal nuisance! She halted for a moment to digest this fact. It was now time for the lunch at the keeper's cottage, and she encountered most of the party on their way to the rendezvous as she once more emerged into the open.

* * * * *

"Lady Mulgrave, is it possible that I see you refusing our standing dish, Irish stew?" said Dudley Deverell.

"I believe I shall have enough elsewhere," she answered, with significance. "What do you think of your new cousin?" she continued, as she helped herself carefully to cutlets.

"I am not prepared to give an opinion at such short notice."

"Then I gather that it is not a case of love at first sight?"

"I don't believe in that humbug; and besides, I saw her in Ireland."

"No!"—suddenly putting down her glass.

"Yes, by chance—as Mary Foley. I had not the smallest idea who she was then."

"And what did she look like?"

"Oh, a pretty, saucy, country girl, with lots to say for herself. I never was so amazed as when I discovered her last night in the drawing-room! You could have floored me with the traditional feather!"

"She does not talk much now," said Lady Mulgrave. "Evidently she has been advised, that silence is best."

"It must be a trial, for I heard a man describe her as 'the gabbiest little divil in the country.'"

"Oh, I expect she will soon find her tongue."

"And her feet?" supplemented Captain Deverell.

"I'm not so sure of that; it takes some time to rub off twenty-one years of the cabin."

"She is not awkward—no, not a bit."

"Except when she spills things over people, and breaks wine-glasses. You don't think her pretty, surely?"

"Yes; very pretty, in an uncommon style."

"A very uncommon style. What a mixture—French, English—reared in Ireland!"

"She has some curious ideas."

"Dear me! I had no notion that she had any ideas at all."

"Oh, yes; with regard to shooting, and idle young men, who won't do a hand's turn!"

"Nonsense! How amusing! You and she must have become delightfully confidential among the laurels! She is a frightful flirt; any one can see that with half an eye."

"Well, I cannot, with two eyes."

"Oh, but you will. Oh, she'll try her prentice hand—and a red hand it is!—on you, of course!"

"How do she and Tito hit it off?"

"Pretty well. You know Tito has the temper of an angel; so unselfish and sweet. She and I are running over to Paris to do some shopping for ten days. Any chance of seeing you, Dudley?"

"Perhaps. The old place, I suppose?"

"Yes; and Joseline and her father will have the house to themselves, and be able to make much of one another."

"He seems immensely devoted," said Dudley.

"Yes. He is full of sentiment, you know. There is, however, one drawback; she is a Catholic."

"Well, I agree with the earl. It is something to be anything in the present day. Personally, I like a woman to have a religion."

"But we all have," protested the lady.

"I suppose you think so. At any rate, you worship the Golden Calf."

"Really, Dudley!" she said, in an offended tone, "you do say the rudest things! Your manners are not improving."

"No, wearing a bit thin. Well, I must run over when you are in Paris, and see if I can't give them a touch of French polish!"

CHAPTER XXVI

The small family party had dispersed, and as the days went by without social events, Joseline began seriously and methodically to accustom herself to the routine, and resolute to become at ease in her new life. She was painfully conscious of her ignorance of the ways of people in society. She felt that she shocked Lady Mulgrave ten times a day; and Lady Mulgrave, for all her sweet smiles, had, as she mentally expressed it, "a pick on her." Yet she was making some progress, and from conversations listened to, she acquired a familiarity with the jargon of her surroundings, and was learning to manipulate just those turns of phrase, best calculated to sustain amiable relations.

Joseline was a great reader, and devoured books. With her, this was not a cultivated taste, but a natural appetite. From books, magazines, and reviews, she was learning with avidity, humbly conscious of her own inferiority, and that her father hoped for her to acquire a polish, and to shine.

When Lady Mulgrave and Tito had departed to Paris she and her father were thrown into one another's constant society. Innumerable small signs of her affection afforded him a happiness such as he had not known for years. He was becoming reconciled to shocks and to strange expressions, and all the best that was in Lord Mulgrave was brought to the surface. Together the pair walked and drove, explored the estate, and visited the cottagers. The girl's manner to their inmates was charming, and many of the elder people remembered and recalled her mother.

"I cannot imagine where you have acquired it, but you have a wonderful way with these folk," exclaimed Lord Mulgrave. "How do you know what is just the right thing to say?"

"It's like this, you see: although I am so awkward and flurried in fine society, and make such awful mistakes—you remember how I shook hands with the head gamekeeper at Lord Dover's, and walked out of the room before the Duchess—I am really at home with the poor. I can enter into their feelings, for I have lived with them all my life. They are the same all the world over, only they talk differently."

"Then in that case you shall be my Lady Bountiful and take on the cottage hospital, the school, and the almshouses. Her ladyship does not care for the people; she never visits them; she says they are uninteresting, grasping, and thankless."

"Well, some are! They can't help it. I knew a funny old woman at home; and once, when a lady gave her a nice stout serge, she just whimpered and said, 'And what about the elegant little grey dress ye had in the spring—where is *that*?'"

Lord Mulgrave laughed and she resumed: "But, after all, we should not be looking for thanks; some of them have so little, and we have so much."

"You talk like your mother, my dear. She was always on the side of the poor."

"Oh, father"—and she blushed vividly—"you make me so happy when you tell me that I am like her in other ways besides looks. Of course I can talk to the people, because I was one of them for so many years. Yet, somehow, these English are different—they are *all* ladies."

"Good gracious, Joseline! What do you mean?"

"I'll explain if I can. Now there is Mrs. Gillson, a widow-woman; I asked her to come up yesterday, and I would find her some warm clothes, but she said, 'I cannot come to-morrow, for a lady I've worked for regular every Wednesday this three years will expect me. I do her washing, and the lady always puts the clothes in soak of a Tuesday, and gives me a hand herself, so I really could not disoblige her!'"

Lord Mulgrave laughed again.

"Now, you see, in Ireland there's none of that. You are a lady born, or you are not. Irish ladies don't do washing."

"As yet; but it will come."

"That's true. Some of the quality are very short of money; the Mulligans, of Carlane, have sold all their old silver and pictures, and the young ladies do lace-work for the shops. I liked the lace-work myself, but I hadn't the time for it. I might do it now, I'm idle."

"Yes, and you seem to be getting on pretty well, and more at your ease."

"I'm not so flustered and awkward with you, or with the poor, or Tito; it's only with Lady Mulgrave and the servants I feel that small, ye might put me in your pocket!"

"You will outgrow that by-and-by."

"I'm awfully afraid of my maid; she is very *nosey* with me, and that's the truth."

"Then send her away, and get another. You must try and be more self-assured. Do you know that next week you will have to stand alone, for I'm going to the north of England on election business, and will be away a week."

"Oh, father, couldn't you take *me* too? I just love elections!"

"No, my dear—impossible."

"Oh, I wish you would. I'd adore the election and the speechifying, and the fun. We had one down in Glenveigh; they nearly tore one another to flittergigs."

"That must have been exciting. I'm afraid I could not promise you anything of that description. It will be rather a good thing to leave you to stand alone and rely on yourself. After I return, I intend to take you over to France to see the Hernoncourts. I have promised that you shall pay them a long visit."

"I wonder if they will like me?"

"I daresay they will, for you have inherited the Hernoncourts' face, and disposition."

"What is their disposition?"

"Gay, vivacious, impulsive, sensitive to kindness or ridicule. There is not much of the Mulgrave in you."

"Oh, what a pity. Is Dudley more of a Mulgrave?"

"Yes. Do you and he hit it off?"

"Oh, pretty well; he is slow."

"But sure."

"Perhaps *too* sure!"

"What do you mean?"

"He takes much for granted—sometimes I fancy he takes *me* for granted"—she added with a mischievous smile. "Now, father, let me race Rap to the little white gate, giving me a start. You must hold him."

"What a child she was!" thought the earl, as he held the struggling dog—a child in some ways; but in others, her sayings were beyond his comprehension.

CHAPTER XXVII

Joseline and Tito stood together in a window watching the departure of Lord Mulgrave. Last words and farewells had been exchanged in the hall, and the girls had ample time to return to the library before the brougham travelled out of sight. As its polished blue panels disappeared round a clump of trees Tito suddenly flung her arms round her companion and exclaimed—

"Hurrah!"

"Tito!" she remonstrated, thrusting her back with angry force.

"Well, Joe, you know as well as I do how fond I am of the pater; but—when the earl's away, the family will play—bridge."

"So you do now."

"Only in a mild form—a couple of quiet rubbers after dinner, at farthing points. The pater looks upon daylight bridge as undignified and unseemly. Now he has departed, the drawbridge is down."

"For mercy's sake will ye talk sense?" cried Joseline.

"Certainly. Don't I always talk sense? Mother is going to have her innings now, and she has invited a party of kindred spirits to spend a week, including—though she does not suspect it—her future son-in-law! Oh, yes, Joe, you may gape, but he arrives by the four o'clock train!" And Tito began to waltz around the room, with her hands on her hips.

"But who is he?" inquired Joseline, suddenly turning her back on the window, and surveying her companion with grave interest.

"Just what you might expect! A bad match, but everything else that is charming and desirable."

"What do you call a bad match?"

"One that will make mother furious. Tony is a third son, in the Foreign Office, with only four hundred a year. His name is Anthony Goodrich, and he is good enough for Tito Dawson."

"But sure, I thought that Dudley——" began Joseline.

"Would kindly throw the handkerchief to *me*?" continued Tito briskly. "No, no. Wait, and you will see that honour lies elsewhere, between Lady Agnes Shutter and"—with a significant smile—"another girl. Lady Agnes is stupid, but she has good manners, and a very clever mother."

"Who else is coming?" resumed Joseline.

"Oh, quite a number. Mother has to crowd them all in now, because the pater loathes them; they smoke and gossip and gamble, and treat the house like a hotel. First of all there is the Honourable Gussie Tripp, a tremendous swell at bridge—they say she clears a thousand a year."

"What, at cards? Ah, you're humbugging me!"

"Yes, at cards."

"Holy Saint Bridget!"

"Then there is Lady Boxhill, a very young elderly widow, rich, and fond of play and admiration. Lady Towton, rather pretty, with the most exquisite frocks—*dreams*! She won't tell where she gets them in Vienna. And of course Teddy Boltover. Then Senor Bambinetto—an Italian prince, they say; but if I saw him behind an organ and a monkey I should not be a bit surprised; he is looking for a rich wife, age and appearance quite immaterial. I fancy he likes Lady Boxhill. I hate him; he pokes his nose into one's face, and paws one! Colonel Wildairs, late of the Greens, a most distinguished officer. Sir Harry Coxford. Two cavalry men from Canterbury, and perhaps the great Dudley himself!"

"I'm glad he is coming," said Joseline. "Anyhow I'll have some one to speak to."

"I'm not so sure of that. If Mrs. Folly Fullerton appears, *she* will talk to Dudley. They have been a good deal talked about. That's the lot, with power to add to their number."

"I expect we shall find them plenty."

"You will, at any rate! They will make you sit up, you little rich and rare specimen from Ireland. However, take my advice, and amuse yourself. I can't look after you because——"

"You will be looking after Tony!"

"How smart! There is a ball on the fourteenth at the Hamptons', and we are going to it in full force; it will be enormous fun. Now remember they will all be here at four sharp. The cart that took the pater's luggage was to wait, also the brougham. Little he knew! Go and get into a smart tea-g. and prepare to receive—shocks." And as she uttered the last word, Tito waltzed to the door, and exit singing.

By five o'clock the expected guests were assembled in the little drawing-room, enjoying tea and sandwiches, drinks and cigarettes, discussing the weather, the latest news, and above all, bridge. Miss Tripp was a tall, talkative woman, with a high nose, a fine figure, and an air of easy assurance. Little Lady Boxhill, a good deal made up, looked about twenty in a certain light, and wore a chestnut wig, and a complexion. Mrs. Folly Fullerton, fair, sylph-like, languid, and insolent, dressed in flowery, diaphanous robes, with a gold cigarette-case dangling at her side. The Colonel, late of the Greens, a loud-voiced, well-groomed gentleman, who seemed to know every one, and be anxious that they should make themselves thoroughly at home.

Joseline gazed at him as he stood with his back to the fire, precisely like the master of the house, and said to one of the cavalry men with an off-hand air—

"Oh, it's all right, Pierrepont—smoking allowed. Try one of these Havanas?"

She had taken Tito's advice, and invested herself in a new tea-gown, and an armour of reserve. Nevertheless she felt frightened among the crowd of supercilious strangers, who appeared to look upon the house as a comfortable private hotel; indeed, she heard Lady Boxhill say to Mrs. Fullerton—

"What room have you this time, Bab? Not the corner one I hope?"

"No, I'm on the big landing."

"That's right."

"Yes. I told Lottie I simply would not come unless I had a suite."

"Oh!"—with a gesture of approval—"when one comes to a country house, the *least* they can do is to make you comfortable. I've brought my masseuse, my secretary, and my dogs."

The company were still discussing racing odds, shares, divorce cases, Yarborough and little slams, and Joseline sat in the background, completely bewildered. All her newly acquired confidence and manners seemed oozing away amid surroundings of inquisitive eyes and languid patronage! Dudley, who on flying visits had been friendly, was now chilly and unsympathetic, and almost ignored her. Tito was engrossed in the company of a thin, clever-looking young man, and she was left to the mercies of strange women, who stared at her in a way that put her out of countenance, and asked such blunt questions.

"And were you really in a cottage in Ireland only three months ago?" inquired Mrs. Fullerton, contemplating her with a look of languid insolence.

"Yes, only three months ago"—and she sighed.

"And is it *true* that you actually sold fowls?"

"Yes"—colouring—"and eggs as well."

"Dear me, how amusing!"—with a sarcastic lifting of the brows; and she replaced her cigarette in her mouth, and took a whiff. "I hear you are tremendous fun," she drawled.

"Who says so?"

"Oh, some one—Dudley I think; but it does not matter. Would you mind reaching me that cushion? Thanks. Now you might fetch me another of those excellent caviare sandwiches."

*   *   *   *   *

The following morning was wet—a hopeless day; and card-tables were set at eleven. People played till lunch, from lunch till tea, from tea till dinner.

After dinner Lady Boxhill said—

"Lottie my dear, my brain feels in a sort of pulp; my ideas are mixed; I've played seventeen rubbers to-day. Do let us have some parlour tricks, or music, as a sort of rest cure."

"Oh, very well, if you like. Yes, Tito"—turning to her daughter—"go and beat up recruits"—and she once more settled herself comfortably among her cushions.

Presently Tito came back, and proclaimed—

"No performance! The Prince has a cold, Lady Boxhill says, and Mrs. Folly simply won't; she is sitting in the little back room with Dudley."

Lady Mulgrave muttered something that may, or may not, have been, "Selfish pig!"

"And," continued Tito, spreading out her hands, "there is no one else."

"Unless we have the pianola?" suggested Lady Mulgrave.

"No, no!" cried Sir Harry Coxford, "I like to look at the fair performer. The pianola is so mechanical, and it does not *sing.*"

"I believe the housekeeper has a gramophone," put in Tito; "it sings 'I won't play in your yard.'"

"Housekeeper and gramophone. That reminds me," murmured Lady Mulgrave, "where is Joseline? Tito, did not your father say she sang, and had a lovely voice?" Then, with a laugh, she added, "She can borrow the footman's concertina!"

"Mother," remonstrated Tito, "please don't ask her. I am sure she would be too shy. She would hate it!"

"Nonsense! Tell her she must! There is nothing to alarm her. Stay—where is she? The library, I suppose. Then I'll go myself," said Lady Mulgrave, rising with unusual energy; and as she swept out of the room in search of her victim, she promised herself that the forthcoming performance would prove a novelty, a draw, and a good joke. Already it was evident to some of her ladyship's guests, that they might laugh at the wild Irish girl with impunity, and in spite of all Joseline's efforts in the way of humble conciliation, her stepmother treated her, in private, as a species of domesticated savage. Whatever blandishments or arguments her ladyship had used, proved successful, for in less than ten minutes a white and stricken figure, clutching a concertina, stood up and faced a critical, and secretly scornful audience.

Many a time Mary Foley had played and sung to five times their number with the confidence born of appreciation and success. Mary's singing and playing of old Irish songs was declared "to beat all," and with her own neighbours she enjoyed a far higher reputation than Madame Melba herself. But here were different listeners, and a different atmosphere. The girl's heart felt like lead; her hands were so icy cold she could scarcely hold the footman's concertina. She glanced timidly about her, half hoping that her cousin Dudley would befriend her or beg her off; but Dudley had dined, he was at peace with his digestion—he was not disposed to exert himself, and if Lady Mulgrave did hustle the girl a bit, it would do her good! She struck a few shaky chords and endeavoured to find her voice and courage. What could she give them? "The three-leaved Shamrock"? "The stone outside Dan Murphy's door"? "The exile of Erin"? Yes. She looked over towards Dudley, hoping for at least his moral support; but there he lounged in the background, with his glass in his eye, sniggering at some remark of Mrs. Fullerton's. "So much for a cousin!" she thought, with deep resentment. "He would stand by and see her baited, the same as a rabbit among the coursing dogs of a Sunday!" At last she began; her sweet full notes were tremulous, and occasionally inaudible. With painful difficulty she brought out the opening bars:

"There came to the beach, a poor exile of Erin;

The dew on his thin robe was heavy and chill;

For his country he sighed, when at twilight repairing

To wander alone by the wind-beaten hill."

The sound of her own voice had given her confidence, and she continued with fuller notes:

"Where is my cabin door, fast by the wild wood?

Sisters and Sire——"

Here an hysterical titter caused her to pause. Miss Tripp held her handkerchief to her mouth, and Lady Towton was convulsed. The girl stood staring for a whole moment; then, with a gesture of unexpected passion, dashed down the unhappy concertina, saying, "Sing for yerselves!" and escaped from the room.

When the commotion, consternation, and amusement, had somewhat subsided, Lady Towton said, in a choked voice—

"I really could not help myself! The *cabin* door was so appropriate, it was too much for me. I'm really awfully sorry."

"'Pon my word, I think you ought to be," interrupted Sir Harry brusquely.

"She has a beautiful voice," added Colonel Wildairs.

"More than we can say for her accent," murmured Miss Tripp.

He turned his back on her, and went over to Tito, who was arranging the pianola.

"Won't you run after her, Miss Dawson, and take her our thanks and apologies, and see what she is doing?"

But Tito found the door locked, and to all her knocking and calling there was no response.

Lady Joseline was Mary Foley once more, and her heart was too sore for even Tito's sympathy, as she lay on her bed sobbing. She wished herself back at the Corner; she went even further—she wished herself *dead.*

* * * * *

Dudley took but scant notice of his new cousin; in fact, he avoided her, and maintained a sort of studied aloofness, determined not to be associated with ridicule. He was fastidious, and easily influenced by a woman like Mrs. Folly Fullerton, who did not see anything to admire in Joseline, and made fun of her continually. Dudley, shameful to say, drifted with the stream, too indolent to swim against it. Poor Joseline seemed to find so many adversaries among the company; she became shy and awkward when people addressed her, and appeared to have a genius for saying and doing the wrong thing. She was, moreover, downright unlucky; she knocked down and broke a piece of china, value untold. And Rap had nearly been the death of Lady Mulgrave's little dog, which he in the heat of the moment had chased, shaken, and mistaken for a rat. Some of her miseries were possibly due to imagination. She was painfully sensitive, and believed the whole of this little world was against her. Certainly she made a few blunders, and two enemies. For instance, one evening, at dessert, there was an animated discussion respecting the conduct of a certain married lady, whose case had been recently in the papers. Her letters had been read to the wide world; her husband had vainly sued for a divorce. Some blamed her, others merely laughed.

"Why, I declare Lady Joseline looks shocked," said Colonel Wildairs, in a loud, full voice, which would have been a fortune to an orator. "She is not used to the manners and ways of such society, eh?"

"No, thank goodness, I am not," she answered, with decision.

"Are you Irish so particular?"

"Among the lower orders—yes. I do not know the other lot; they may be as bad as yourselves, but the common people have conduct, and they *have* to behave themselves. I knew a girl—a married woman—and her husband thought she was speaking too free to a young boy, and he punished her proper."

"How?" inquired Miss Tripp, leaning forward as she spoke. "Do tell us how he punished her 'proper' for improper behaviour."

"Well, he tied her up by her two hands in the cowhouse, and he bet her with a car-whip till he could stand over her no longer, and she was half-killed. I heard the screeches of her myself, and it served her right."

"You think so?" said Lady Boxhill sarcastically.

"Certainly, and to be sure I do. What does a married woman want with a sweetheart? Will ye tell me?" Here she inadvertently fixed her eyes upon Lady Towton, and the question seemed to be shot at her from the girl's impetuous lips.

The stupid creature did not know how her arrow hit the goal—the only one at table who was ignorant of its effect. Lady Towton became white, then crimson, and Joseline's bitter enemy to the end of her life.

Dudley Deverell had witnessed the scene with a mixture of dismay and amusement. What a dangerous young woman. She seemed to have a knack of dropping bomb-shells into people's laps! The very same evening she surpassed her previous effects. She was looking on at a game of roulette—indeed, she was actually playing, and occasionally placing a timid shilling here and there (as no knowledge or practice is required). Suddenly Lady Boxhill announced—

"Well, now I'm going to plunge and put a sovereign on my *age*!" And she surveyed the circle with her crafty, made-up old eyes.

"But you can't do that! How can you?" remonstrated Joseline, in her soft, sonorous tone. "Your age is not on the board within twenty years. Why, the highest is thirty-eight."

Joseline's protest and faux pas were immediately drowned in a loud buzz, and she felt herself severely pinched by Tito. The miserable girl had made another enemy, and Lady Boxhill in future spoke of her as "that fearful Yahoo," and snubbed her ruthlessly whenever it lay in her power.

"The fearful Yahoo" was painfully sensitive. She knew that she was unpopular, and was quick-witted in her own unpolished fashion. She caught stealthy looks and smiles exchanged on her account. Lady Mulgrave frankly ignored her (unless she found occasion to exhibit her as a curiosity). Dudley held aloof, in chilling disapproval; he was a coward, and ashamed to be identified with the public laughing-stock, whose ignorance of the social code was displayed at every turn. Sir Harry Coxford, however, paid her many stupid compliments; Colonel Wildairs assumed bluff, fatherly airs. Yes, these two were her friends; but Teddy Boltover was stolidly rude, and the Prince pursued her with detestable attentions; he brought his face so close to hers when he addressed her, and surveyed her with such a detestable expression that she hated him.

Naturally, Joseline was gregarious and fond of life and company; had she not for many years been "Mary of the Corner," accustomed to continual homage, and acclamation? Better be a success in a cottage, than a failure in a castle! Gradually she withdrew into her own company; she went for long walks with Rap, or sat up in her little boudoir, keeping the fire warm as she crouched over it, meditating on her many blunders and the hostility, or indifference of her associates. She did not play bridge, she disliked motoring, she had no friends or tastes in common with the party, nor any claim to be remembered or considered; her heart was filled with bitterness and revolt. Oh, if her father were at home!—never, never again would she remain behind alone as an experiment, and for the sole benefit of her education.

But her enemies within the gate had a strong case against Joseline, and Lady Boxhill voiced the sentiments of her friends when she said—

"Did you ever notice the way that girl sits huddled over the fire on a low stool, as if she were still in her kitchen? What a frightful trial to poor Lottie! She plants her elbows on the table, her hands on her hips, she pushes before people, and in her clumsy haste to be obliging she gets flustered, drops things, falls over footstools, and treads on every one's toes."

"Yes," put in Lady Towton, "and asks such odd questions; and I declare her scarlet blushes, are positively indecent."

Alas! Poor Joseline was, in some respects, an Ishmaelite; her hand against her associates, and their hands against her.

One afternoon, as Joseline sat by her fire knitting a sock, with Rap, the criminal, luxuriously extended beside her, the door opened quickly, and Tito entered. She looked rather pale and agitated. Without preamble she came up to the hearthrug, spread out her hands before the blaze, and said—

"I've had an awful time!"

"How? Where? What is the matter?"

"I've been playing bridge since two o'clock, and my brain is buzzing. My partner was Colonel Wildairs, against Sir Harry and Gussie Tripp. She *is* a beast; she riles me! So hatefully sharp and on the make. The way she slaps down a good card, with a sort of jerk, is just maddening, even when I *knew* she had it all the time. She made me lose my temper, and what's worse—my money. Joe, you will have to lend me thirty pounds?"

"Arrah! Is it for card-playing? Go on with ye!"

"It's true. I've lost forty pounds."

"The saints preserve us!"—lifting her hands and eyes in protest.

"Yes, it's a fact. I went no trumps, and she redoubled: my partner had nothing, and I was weak in diamonds. She got in with her ace, and made the little slam. Colonel Wildairs was furious; he pays Sir Harry, and I pay *her*; she was so nasty about it, too. She said—'Forty pounds, dear Tito! You should *never* double until you are more experienced. It is a shocking sum, but I won't press you. Pay me next week.' And of course, I'll settle up this very night."

"I don't understand the quarter of what you are saying; only that you are short of money."

"Yes. I've only ten pounds. I should hate Tony to think I was a defaulter, and she is so mean, and would talk at the Women's Clubs, and say awful things of me."

"Oh, would she?"

"Yes. She has her knife into most people."

"I've not much money left," said Joseline, "but whatever I have you are welcome to"; and she rose and went to a writing-table.

"But my dear, what *have* you done with it? The other day you said you had a hundred pounds."

"Well, ye see, being near Christmas I sent some over to Father Daly to lay out; they'd take it kinder from him, than me."

"Take what?"

"Well, my old friends. Mikey Mahon would be the better of an ass and car, I know, and Mrs. Curran is lost for a good pig, and Larry Duff's cow went and died on him, so I've told them to buy a nice little young Kerry; and there was coals badly wanted, and I sent Peggy Curran a dress piece, and Mrs. Hogan a weather-glass and a visitors' book, for the last one was spoiled on her, and full of impudence and poetry."

"What have you left?" interrupted Tito impatiently.

"Here it is—twenty-five pounds"—and she held it out. "I am sorry I'm short. What will you do for the rest?"

"I'll borrow from Robins the butler."

"Goodness, girl alive! Isn't that queer doings?"

"Oh, Robins knows me; he is a family friend, and rolling in tips. Well, Joe, you *are* decent. I'll pay you next quarter."

"No, no, let me give you the money; I really don't want it. I wish you would promise me not to—I won't say play bridge—I'm not a born fool; but not to play for so much."

"I'll promise farthing points with pleasure; I will indeed," said Tito emphatically. "I'm sick of the whole thing. I love the game, but I loathe losing my money, and I'm not a very good player, for I'm too hasty and emotional, like you! By the way, why do you sit up here all by your little lone?"

"Where else would you have me sit? They are not missing me downstairs, are they?" she asked, with a sarcastic laugh. "And when I'm here, I'm not making a show of myself."

"They *are* a horrid pack, most of them! Old Lady Boxhill—I suppose she'll take the Prince—Lady Towton, Mrs. Folly, and Gussie Tripp—

hateful! But you should not let them draw you out about wakes, and dances, and your schooling, and so on."

"Sure, I see that, and I'm getting wiser now. I thought they wanted information, they all seemed so eager with questions. Now, I know 'twas only laughing they were."

"Tony disapproves of them; says they are—well, no matter; and he was horrified at my losing this money"; and she held up the notes. "He never plays high now; he simply refuses anything more than half a crown a hundred. You can lose quite enough at that."

"Can ye now?"

"Once, he told me, he played with a very smart woman, who said, 'What shall we have on?' And she named quite a big stake—something like half-crown points. He was ashamed to refuse. However, he won, and won, and had great luck. He won about a hundred, and they stopped. She said, 'I'll settle at once.' 'Oh, no, no hurry,' he said, thinking it was such a big sum, he would give her time. 'I always pay money down,' she said, and handed him ten shillings. 'What is this for?' he asked. 'What I've lost to you,' she answered, as bold as brass, naming some decimal points. He was struck dumb. Of course, being a woman, he could not argue with her. Afterwards, he heard, that it was a habit of hers to play this trick, and that if he had *lost*, she would have come down on him for her hundred pounds."

"Then she is a cheat!" cried Joseline.

"Oh, yes," rejoined Tito triumphantly, "of course she is! and I only hope she will be run in some day. Now I must fly and dress."

CHAPTER XXVIII

In spite of all her excuses, protestations, and pleadings, Joseline found herself *en route* to the Hamptons' ball, packed into the omnibus along with seven others, and being carried to the scene of action as fast as a pair of fine steppers could take her. Figuratively speaking, the vehicle was almost bursting with high spirits; the clatter of chaffing tongues was incessant, and, as some so-called "wit" had extinguished the lamp, semi-darkness promoted hilarity.

Joseline sat at the far end next to the Prince, who made a gallant attempt to hold and squeeze her hand, under the impression that she was Lady Boxhill—which endearments she forcibly returned by a sharp and vicious pinch. Now and then she was drawn into the conversation, and forced to reply to questions.

"Will you give me a dance, Lady Joe?" said Colonel Wildairs, who was her *vis-à-vis*.

"Thank ye, but I can't dance—only jigs and reels."

"Well, I cannot imagine any one going to a ball that can only dance jigs," said Gussie Tripp, "especially when she is not old enough to care for supper."

"Signs on it, I agree with you with all my heart," declared the brogue in the corner. "I wanted to stay at home. I don't know why Lady Mulgrave was set on bringing me, seeing I can't dance a step, and I never eat supper."

"There is such a thing as looking on," suggested Sir Henry Coxford.

"And—sitting out," supplemented Tito.

"That's true," said Sir Henry. "Lady Joe, you and I will sit out a couple of dances, eh? Here we are, and a bit late too," he added, as they drove under an illuminated porch, descended, and joined the rest of their company—a party of no less than twelve.

"Quite an invading force, are we not, dear Mrs. Hampton?" said Lady Mulgrave, as she shook hands with her hostess. "I think you know most of them, except my stepdaughter, Lady Joseline, and Prince Bambinetto"—presenting them as she spoke. "I am afraid we are a little late."

"The third waltz; but you do not dance, I know. There is bridge—in the end room, and you will, I hope, get a rubber."

The party moved on and presently dissolved among the gay company. Joseline, who was not sorry for Sir Henry's escort, made her way with him into a wide corridor hung with tapestry lined with splendid furniture, and priceless inlaid cabinets.

"This is as good a perch as any; I know the house well," he said. "You can see and be seen; they all pass by in review order"; and he nodded or bowed to several acquaintances. Finally, he got up to speak to a lady in reply to an imperative summons, and Joseline for the moment was alone. How strange! She did not see one familiar face. How different to her former dances: when she took the floor—a mud floor—with Tom Kelly or Patsy Malone, an enthusiastic audience of friends and admirers lined the room, and greeted their performance with uproarious applause—applause so vigorous and infectious, that the very soot came tumbling down the chimney!

As she sat a little aloof and distrait, looking vacantly before her, her mind filled with other images, she recalled her sole previous experience of a society gathering—the great concert at Kilmoran, and Mr. Ulick singing the bull-fighter's song. These reflections were interrupted by her hostess, who had been attracted by her lovely face, and now approached her, followed by a tall, soldierly-looking man.

"I hope you are dancing?" she said. "I have brought you a partner—Major Doran."

Behold the hour and the man!

Had Joseline's thoughts summoned him?

Since we last came across Ulick Doran he had served in India and South Africa, had won laurels, and seen the world. With many matters to occupy his attention and fill his time, he had never forgotten Mary Foley—she held her own against the various pretty visitors who had knocked and rung at the door of his heart. From the animated Indian spin; the South African grass widow; the charming American girls;—his thought invariably turned to a slender red-haired maiden, with a soft, insinuating brogue, and a pair of bewitching brown eyes.

The astonishing history of her exaltation had recently come to his knowledge. It sounded like a fairy tale! Well, she was now nearly as much out of his reach as before—and for an exactly contrary reason.

When Mrs. Hampton (an active and admirable hostess) had said, "I want to introduce you to a beauty," Major Doran, who had no idea of what was in store for him, obediently accompanied her into a gallery, where sat a young lady in a high-backed chair, with her eyes bent on the ground.

As Mrs. Hampton addressed her, she lifted them and looked from the image in her thoughts on the real man, Ulick Doran—browner, graver, older, otherwise unchanged. In a moment her face became transfigured, and wore a smile of radiant surprise and joy. The recognition was not mutual, until Mrs. Hampton added—

"Major Doran—Lady Joseline Dene."

He stared at her blankly, incredulously, as she sat in the ancient chair, with its great carved crown showing above the masses of sunny hair, her delicate hands resting on its massive arms, her graceful slimness thrown out into relief by its broad leather back.

She looked dazzling in her mother's pearls and a silver spangled gown. Almost like some stately young sovereign, enthroned among her subjects.

And yet it was the same little face that had haunted him all these years—the same that had been pressed against the window-pane one April night, in passionate farewell.

"May I have the pleasure of a dance?" he asked, after a moment's hesitation.

"Thank you, I don't dance," she answered inarticulately, as she pressed on the knobs of the arm-chair with trembling hands.

"Then may we sit it out?"

She bowed, without raising her eyes.

"What a queer, nervous sort of girl!" thought Mrs. Hampton, as she moved away.

To Major Doran it seemed almost incredible. But these delicate patrician features, and the rich, soft brogue, both belonged to Mary Foley. She was curiously reserved, and cold. Had her sudden uprise turned her head? Did Lady Joseline Mulgrave hate to recall the old days, when she was the inferior, and dropped curtseys to *him*?

"Lady Joseline," he said, on a sudden impulse, "may I ask you a question?"

"You may if you like," she answered, almost under her breath.

"Do we meet now for the first time? or—have we known one another all our lives. It is for you to say?"

"Me to say," she repeated, raising her eyes to where he stood, humbly awaiting her decision. "Why, to say the truth, and what else?—wasn't I your mother's egg-huxter?"

"Well, perhaps we need not recall *that*—only—other things?"—and he studied her pale, uplifted face, and her brilliant eyes, with a keen and intimate interest. "Do you know that I've always had a presentiment, that we should come across one another some day. Of course I have heard your story."

"Yes," she answered, with regal equanimity, "I believe it was on the papers."

"I was not as much surprised as other people. You were always different to your surroundings."

"I suppose I was," she acquiesced. "I never had much heart for work."

"But you had for play. You seem to have left your spirits in Ireland?"

As he spoke he took a seat and continued.

"It is six years since we met. A good deal of water has run under the bridge——"

"Oh, for the Lord's sake," she interrupted, with unexpected passion, "will ye not be talking of bridge! I'm fair sick of it!"

"I am not alluding to cards, but to events. Many things have happened since we said good-bye to one another."

Did she recall the episode? Yes, for her face flamed.

"You remember?"

She moved slightly in her regal chair, and made no reply.

"Do you?" he urged, with low persistence.

"Oh, I've a pretty good memory," she answered at last, her face aglow, as she raised her eyes to his with a glance of proud defiance. "There's been changes—the death of Mrs. Foley; the break-up at the Corner; some going to America, and some getting married."

"I was told that you were going to be married," he said.

"I?"—and she laughed derisively. "I might be married years ago, if I'd liked."

"I don't mean over in Ireland," he protested; and his glance wandered to where Dudley was permitting a pretty woman to entertain him.

"Oh, that!" A pause; and she added, with a touch of her natural impulsiveness, "I wouldn't marry him if he was hung in diamonds, nor he me; he is afraid of his life of me."

"Why, what have you been doing to frighten him?"

"Always saying and doing the wrong thing. You see, I'm so ignorant, and when people make signs at me, 'tis worse I get."

"What do you call the wrong thing? Can you give me a specimen?"

"Well, talking to Lady Boxhill of wigs, and age, and to Mrs. Fullerton of divorce, and to Sir Harry Coxford of debt and people owing money. I mean no harm, God knows! but I frighten people, and I make them hate me"; and her lip trembled, and her eyes were brimming.

"I am sure no one could do that," he protested.

"Oh, but they can! I'm such a clumsy fool. And faix, your own mother wasn't too fond of me! All the same, I hope she is getting her health?"

"Yes; but I'm sorry to say Barker is giving her a lot of trouble."

"Well, she has him as she reared him! I suppose about the big lump of a girl that's barmaid over in Killarney?"

"He has married her."

"I am glad he had that much decency."

"And he insists on bringing her home. It's a terrible trial to my mother."

"Well, if I'm not mistaken there will be two of them in that trial. And what have you been doing with yourself?"

"Soldiering in India, and other places—and twice to America, to see my aunt Nora. I am going over again immediately. She is a widow now."

"That was she that came in one soft evening in the old blue cloak. I took her down to 'The Arms.' Mrs. Hogan told me about her. She must have got a queer sort of shock when your mother chased her out of the Castle."

"I think she has forgiven and forgotten. Now would you like to take a turn, and see the other rooms and the dancing?"

"Yes, I would"—rising with graceful alacrity.

"I suppose this is your first ball?" he continued, as they stepped into the stream of moving figures, a remarkably distinguished-looking pair. Joseline held herself well, and looked every inch the daughter of a hundred earls. Not a few people remarked her, and asked, "Who was the beauty?" In fact, she made a sort of triumphal progress, as she moved about the rooms, the loveliest of visions. The fame of her remarkable story, and the presence of her beauty, filled the air. No one who saw Lady Joseline, would believe that she was stupid, common, uneducated, and muddleheaded.

Ulick Doran, her escort, was conscious of the sensation caused by his companion. Admirers crowded about Mrs. Hampton, clamouring for an introduction to the charming heroine of a romantic tale; but among them her cavalier still held his ground, and would not yield his place.

"I say, what a find for Mulgrave!" muttered one county magnate to a neighbour.

"Yes. I'm not sure that Lady M. is delighted with his discovery. Where is she?"

"Need you ask? In the bridge-room, of course."

"I wonder what she would say to the stir the girl is making? By gad!"—watching her as she passed by. "And who is the fellow with her?"

"Lady Barre's nephew; his name is Doran."

"Irish! Well, no Irish need apply—her ladyship is booked for Dudley Deverell. By the way, I see him here playing the fool with the Fullerton woman."

Dudley Deverell observed from afar, and marvelled. So Joseline had got hold of Doran. Such a smart, good-looking chap—and Joseline was undeniably admired. Oh, yes, she was all very well—until she began to talk!

"It is a pity you can't waltz," remarked Ulick, as they looked on; "but you will learn in no time."

"I'm no good. I can do nothing like other people. I can't ride, or dance, or play bridge, or tell pleasant lies to people's faces without turning a hair, or even pretend I like those I can't bear."

"Oh, all those things will come easy to you, bar the hypocrisy. It was strange our meeting here to-night," he said.

"Our meeting—and parting," she added quickly.

"Why parting?"

"Because you are going to America, and I am going to France. Yes"—in answer to his look—"as soon as my father returns, next week, I believe. You know, I'm half French and half English."

"Yes, and half-hearted."

"Why do you say that?"

"Because you don't seem happy."

"That's true. Ye see how it is; I'm neither fish, flesh, nor fowl. Too fine for the folks in Ireland, and not up to the mark over here. I was twenty-one years too long in a cottage. I will never be a lady."

"Would you like to return to the Corner, and be Mary Foley?"

"Oh no, I could never go back to that," she answered with emphasis. "There is my father, who is more than good to me; and Tito too. But I'm not denying, that I don't care very much for the crowd in the house."

"I daresay not. I know the set; you are a bit out of it?"

"I am so—and so best! In Ireland the people laughed with me. Here they laugh *at* me. Oh, it's a sore change!" she concluded, in a miserable voice.

"Surely you need not trouble your head, or think about them."

"But I've not much else to think of just now, being hand-idle. Tell me," she added eagerly, "what did *you* think now, when you saw me?"

"My first impression when I caught sight of you was, 'Splendid isolation.' Then I had a curious sense, of something foreseen."

"I can't understand them grand words."

"Are you aware, Major Doran, that you have cut my dance?" said a sharp voice, and there was Miss Tripp and her partner standing beside them.

"Number eleven, I think," he faltered, hurriedly pulling out his programme.

"No, number ten. I see that you agree with Lady Joseline, who simply came to the ball to sit out"; and she accorded the girl a deadly glance.

"I'm sorry, Miss Tripp," he said. "Pray accept my most abject apologies."

"Oh, well, if you really are repentant, you may have the next instead," said the lady, releasing her cavalier with a nod. "It's going to begin, so come along—I hate to miss even a bar."

"But—Lady Joseline"; and he looked at Joseline, resolved that he would not desert her.

"Oh, *she* will be all right! Here comes Colonel Wildairs, only too pleased to take her off your hands"; and before Major Doran could remonstrate, the tall, masterful lady had carried him away.

"I am delighted to step into his shoes, Lady Joe," declared the gallant officer, who was keenly alive to the fact that he was escorting the beauty of the evening—a beauty, too, who had no honour in her own home.

"I see you know Doran," he added, as they made their way into the ball-room.

"Yes."

"He is a good sort. I knew him in Natal; he did very well in the mounted infantry—a nailing rider."

"Oh, he rides well," she assented, as she watched him dancing with his captor.

"And is able to keep fine horses; he is rich."

"Oh, no, indeed."

"Sorry to contradict, but he is a wealthy man; an uncle in America left him tons of dollars. I'm surprised he stays in the service; but money is useful everywhere. It was rather amusing the way Miss Gussie carried him off; perhaps she will manage it for good and all!"

Joseline was enjoying the scene; the fact was written in her speaking eyes, and brilliant colour, also she was aware that many glances followed her; she knew that she was discussed and admired. The knowledge that she was a success restored her shattered self-confidence; her spirits rose to their former pitch, and her heart throbbed with alternations of hope and fear. Mr. Ulick!—*Ulick!* Oh, she could hardly believe that she had seen him and spoken to him! Old recollections came surging through mind and memory, and beating in her brain; everything connected with that poignant, uncertain, happy, and agonised time was coming back. Joseline realised that she was unchanged. Was he?

As she stood beside a pillar, surrounded by a little court, which now included Colonel Wildairs and Sir Harry, distributing smiles and "Ah, sures," and "I don't rightly knows" among her circle, all the time she was in a state of seething impatience; a voice was muttering, "Will he come back? Shall I see him again to-night? Yes"—he had effected his escape, and joined the group. Her face kindled and looked radiant as their eyes met, and he said—

"Lady Joseline, I have come to carry you off to supper."

Was it but an excuse to release her? No; they proceeded towards the supper-room in real earnest, (followed by the attentive observation of the crowd,) where he secured a little table and the services of a brisk waiter.

"I'm not a bit hungry," she protested, refusing several proffered delicacies.

"But I am," he said, "and I hope you will keep me in countenance. Let me help you to some of this salmi. My cousin, Freddy Barre, and I motored over here, thirty miles, after dinner."

"That was a long way."

"So I thought, and I wanted to cry off; but then I'd no idea I was coming to meet you. Have some champagne?" he added.

"No, no, please; I do not care for it."

"Just a little"—pouring it out as he spoke—"to drink to ourselves and old times"; and he lifted his glass and touched hers. "But," he added, seeing that she had suddenly become extremely pale, "perhaps we should forget! Now that you know your place in the world, and I may be presuming on mine."

Joseline's face expressed bewilderment; and then, as her eyes were drawn to his, the colour flowed back into her checks, for she had divined, by some infallible instinct, that Mr. Ulick had not changed. It was the same Mr. Ulick who had sent her the poetry, and kissed her through the pane.

"Miss Tripp introduced me to Lady Mulgrave," he continued; "she knows my aunt, Lady Barre, and she has asked Freddy and me over to-morrow for a bridge drive, to dine and sleep."

"Are you coming?"

"Yes, we will motor over—forty miles."

"Just to play cards?"

"That may be Freddy's inducement; mine, you know, is to see you."

"And Rap?" she added. "I wonder if he will know you?"

"Rap"—colouring—"the red terrier? Why, you don't mean to say you have him still?"

"Sure, six years isn't long for a dog to live!"

"And you brought him over?"

"How could I leave him after me, when I knew he'd never be happy with any one else?"

Major Doran nodded. "And how does he like the change?"

"Oh, finely; he is very proud in himself, and great company for me just now—him and books."

"You got the one I sent you?"

"Yes, I did so. Oh, it was beautiful poetry; I have it off by heart."

"Do you mind the day that's over,

And bless the day that's here?"

he quoted, leaning suddenly towards her, and lowering his voice.

She was on the point of answering, when she caught sight of Lady Mulgrave approaching.

"Joseline," she said, "we have been looking for you everywhere. What *have* you been doing with yourself?"—and she gave Major Doran a quick, sarcastic glance. "We are going at once. Now, don't sit staring, my dearest girl," she added peremptorily, "but run away and get your cloak."

CHAPTER XXIX

It was the last day of Lady Mulgrave's house-party. They were to scatter on the morrow—and the assemblage was to conclude with a brilliant finish: a gathering of neighbours at lunch, skating on the ornamental water, a festive dinner, and a bridge drive—such was the programme. Captain Barre and his cousin were among the guests, and the latter naturally singled out Lady Joseline for his companion when they all set out for the lake. She was accompanied by Rap, who, though he failed to recognise his former owner, accorded a searching investigation, and a civil reception. With her bright colour—the complexion of a true country girl—and her becoming sables, Lady Joseline confirmed the sensation she had created at Mrs. Hampton's ball. Unfortunately she did not skate, and was left among the dowagers and lookers-on, whilst most of the company took to the ice, figuratively, as young ducks do to water. Here was an opportunity of which Ulick Doran was not slow to avail himself. Together (and attended by Rap) they accompanied a self-conducted party in a brisk walk across the park, explored the frost-bound gardens and the sultry stoves. On the present occasion their talk was confined to the commonplace, and to old times; it never once soared into the region of Romance, for Ulick Doran had taken himself sternly to task, and his inner mind was filled with anxious debate. Years ago he had kept aloof because he had loved the girl too well to drag the poor child into a position which would entail misery—a ceaseless combat with prejudice, with his mother, and the world at large. Now, by a strange stroke of fortune, she was elevated to a position above his own. Did it not seem mean and despicable to ask her to descend to his level? On the other hand, he was well born, he was rich, he had been first in the field; why should he not take his chance? If Joseline was of the same mind as Mary Foley, why should they not both be happy? He honestly believed that he would make her a better husband than that faineant, Dudley Deverell, with his drawl and his dyspepsia.

As they walked in the wake of others he talked of his travels in Asia, Africa, and America, remembering her keen interest in foreign countries. He told her many amusing anecdotes, gave little sketches of people, and one or two sensational experiences. For her part, she described the chief local events (as seen from Foley's Corner). She also surprised him by her shrewd comments on her new life, intelligent criticism on books she had read, and questions she had heard debated. One moment she was Lady Joseline discussing "Helbeck of Banisdale"; the next, as Mary Foley, she accosted a gardener's kitten as a "poor angashore" whom she eloquently harangued in Irish.

After dinner the bridge drive was arranged in the great drawing-room; a few repaired to billiards, but most people declared for cards.

"Of course you'll play, Major Doran?" said Lady Mulgrave. "We will make up six tables."

"No thanks," he rejoined. "I am rather out of form, and if you will allow me, I'll just have a look round the pictures. I've heard so much of the Ashstead Romneys."

"Oh, of course"—and she raised her eyebrows in apparent amusement. "I daresay Joseline will be pleased to introduce you to some of the ancestors. Mr. Baines will take your place—*he* is very keen."

It flashed through her mind, what a good thing it would be if this Major Doran, who was Irish and rich, would relieve her for life of "her young girl from over the sea."

Presently everybody in the drawing-room resolved into silence, and tricks; whilst Joseline and her companion strolled through the empty reception-rooms into the little boudoir. Ulick Doran was turning over in his mind how he would approach the subject, when Joseline herself made an opening.

"To think of all the travelling you have done," she exclaimed, "and the countries you've seen, and your never once coming home!"

"But I did return once, just for a couple of days."

"Yes, but never to stop. Why was that?"

"Surely you need not ask. You know the reason."

"I—Mr. Ulick?" she exclaimed, thrown off her guard.

"Don't call me Mr. Ulick."

"Well, what will I call ye? Oh, of course—Major."

"I know what I hope you'll call me," he interrupted; "but I daresay you won't."

"Ah, what's that?"

"Ulick."

"Oh"—colouring—"how could I do that? Oh, no, I really couldn't—never."

"Do you really mean—*never?*"—and his face was serious.

She hesitated for so long, his expectation became intense; at last it was positively painful. "Well"—drawing a quick breath—"any way—not yet."

"And when?" he persisted.

She made no answer.

"In six months?"

"Ah, sure ye know I'm not fit," she faltered, and her eyes were filled with tears. "Although I'm dressed up like this"—and she glanced at her dainty gown of white chiffon—"I'm only a common girl, and faix, no one knows that, better than yerself."

"Once upon a time you were very fond of me, and I have never forgotten you. Mary, I believe you have been constant to that time."

"In a way, only," she said, rising suddenly, "I tried my big best to put you out of my mind, and I'll tell ye no lie, but you would not stir—no, strive as I would, I could not get shut of ye, for three long years. Then I began to think ... I was a fool"—and she paused and put her hand to her long, slim throat—"and if any boy I fancied, had asked me to marry him, I'd have said 'Yes'; but I never did see one I could like in the same way as you—no one that made my heart ache, and kept me pining and fretting, and wishing I was dead—the same as *you* did, Mr. Ulick."

"Ulick!"

"Well, then, Ulick."

"And I believe people will say it is tremendous presumption to lift my eyes to your father's daughter. You know I'm only just a major in the service, and he will expect you to make a splendid match."

"I don't think he wishes me to marry at all—any way, for a long while. You see, he has only *had* me for a few months."

"Yes; it would be hard lines on him—and I will wait, if you will marry me in the end.—Mary, will you?"

"Ye were always terribly set in getting your own way, Mr. Ulick"; and she looked up at him with a tremulous smile. "I remember it with horses, and how once the black hunter stood with ye on the road for five mortal hours—and ye waited, and won the day."

"I'll wait on you for five years if necessary. May I speak to your father when he returns?"

"About what?"

"Why, about you, of course. I shall ask him to give you to me."

"Yes; but not for a good while—I am so awkward, and ignorant, I'd shame ye."

"No, never. I shall always be proud of you!"

"An' ye may think it strange, but he is real fond of me."

"Not as fond of you as I am, Mary"; and he slipped his arm round her waist, and kissed her—this time without the intervening pane of glass.

Five minutes later, and the door was pushed open, and Lord Mulgrave entered, in the act of taking off his muffler.

He started when he saw Major Doran and Joseline standing together by the fire; and, unless he was losing his wits, the fellow's arm was round her waist. In a flash he recalled a whispered secret one dim evening in the "Shelbourne"—the *real* gentleman, who was Irish, and had given Mrs. Foley a dog.

Here they were, the very trio—the red terrier, the lover, and the girl.

As Doran was no stranger to him he came forward, with a rather constrained "Hullo, Doran!"

"Oh, father!" cried Joseline, "we did not expect you till to-morrow. How did you come?"

"In a fly from the station, my dear. I got away earlier than usual. Not playing bridge, eh?"—turning to the man.

"No. The fact is, Lady Joseline was good enough to offer to show me the pictures; but we—er"—and as he glanced at his companion, she vanished through the door.

"I see, you had forgotten all about them," said Lord Mulgrave, hastily finishing the speech.

Well, there was no time like the present moment; here was his opportunity. Lord Mulgrave was not allowed to take off his top-coat, much less to think of his supper, before Ulick Doran was in full career.

In two or three pithy sentences he told his story. For a few vital moments they talked squarely, man to man. Lord Mulgrave knew all about Major Doran—his reputation and his fortune.

When he had divested himself of his great-coat, he said, "I will not part with Joseline yet, and we will take no one into the secret for six months. The girl has seen nothing so far, but Joseline is not like young women of her rank. She has a past of twenty-one years behind her. She loved you in that other life; you belong to it, and, I suppose,—she belongs to you."

*   *   *   *   *

"I say!" said Tito, as she encountered Joseline in a corridor, "what has happened to you? Why this radiant air of 'I fear no foe in shining armour'?"

Joseline did not wait to be cross-examined, but threw over her shoulder the misleading statement, "The pater is home!"

Lord Mulgrave escorted his daughter to France, and presented her to her mother's family, who received her with open arms, and were enchanted with l'Irlandaise, their kinswoman. Here the brogue and her occasional solecisms did not matter, since the child had her mother's face, and her mother's heart. She spent six months in the valley of the Oise, and returned to Ashstead Park a much improved and polished young woman; for her cousins had found her a ready pupil, and had taught her ease, self-confidence, and fluent French.

*   *   *   *   *

Ashstead always looked its best in August. The gardens were perfect, the green sward like rich velvet, the old trees dense, massive, and picturesque, and the surroundings silent and restful. On a certain warm afternoon, the sound of croquet-balls and voices woke the sleepy grounds. A game had just been concluded, and Joseline strolled off towards the shade, followed by her cousin and partner; they had been defeated by one stroke.

"What is the meaning of 'Bad scran to ye'?" he asked. "I heard you addressing the blue ball in those terms."

"Oh, it means 'bother take it!' and is just one of the old expressions I want to forget. I was so vexed that I lost the game. The words slipped out. I hope Miss Usher did not hear me."

"What matter if she did? Come and let us find a seat."

"Tired?" she asked. "Oh, poor cousin Dudley!"

"Tired? Yes, of a good many things."

"If I am one of them, please don't hesitate to say so."

"No, I'm never tired of you, Joseline. On the contrary, I should like to have more of your society."

She turned, and made him a little curtsey.

"And so Tito is going to marry young Goodrich?" he remarked.

"Yes, father has consented at last."

"Which means he has given Tito a dot."

"It means that he likes Tony, and so do I."

"You will miss Tito, won't you? You and she pulled together from the first."

"Yes, I shall miss her, but, of course, they will often run down."

"By the way, talking of 'running down,' you seem to see a good deal of that fellow Doran. How does he get leave?"

"Oh, pending retirement."

"Ah, so he is going. I wonder what he will do with himself? It's rather a bore to be a rich man with nothing to do."

"Like yourself, for instance?"

"Yes."

"But, cousin Dudley, you have lots to do if you like; you could go about your property, and see things for yourself. You'd really like it after a bit; you would know what to do, and what to give, and what to take away."

"Yes, yes," impatiently, "I know. You are always preaching."

"And you won't practise!"

"Well, perhaps, your sermons may do me good; but I can't say there is much jam in the powder! I am aware I'm an absentee landlord, but not a hard one."

"Pray, how can you tell?" she asked.

"Well, I let fellows off, and I subscribe to things that are necessary."

"That costs you little!"

"There now, don't go on rubbing it in," he said resentfully. "I've told you often that Harrowside is a great big black rookery of a place. I can't stand it! No, I never go near it."

"It is your duty; you have responsibilities. 'Noblesse oblige.'"

"Since I've been in bad health——"

"That's an old story," she interposed. "You are as strong as a horse now."

"Well, Joseline, you talk of my responsibilities; what would you think of taking charge of them, and me?" He turned his head suddenly and looked at his companion with a complacent, proprietary air. Then he added, in his usual drawl—

"What would you say if we were to get married?"

"Say!"—and she dug her mallet into the turf. "That we would lead a cat-and-dog life!"

"And which"—sitting erect—"would be the cat?"

"I—I suppose a woman is always a cat! You never call a man a cat, or an old cat."

"No, I'm a dog—the unlucky dog."

"No, a lazy dog," she corrected. "There are always puppies, and lap-dogs."

"Do you infer that I am one of these?"

"Well, you are petted enough. You live in the lap of luxury—I believe you don't even shave, or open your own letters."

"What else?" he demanded shortly.

"You won't take the trouble to, what's called make love! You say to a girl, 'Shall we get married?' and the girl says, No."

Dudley again turned his head, and looked at her steadily. Was she in earnest? Of course not! She was smiling. To her, everything was a joke; it was one of her silly habits imported from Ireland, and not yet abandoned.

Well, he was in no hurry; he did not wish to settle down at present. Joseline was amazingly improved—a handsome, amusing, much-admired girl, clever in her way; even Lady Mulgrave was reconciled to her.

To suppose that any sane young woman would seriously refuse him, Dudley Deverell, never dawned on his mind. He decided to postpone the question.

"I say, here is your father coming over with that fellow Doran," he announced. "I hear his brother has married a dairy-maid, who turned his mother out of doors."

"I'm sure she could not manage that,—from what I knew of her."

"Do you mean that *you* knew Mrs. Doran?" he asked, with quickened interest.

"Yes, I was reared on the land."

"I declare, one would suppose you were talking of a lamb."

"I *am* a lamb—sometimes. I sold her eggs."

"Ah, now I begin to see light," exclaimed Dudley—"to see—many things."

"To see further than your nose?"

"Yes"—rising to his feet—"I have it! Lady Mulgrave gave me a hint, but I laughed at her. Is this Doran the son who did *not* present you with the locket and chain?"

"He is," and she sat up abruptly.

"And perhaps he would like to offer you something instead; for instance, a ring?"

Joseline coloured, and nodded assent.

"Ah! I understand where I've been remiss, and he has been successful. These Irish fellows are tremendous hands at making love!"

He paused, momentarily overwhelmed with the shock of his discovery.

"Well, as to making love," said Joseline at last; "love should be real—and grow. But it is right that I should tell you, that Ulick has cared for me for seven long years, and that I have loved him—ever since I was in pinafores."

CPSIA information can be obtained
at www.ICGtesting.com
Printed in the USA
LVHW040611020223
738427LV00006B/527

9 789356 907942